THE INTERNAL POLITICS OF CHINA 1949–1972

JÜRGEN DOMES

The Internal Politics
of China
1949-1972

Translated by Rüdiger Machetzki

C. HURST & COMPANY
LONDON

First published in English by
C. Hurst & Co. (Publishers) Ltd., London, United Kingdom

German edition (*Die Ära Mao Tse-tung*) © 1971
Verlag W. Kohlhammer, Stuttgart, Berlin, Köln, Mainz

This translation © 1973 C. Hurst & Co. (Publishers) Ltd.

SBN 90096692 0

Printed in Great Britain by
Billing & Sons Limited, Guildford and London

Contents

PART ONE: RECONSTRUCTION 1949–1957

PART TWO: EXPERIMENT 1957–1965

PART THREE: CRISIS 1965–1972

Tables

Abbreviations

APC	Agricultural Production Co-operative
APD	Association for Promoting Democracy
AS	*Asian Survey*
BSF	Brandt-Schwartz-Fairbank
CB	*Current Background*
CC	Central Committee
CCP	Chinese Communist Party (Kung-ch'an Tang)
CFCP	*Chieh-fang-chün pao*
CKCNP	*Chung-kuo ch'ing-nien pao*
CKT	Chih Kung Tang
CKYC	*Chung-kung yen-chiu*
CNA	*China News Analysis*
CPSU	Communist Party of the Soviet Union
CQ	*China Quarterly*
CRG	Cultural Revolution Group of the CC of the CCP
CSS	Chiu-san hsüeh-hui
DL	Democratic League
DNCA	Democratic National Construction Association
FEER	*Far Eastern Economic Review*
HC	*Hung-ch'i*
HHYK	*Hsin-hua yüeh-k'an*
JMJP	*Jen-min jih-pao*
JMP	Jen-min pi (People's Currency)
JMST	*Jen-min shou-ts'e*
JPRS	*Joint Publications Research Service*
KJJP	*Kung-jen jih-pao*
KMJP	*Kuang-ming jih-pao*
KMT	Kuomintang (Nationalist Party of China)
KMWH	*Ko-ming wen-hsien*
NCNA	*New China News Agency*
NFJP	*Nan-fang jih-pao*
NPC	National People's Congress
NZZ	*Neue Zürcher Zeitung*
PLA	People's Liberation Army

PR	People's Republic
PWDP	Peasants' and Workers' Democratic Party
RC	Revolutionary Committee
RKMT	Revolutionary Committee of the KMT
SCMM	*Selection from China Mainland Magazines*
SCMP	*Survey of China Mainland Press*
TDSL	Taiwan Democratic Self-Government League
TKP	*Ta-kung pao*
URI	*Union Research Institute*
URS	*Union Research Service*
WHP	*Wen-hui pao*
WYP	*Wen-yi pao*
YCWP	*Yang-ch'eng-wan pao*

Preface

Experts in growing numbers have been observing the entry of the People's Republic of China into world politics. But the results of their observations remain controversial. Condemnation, scarcely veiled admiration and passionate commitment have been in conflict with each other. Yet the body of those who attempt to formulate dispassionate analyses detached from the object of their studies is also growing.

There has been much research of great informative and analytical value on the role of China in international politics, its conflict with the Soviet Union and its influence on South and Southeast Asia. Such are the works of Richard Lowenthal, Donald S. Zagoria, Morton Haperlin and Helmut Dahm, while the writings of – among others – Stnnrt R. Schram, Franz Schurmann and Gottfried-Karl Kindermana have interpreted the political theory of the Chinese Communists.

In the realm of internal politics, there have been monographs on specific phases of development, aspects of decision-making structures and the political system in Communist China, especially in the United States. Such descriptions contribute towards our understanding of the People's Republic of China. However, an informative summary of the development of internal politics in China since the Communist take-over in 1949 has been lacking. This book attempts to provide such a summary. We shall, of necessity, confine ourselves to major issues and the main lines of development.

No attempt will be made to expound and discuss the theoretical claim of the Chinese Communists to have created a new society. The focus of interest of this study has been determined rather by the development of political reality in Communist China. The strict adoption of theoretically descriptive models, which permit an external approach to the problem, will not be undertaken either. In the last five years, particularly in the realm of political science, comprehensive methodological discussions, often previously neglected, have supplanted reflections on methodology. Sometimes such disputes seem to have served the progress of our objective understanding less than this development of our specialised abilities to juggle with esoteric terminology. Thus the description of what really happened often falls victim to the discussion of alternative cognitive approaches. However, if this is to be avoided, the author must present his *a priori* understanding, moulded perhaps by scepticism of any ideological claim and by the conviction born of experience that although political leadership groups rarely acquire and defend their ruling positions for the sake of rule alone, their own justifications offer unsatisfactory information about their basic motives. If one considers politics from the point of view of this *a priori* understanding, then one wishes to describe and interpret, not praise or blame. The question of sympathy or antipathy for the object of study is therefore not important. I regard myself as a friend of the Chinese people, who have suffered more in the last hundred years than most other peoples. However, this fact does not force me to sympathise with any of the leadership groups which have ruled this people in these last hundred years. With regard to political systems, my first preference belongs equally to the greatest possible participation of the people in the political decision-making process and efficiency in development. My interest lies secondly in avoiding physical violence internally and externally, thirdly in the change of social relationships and only lastly in maintaining traditional material and spiritual cultural values.

According to this *a priori* understanding and in conscious obedience to this order of preferences, I will attempt first to determine the process of development of internal politics in China since 1949. Then I shall present some possible future perspectives. However, this study does not discuss alternatives, although this is certainly among the important tasks of political science. This study will have achieved its aim if it offers some useful material for such discussion.

I wish to thank in particular the Ford Foundation, whose generous support made this study possible. This was made available through the Koordinierungsstelle für gegenwartsbezogene Ostasienforschung, which has now been amalgamated with the Deutsche Gesellschaft für Ostasienkunde.

The political scientists Dr. Marie-Luise Näth and Dr. Ulrich Gründler, as my research assistants, have made substantial contributions to the collection of source materials, and the manuscript has greatly benefited from their criticisms. The help which I have received from my colleagues Dr. Erik von Groeling and Werner Pfennig were of considerable importance in the course of work on the manuscript. I wish to thank them especially, and also all the other members of the Arbeitsstelle 'Politik Chinas und Ostasiens' at the Berlin Free University.

I gained many valuable insights through exchanging ideas with my respected teacher, Professor Richard Löwenthal, and my colleagues Professor Gottfried-Karl Kinderman, Dr. Joachim Glaubitz, Dr. Bernhard Grossmann and Dieter Heinzig who, together with the political writers Harry Hamm and Dr. Fritz von Briessen, have worked for the recognition of the study of contemporary China in Germany.

However, scholarly concern with present-day China achieves

nothing without the continual international exchange of ideas. Many
foreign colleagues offered suggestions in critical discussions, without
which my work would not have been possible. I mention here, with
particular gratitude, W. A. C. Adie, Thomas Bernstein, Cheng Chu-
yüan, Audrey Donnithorne, Daniel Ellegiers, Harold Hinton, Donald
Klein, Roderick MacFarquhar, Franz Michael, James Myers, Michael
Oksenberg, Dwight Perkins, Ralph Powell, Robert Scalapino, Stuart
Schram, Richard Solomon, Ezra Vogel, Richard Walker and David
C. Wilson. They are representative of the large group of China experts
throughout the world whose controversial but always important
contributions facilitate the understanding of Chinese politics.

In Hong Kong and Taiwan, many Chinese scholars have contributed
invaluably to my work. I am especially indebted to Huang Chen-hsia,
Hsiang Nai-kuang, Hai Feng, Liu Chieh, Ting Wang and Wu
Chün-ts'ai. But above all I wish to thank the many young Chinese
intellectuals who were willing to have long discussions after escaping
from their mother-country, China, and whose information and
criticism became increasingly important for this study over the years.

For the transcription of Chinese names and terms I have used the
Wade-Giles system which is the most customary in international
political science, with the exception of well-known geographical names
for which I have used the transcription of the World Postal Union.

This book is dedicated to Dr. Ladislao La Dany. The dedication is
intended as a modest expression of gratitude for the comprehensive
analytical work with which he, more than anyone else, has promoted
the international study of Chinese politics in the last twenty years.

Berlin
Autumn 1971–Autumn 1972   JURGEN DOMES

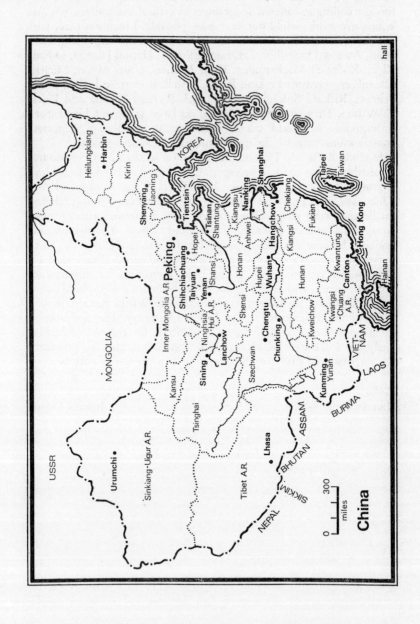

China

Introduction

Western works on Chinese Communism are often inclined either to uncritical praise of the considerable developmental and organisational achievements of the Chinese Communist Party (Kung Ch'an Tang) or to *a priori* condemnation of anything that has been happening in China. This twofold danger is linked to a third: in order to determine the place of the theory and practice of government by the CCP within the context of the whole of Chinese history some observers have been tempted to interpret China's Communism mainly as the outcome of her social tradition. Others, however, have denied any continuity between China's philosophical history and contemporary developments. They regard Communism as a complete disruption of the course of Chinese history. In the introduction to his documentary collection, *Confucianism, Sunyatsenism and Chinese Communism*, Gott-fried-Karl Kinderman has avoided this danger. He points out that Marxist–Leninist ideology, as well as traditional Chinese socio-political theory, did not know the concept of a personal God, and that both expressed a belief in an 'immanent cosmic law'. Apart from this there were striking differences in evaluating the role of the family and educational methods. The thesis that Chinese Communism is rooted in Confucianism is therefore hardly tenable.[1]

Reports from journalists who have travelled in China frequently offer interesting suggestions about the political situation of the country. But many of these authors tend to generalise their subjective observations which are limited to a certain point in time. Moreover, the Chinese Communists have repeatedly proved themselves to be masters in the art of deluding their foreign visitors.

Journeys in China are mostly guided by 'translators' from the security and propaganda apparatus, and the objects shown to visitors are 'showpieces'. It has been noted that most Western visitors to China saw the same producers' co-operatives or people's communes and the same factories and dyke constructions. They were permitted to talk to the same 'democratic capitalists'.[2] A lack of historical knowledge and language skills frequently prevents the formation of impressions which are not in the interest of Chinese Communist public relations policy. The real value of the numerous travel books on the Chinese People's Republic is comparatively low. The few descriptions which carefully consider and vividly reproduce travel impressions based on

I

intensive studies of the literature of political science relating to China are therefore all the more important. These are, above all, the works of Harry Hamm,[3] Lorenz Stucki[4] and Edgar Snow.[5] In contrast to Hamm and Stucki, Snow was a personal friend of Mao Tse-tung and other leaders of the CCP, but nevertheless a critical friend.

The conscientious journalists would not deny the relevance of sustained academic research if we wish to safeguard a broader range of information. In this way we shall avoid the intellectual racism of those who regard China solely as an enemy of the whole world order and propagate the unreflecting and unsubstantiated slogan of the 'yellow peril', as well as that of those who think that the Chinese, in contrast to Europeans, necessarily require governmental coercion. Furthermore, we avoid the intellectual colonialism of those who, remaining aloof in their European studies and lecture rooms, are arrogant enough to know the 'real needs of the Chinese masses'.

Research in political science contains no judgement, apologia or uncritical championing. It regards Communist China as one state among others, and its leadership as an élite committed to a certain modernisation programme and to the exercise of power. Political science ought to be – given a variety of approaches – nomological and analytical, but not hermeneutic and 'intuitive'. Its duty is neither to justify political systems ideologically nor to attack them. It is an integrative science and by its nature does not permit any monocausal approach; indeed it requires multi-causal work and theories. The victory of the CCP in 1949 in China cannot be completely conceived of simply as part of an inevitable global development. Rather it was the outcome of various factors not necessarily dependent on each other, which would not necessarily lead to comparable results within different historical entities.

Research in Chinese politics means the study of the political system and processes of a foreign region and of a country of totally different cultural and political traditions from those of any other country. Furthermore, the Chinese People's Republic constitutes a political system which makes the gathering of reliable data extraordinarily difficult. So we are forced to do more interpretative work than would be necessary in describing a system more open to study. The dangers which such interpretations entail may be reduced by the exercise of the greatest intellectual discipline and the simultaneous and mutual control of our interpretations and descriptions. Four aspects which are rooted within the intellectual traditions of China have to be specifically considered:

1. Traditions emphasised by communities which governed themselves for centuries developed largely passive types of resistance against governmental actions which impaired this autonomy. The Chinese,

therefore, show totally different reactions to exogenous stimuli. We have to take into consideration these traditions, yet we must not forget that men everywhere resemble each other to a great extent. We should be conscious of the phrase: Many things are different in China. If we understand it aright we will be safe from the primitive concept: Everything is different in China.

2. Personal relationships arising out of family, birthplace, common education and common work exert even greater influence on political processes in China than in other countries. They represent an extremely relevant factor in political studies of China.

3. A monosyllabic language favours playing on words, the contraction of explanations, reduction to slogans, and the use of veiled terms. The terminology of Chinese communication has acquired a value of its own which has to be considered in order to decode those messages.

4. Chinese tradition has deeply formalised social and political relationships. Ceremonial writings and actions are of greater importance than in the West and sometimes achieve a political influence such as to make them useful as data.

Finally, the very study of *Chinese* politics calls for a warning. Scholars and others who have had no empirical experience of the area are sometimes tempted to abstract concrete events in Chinese life and thought. This does not mean embarking on a study having adopted a preconceived theoretical conception of the state and the political system of China.[6] More common is the dangerous tendency to interpret the communications of Chinese institutions and politicians mechanically according to their Western word-for-word translations, or to apply our institutionally oriented political thought to China without further inquiry.

With these reflections in mind we shall attempt to project the internal development of the Chinese People's Republic from the autumn of 1949 when the CCP came to power up to the decisions of the Ninth Party Congress which completed the period of the 'Cultural Revolution'. No personality moulded these two decades as decisively as Mao Tse-tung, the leader of the Chinese Communists, and they can therefore with justification be called the 'era of Mao Tse-tung'. Some symptoms indicate that Mao's personal influence on the process of political decision-making waned and that this era came to an end with the close of the second decade in spite of the intense personality cult. An initial summary of this phase of Chinese history has therefore become possible. I shall consider the following questions in regard to internal policy.

– How and why did the CCP come to power in China?

- What economic and social conditions prevailed when it came to power?
- What kind of programmes were projected to change these conditions?
- What was the nature of the concrete concepts of development designed and practised by the CCP?
- To what extent has the CCP's development policy succeeded since 1949?
- What were the problems of government rule with regard to the structure and actions of the CCP and of the apparatuses controlled by it?
- What types of groups developed and are discernible in the course of the internal disputes of the CCP since 1949?
- What items of evidence point to such intra-Party disputes and what were the relationships between these items and types of group formation?
- How and with what results did such intra-Party disputes cause changes among those in control of government?

Finally, there is the basic question of Communist rule and its role within the historical dimensions of the Chinese Revolution. The term 'Chinese Revolution' describes the comprehensive transformation which has taken place in China since the second half of the nineteenth century. This transformation process is usually described as 'development'. It is in fact nothing but the enduring, problem-ridden and deeply painful process through which Asian, African and Latin American countries enter the modern state system.[7] It delimits the conditions of the Chinese Communists' governmental behaviour and of the problems which they wished to resolve and will have to resolve. The question arises as to whether the coming to power of the CCP meant the beginning of the last phase of the 'Chinese Revolution' or whether its rule is a temporary phenomenon of this revolution.

Because of disruptive crises, periods from 1949 to 1957, from 1957 to 1965 and from 1965 to 1969 are clearly discernible. According to these periods the development of internal Chinese politics in construction, experiment and crisis will be drawn up. In the end an attempt will be made to evaluate the developmental successes and failures of the CCP and to show the relationship between the ideological claim of 'Mao Tse-tung's Thought' and the reality of the exercise of Communist rule. Medium-range perspectives of Communist rule in China will be discussed and related to initial reflections on the CCP's role in the Chinese Revolution.

Although comprehensive material has been evaluated, no claim is made for definitive historical reliability. A number of essential documents have not yet been made public. Some problems therefore cannot be explained. Nevertheless, this study is presented because I believe that the basic tendencies of this development are already discernible. But it is likely that later historical studies will have corrections to make.

References

1 Gottfried-Karl Kindermann (ed.), *Konfuzianismus, Sunyatsenismus und chinesischer Kommunismus – Dokumente zur Selbstdarstellung des chinesischen Nationalismus*, Freiburg Brsg., 1963, pp. 19–30.

2 Cf. the evidence of the author in *Bücher zur chinesischen Revolution, Teil II – Politische Vierteljahresschrift*, Köln and Opladen, 2 Jahrg., Heft 1, March 1961, pp. 91–100.

3 Harry Hamm, *Das Reich der siebenhundert Millionen – Begegnung mit dem China von heute*, Düsseldorf and Vienna, 1965.

4 Lorenz Stucki, *Land hinter Mauern – China heute*, Zürich, 1964.

5 Edgar Snow, *The Other Side of the River*, New York, 1961.

6 One example is Edoarda Masi, *Die chinesische Herausforderung*, Berlin, 1970.

7 Jürgen Domes, *Vertagte Revolution. Die Politik der Kuomintang in China, 1923–1937*, Berlin, 1969 (hereafter cited as Domes, *Revolution*), p. 1.

Part One
Reconstruction 1949–1957

I. The Chinese Communists Win Power

When Mao Tse-tung announced his seizure of power and proclaimed the People's Republic of China (*Chung-hua jen-min kung-ho-kuo*) on October 1, 1949, twenty-two years of armed struggle came to an end. The CPSU needed five years to bring Russia under its rule, and the Yugoslav partisans' struggle lasted four years. These comparisons show the heavy burden which the protracted revolutionary war had laid on the country and the victorious Party. The CCP had been founded as an organisation of revolutionary intellectual youth. Large sections of Chinese intellectual youth had renounced Confucian traditions and turned to European and American ideologies during a far-reaching intellectual modernisation movement which culminated in the nationalist student demonstrations of May 4, 1919, and was therefore termed the 'May Fourth Movement' (*Wu-ssu yün-tung*).[1] The influence of these ideologies was soon weakened, however, under the imprint of the Russian October Revolution and the fascination of Marxism. Already in spring 1918 the Peking economist Li Ta-chao, had founded a 'Socialist Study Group' (*She-hui chu-yi hsüeh-shuo yen-chiu-hui*) in which a number of students and also the library assistant, Mao Tse-tung, took part.[2] In spring 1919 Ch'en Tu-hsiu, a literary historian and one of the most important leaders of the intellectual modernisation movement, approached this circle,[3] out of which a 'Marxist Study Group' (*Ma-k'o-ssu hsüeh-shuo yen-chiu-hui*) had grown in March 1920 after Li and Ch'en had openly professed Marxist ideology.[4] The leadership of the Communist International (Comintern) was therefore convinced that the preconditions for founding a Communist Party in China existed, and in May 1920 it sent Grigori Voitinski as its representative to China. With his assistance a number of Marxist circles were convened in Shanghai and other provincial capitals. At the same time Chinese Communist cells were founded in Europe: in 1917 and 1918 many Chinese students went to Europe, especially France, to study and work in factories. In spring 1920 several of them came together in Paris in a 'Socialist Youth Corps'. Among them were young intellectuals who were later to play a leading role in the Communist movement in China; they included Chou En-lai, Teng Hsiao-p'ing, Li Li-san, Li Fu-ch'un, Li Wei-han and Ch'en Yi.[5]

9

These groups came together to form the CCP during the First Party Congress on July 1 or 20, 1921, in Shanghai. The twelve delegates to this Party Congress represented only fifty-seven members, and even this small group was a mixed association of Communists, Social Democrats, Anarchists and radical Nationalists. Some of the delegates wanted to postpone revolutionary activities and continue academic studies of Marxism, but the majority decided to form a central leadership and elected Ch'en Tu-hsiu as Chairman of a three-member 'Central Committee' and as the new Party's Secretary-General.[6] In the two years following the foundation of the Party the Chinese Communists began to build up an autonomous labour movement and to criticise severely the Nationalist Party, Kuomintang (KMT). But soon after the Soviet Union and the Chinese Nationalists had sealed an alliance they were pressed by Comintern to build a United Front with the KMT in the form of the so-called 'Inner Bloc'.[7] This meant that members of the CCP joined the KMT as individuals while retaining their own Party organisation. Co-operation with the Nationalists forced the Communists to abandon temporarily their revolutionary socialist programme, but already during the First Party Congress of the KMT in January 1924 they succeeded in occupying key positions in the united Party.[8] This alliance with the KMT and a broad, nationalist movement conditioned their first major success in the summer of 1925.[9] Within a few months membership of the KMT rose from nearly 1,000 to more than 10,000. Moreover, they were able to broaden their influence during the struggle for succession in the KMT following the death of the Party leader, Sun Yat-sen.[10] They already dominated the Organisation Department, the Propaganda Department, the Peasant Department and the Worker Department of the KMT's Party Central, and they controlled considerable sections of the political machine of the Party army which was led by the young General Chiang Kai-shek who, on March 20, 1926, ventured a first blow against the CCP in the capital of national revolution, Canton.[11] Several Communist leaders were arrested, the KCT trade unions' militia disarmed and the Soviet chief adviser, Borodin, was forced to leave Canton temporarily. By this time some of the CCP leaders were demanding a withdrawal from the 'Inner Bloc', but Stalin and the Comintern leadership forced the Chinese Party to continue the alliance. Moscow's decisions to continue the United Front at first proved justified. When, in July 1926, the Nationalist army led by Chiang Kai-shek started its offensive to liberate China from the rule of warlords, the Communists were able to strengthen their influence considerably in the wake of the military in the newly conquered areas of South China, especially among the impoverished peasants of Hunan province. So up to the time when the Nationalist troops conquered Shanghai and Nanking in the first months of 1927 the CCP's alliance had been largely successful. The number of Party members had increased from 1,000 in 1924 to 58,000[12] and the Communists occupied the Ministries of Agriculture and Labour within the National Government which had been transferred to Wuhan.[13] The Communist-led 'All-Chinese Federation of Trade Unions' numbered 2.8 million members and the peasant associations led by Mao Tse-tung in the province of Hunan alone had more than two million members.[14] The time seemed near when the 'bourgeoisie' would be removed from the revolutionary front and the dictatorship of a 'bloc of petty bourgeoisie, peasants and workers' would lead to the 'dictatorship of the proletariat', i.e. to a Party rule of the CCP after the petty bourgeoisie had been repressed. However, the right-wing and centre forces of the KMT under Chiang Kai-shek struck first: on April 12, 1927, they broke with the Communists, disarmed the Shanghai workers' militia and destroyed by mass terror the CCP organisation in Shanghai and in most of the South China provinces soon after.[15] In July 1927 the left wing of the KMT in Wuhan broke with the Communists too. So the United Front policy which Stalin had supported up to the last had failed. After several ineffectual revolts by Communist troops and workers' militia in Nanchang and Canton the Party seemed to be paralysed for a long time.[16]

But Mao Tse-tung, who in September 1927 had led the 'Autumn Harvest Uprising' of soldier, miners and landless peasants in some areas of Hunan, was able to escape to the mountains with a group of followers.[17] In spring 1928 he and the Communist General Chu Te formed a guerilla army in the Chingkangshan mountains on the border of Hunan and Kiangsi, establishing small revolutionary bases.[18] The official CCP leadership carried out subversive work in the cities and soon wore itself out in factional struggles.[19] So the actual centre of the Communist movement shifted gradually to the Soviets which were growing in South China from 1928 to 1931 and could withstand the offensives launched by Chiang Kai-shek's Nationalist army. Under the influence of Mao and through extensive land reform measures the guerilla army was successful in securing the support of tenants and landless peasants, especially in Kiangsi, and in strengthening its forces. Finally, areas of some sixty million inhabitants were under the control of the CCP. Yet in spring 1934 the National Government mobilised 550,000 troops, under the personal command of Chiang Kai-shek, to undertake an 'Extermination Campaign' (*Chiao-fei*) against the Soviets. In October 1934 they encircled 100,000 Red Army troops in a narrow area of southernmost Kiangsi. The guerilla army was threatened with complete destruction.[20] So its leaders decided to attempt a break-out, and on October 16, 1934, 90,000 guerillas pushed through the encirclement and escaped to southern Hunan.

This was the beginning of the heroic phase in the history of the CCP, the 'Long March' (*Ch'ang-cheng*).[21] The Red Army, continuously fighting troops of the National Government, provincial armies and native tribes, marched nearly 7,000 miles in one year, crossing Kweichow, Szechwan, East Tibet, the Gobi Desert, and Kansu, and finally reached the area around Yenan in the north of Shensi province. Ninety thousand had started out; between 15,000 and 20,000 reached their destination in the autumn of 1935, forming a tight élite of revolutionaries, hardened by a long period of suffering. During the march an enlarged Conference of the Politburo was convened in January 1935 at Tsunyi (Kweichow) which criticised the existing leadership and brought Mao, as provisional Chairman of the Military Commission of the Central Committee (CC), to the top of the Party which at this time was *de facto* identical with the Red Army.[22] In the winter of 1935–6 Mao gathered anew the decimated forces of the Communist movement in the economically poor and remote base of northern Shensi, where the CCP augmented its membership to about 80,000 in the spring of 1937. But already in January 1936 the National army had started new operations against the Soviet. However, the CCP needed a respite in order to survive. This respite was gained by once more co-operating with the KMT in the 'Anti-Japanese United Front' which had been agreed upon after the outbreak of the Sino-Japanese War on July 7, 1937.[23] The Soviet was renamed the 'Democratic Shensi–Kansu–Ninghsia Border Region' and the Red Army, the 'Eighth Route Army' (*Pa-lu-chün*), was officially placed under Chiang's supreme command. But in reality there was little change. The Communists retained their territorial base, their administrative autonomy and their own military forces, even if they wore the badges of the National army.

The KMT troops fought desperate defensive battles, trying to prevent the total conquest of China by the Japanese, and with heavy sacrifices they succeeded in holding the major part of West China to the end of the war.[24] The Communists, however, soon proceeded with guerilla activities, and Communist administrative areas were established behind the Japanese lines in North China and Manchuria (Tungpei).[25] The guerilla struggle never constituted a strategically serious threat to the Japanese, but it considerably strengthened the position of the CCP in North China. Whereas the Communists controlled an area of four million inhabitants with their 80,000 Party members and 100,000 troops at the beginning of the war, in 1945 the Party numbered more than a million members, and had 910,000 troops and 2·2 million local militia (*Min-ping*) at its disposal. The areas controlled by the

CCP encompassed more than 95 million inhabitants;[26] most parts of rural North China and of northern and central Manchuria (Tungpei) were in its hands. Only the big towns and small rural corridors along the railway lines could be occupied by KMT troops in autumn 1945 after the Japanese surrender. While the special envoy of the US President attempted to bring about a coalition government of the rival forces,[27] the Soviet troops who had occupied the major part of Tungpei during the last two weeks of the Pacific war violated the treaty concluded with the National Government in August 1945, and for a long time prevented the entry of KMT troops. Furthermore, they ceded to the Communists the entire equipment of the 700,000 Japanese troops who had surrendered to them.[28]

At the beginning of this decisive struggle for control of China the KMT troops were superior to the Communists in numbers, but were in an unfavourable strategic position in the north and north-east of the country. In spite of this, Chiang obstinately insisted on defending the position of the Government troops in this part of the country, thereby sacrificing essential parts of his forces with no reasonable chance of success. Nevertheless, the National army initially achieved considerable success in Tungpei,[29] but the US Government enforced a weapons embargo against the Chinese National Government and consequently a temporary armistice ensued. However, the renewed negotiations called for by President Truman's special envoy, General George C. Marshall, also ended without any result, for neither the KMT nor the CCP was willing to make substantial compromises. On January 7, 1947, Marshall declared that his mission had failed, and he returned to the USA.[30]

Then open civil war started throughout China. For one and a half years it was conducted with varying degrees of success and with no definite outcome, although the KMT troops suffered mounting losses. They had already been gravely weakened when the Communists – ideologically consolidated and imbued with passionate confidence in victory since the so-called 'Cheng-feng Camapaign' of 1941–2 – began their general offensive in Tungpei in the summer of 1948. By October they had encircled about 400,000 KMT crack troops in Shenyang (Mukden), and on November 1 the city surrendered.

After this decisive victory in Tungpei the situation became turbulent for the National army in the villages of the Huang-ho plain in North China. In November and December 1948 the Communists destroyed further Nationalist crack divisions in a bloody battle at Hsüchou in North Kiangsu. Now the big cities of North China could no longer be defended. On January 15, 1949, the Communists entered Tientsin; on January 31, 1949, Peking surrendered. At the same time Chiang ceded the office of President of Nationalist China to his deputy, General Li Tsung-jen, who hoped to achieve a peace agreement with the CCP. Yet these efforts to achieve an armistice failed, as did the desperate resistance of the National army to hold at least a line along the Yangtze. On April 21, 1949, units of the Red Army, now called the 'People's Liberation Army' (*Jen-min chieh-fang-chün*: PLA), crossed the river. During the following months they gained control of major parts of South China, and without substantial military efforts captured Nationalist divisions. On April 23, 1949, Nanking surrendered, followed by Wuhan on May 16, Shanghai on May 27, and Lanchou, the capital of Kansu, on August 26. On October 14, Communist troops entered Canton and on December 3, Chungking. Remnants of the Nationalist army and the KMT leadership escaped to Taiwan and over the border to Burma and Tonking. The CCP had now gained control of the whole country after twenty-two years of civil war, interrupted only by the eight years of dubious co-operation with the KMT in the 'Anti-Japanese United Front'.

The reasons for the KMT defeat and the Communist victory have always been controversial. The Nationalist leaders and their foreign apologists have tried to place the blame on America's China policy. Their critics and opponents make reference to governmental corruption and Nationalist inability to win the support of the intellectuals. Both of these interpretations are correct to a certain degree, but they are incomplete. At least eight different factors contributed to the Communist victory:

1. Eight years of devastating war with Japan upset the still weakly developed economic infrastructure of the economically dominant regions along the coast and in the Yangtze Valley. This led to inflation which prevented the National Government from taking effective action. While in 1937 3·41 yüan exchanged for one US dollar, it was 1,701 in 1945, 450,000 in March 1948 and more than 8·6 million in mid-August of the same year. At this time the National Government made arrangements for a radical monetary reform. On August 19, 1948, a new yüan was issued which was based on gold and had an exchange value of a quarter of a US dollar. But the government's attempts to effect centralised control of the country's gold reserves failed. Not without the support of some leading Nationalist politicians, smuggling and speculation destroyed the basis of the new currency too. So in March 1949 17,700 new yüan had to be exchanged for one US dollar, and in mid-May the exchange rate had risen to 23·3 million.[32]

2. Inflation caused extensive corruption within the administrative apparatus. Badly paid and undernourished government officials had to take bribes in order to survive. Others used the greater part of their working day to conduct lucrative private enterprise. So the

administrative apparatus became more and more inefficient, and was no longer capable of winning the respect of the population. But we have to beware of unqualified accusations of corruption raised indiscriminately and without solid proof by some Western observers. Within the higher levels of the governmental hierarchy there were many able and uncorrupted men. Corruption by itself could hardly haved caused the defeat of the KMT.

3. Since 1927 the KMT had suffered from a permanent lack of development and military cadres. This weak, residual cadre had been decimated further during the war with Japan. More than 100,000 officers were among the victims of the war – a loss from which the KMT army did not recover until 1949.[33] Among them were two-thirds of the graduates of the Central Military Academy and 19,000 of the 24,000 members of the 'Special Units' (*Pieh-tung-tui*) trained for development and mass mobilisation tasks.[34] Because of these losses the Nationalists lacked the cadre structure which the Communists had efficiently developed during the war.

4. Even before the war the KMT had not been able to accomplish overdue social reforms. This was especially the case with regard to the necessary redistribution of land. To stabilise his rule and to resist the Japanese aggressors successfully, Chiang Kai-shek thought it necessary to co-operate with ultra-conservative warlords and different landlord lobbies. This alliance prevented thorough-going improvements in the social structure. Even after the war he was not able to dissociate himself from these forces. When the civil war intensified, there were new efforts to start reform, but due to the lack of mobilisation cadres and military events the KMT could not compensate for delays in this area.

5. The KMT was an amalgam of diverse political and social forces, and was strongly impaired by factional disputes. Even during the last years of civil war these factions were unwilling to co-operate unconditionally. Unity in the ruling party – a precondition for successful operation in the civil war – could not be arrived at. Some of the rival factions were more energetic in their internal disputes than in attempting to develop an extensive strategy which might have decided the war in favour of the Nationalists.

These five factors were of a domestic nature, but foreign policy and military strategy, in a narrow sense, played a decisive role as well.

6. Soviet support in 1945–6 provided a large territorial base and the necessary modern weapons for the Communists in Tungpei to equip strong, conventional military forces. Although there is no doubt that the Communists achieved final victory by themselves and through their own endeavours, the foundations of success were partly built

up with assistance from the Soviet Union in the first months after the end of the Pacific war.

7. The attitude of the USA towards China in summer 1946 caused considerable damage to the Nationalists. When the KMT army achieved its remarkable victory in Tungpei, Washington forced Nanking to conclude an armistice and further reinforced its pressure by a weapons embargo. These measures psychologically (and materially too to a certain extent) broke the backbone of the National army.

8. Since the beginning of 1947 Chiang had committed several grave strategical mistakes. Instead of fighting the Communists in their base areas near the Central Plain he risked a considerable part of his army in spring 1947 in advancing the spectacular but strategically useless conquest of Yenan. Instead of evacuating the élite units in Tungpei he forced them to hold encircled defensive positions until they could not but surrender. Instead of retreating at least south to the Yangtze after the defeat in Tungpei and building up a strong defensive line – which would not have had any sizeable Communist guerilla bases behind it – he threw his best troops one after the other into the grinding battle of Hsüchou. These three decisions were exactly what the Communists had expected, and they had developed an efficient counter-strategy. Chiang's conventional prestige thinking and trench warfare thus essentially contributed to his defeat.

Among these eight major reasons for the Communist victory, the economic crisis, the decimation of KMT cadres, the incapability of the administration and the corruption of the KMT rank and file, as well as the early Soviet assistance to the CCP after the war proved to be the most important.

On taking up the reins of government, China's new leadership was confronted with the very problems which had led to the downfall of its Nationalist predecessors. During the eight years of the Sino-Japanese War and the four of civil war a great part of the embryonic Chinese industry had been destroyed or at least temporarily closed down. The transport system had suffered considerable damage. Many of the dykes along the big rivers were in a state of disrepair. Arrangements for food supply between agriculturally abundant regions and regions of scarcity had been impeded by the insufficient means of transport. In the course of the civil war many millions of people, fearing war and reprisals from one of the parties, had fled their homes. Masses of people crowded into the cities, especially on the East Coast. They did not find work nor could they be maintained. Galloping inflation had destroyed the national currency and basic consumer goods were mainly exchanged on the black market.[35] Above all there were still wide areas of South China where remnants of the Nationalist army fought as partisans or had degenerated into vagrant bandit troops. In 1949 only four million Party members were on hand to penetrate the 500 million Chinese organisationally. Co-operation between the new leadership and as many sections of the population as possible was necessary in order to advance. The Party theory of revolutionary phases offered a useful rationale for this kind of co-operation. In contrast to foreign observers the CCP did not speak of the 'Victory of Communism' in China in 1949. The coming to power was, in its opinion, only the victory of the 'national bourgeois-democratic revolution', although this had been guided from the beginning by the Party. This first stage in the revolutionary process was to create the state of 'New Democracy' where different classes had to support the governmental system jointly and where capitalist modes of production were to be allowed to continue. Only during the second stage was a transformation to 'Proletarian Socialist Revolution' and a transition to a socialist and finally to a Communist social order to be accomplished. In 1949 the CCP and its leaders were still attached to an orthodox Marxist–Leninist conception which made industrialisation of China a precondition for achieving this last stage of revolution.

However, apart from these ideologically determined perspectives, the Chinese Communists were confronted with highly concrete and practical tasks as well.[36]

1. Extensive control over the whole country had to be established. To guarantee this control any potential resistance which might grow out of China's social traditions had to be overcome: for instance the extended family system and the manifold instruments of rural and regional autonomy.

2. Reforms in the system of agricultural ownership and production, the implementation of modern methods of production and the utilisation of new agricultural land had to be put into practice to secure the maintenance of 500 million people.

3. The extensive reservoir of human labour, often regarded as one of the most important, positive aspects of China's development, had to be mobilised and trained in a larger and better educational system to master the tasks with which a society is confronted during the process of industrialisation.

4. The infrastructure had to be built up, not least in order to connect the centres of the industrial economy and the areas of mineral wealth which hitherto had been barely accessible, and to stabilise food supplies.

5. Finally, industrial and technological foundations had to be erected in order to satisfy the needs of mass consumption and investment as well as those of re-armament.

An essential part of the mechanism with which the Chinese Com-

munists began to accomplish these tasks was the principle of centralised planning in investment, production, distribution and consumption,
adopted from the Soviet Union. A system adjusted to this principle
could not but stress the consolidation of a highly organised control
apparatus and the mobilisation of the people to attain the transformation of consciousness.

References

1 Cf. Chow Tse-tsung, *The May Fourth Movement, Intellectual Revolution iu
  Modern China*, Cambridge Mass., 1960, pp. 30–2, 98, 197, 309–11; Wolfgang
  Franke, *Chinas Kulturelle Revolution – Die Bewegung vom 4 Mai 1919*, München,
  1957.
2 Chow Tse-tsung, *op. cit.*, pp. 74, 244. Cf. also Stuart R. Schram, *The Political
  Thought of Mao Tse-tung*, New York, 1963, pp. 17–19; Martin Wilbur,
  Julie L. How, *Documents on Communism, Nationalism and Soviet Advisers in
  China* (hereafter cited as Wilbur-How), New York, 1959, p. 38; Edgar
  Snow, *Red Star over China*, New York, 1938, pp. 149, 151.
3 Chow, *op. cit.*, p. 216; cf. also Benjamin Schwartz, *Chinese Communism and
  the Rise of Mao*, Cambridge Mass., 1958, pp. 12–27; Ch'en Tu-hsiu, 'Chu-i
  yü nu-li' (Principles and Endeavours), in *Hsin Ch'ing-nien* (*New Youth*),
  December 1, 1920.
4 Chow, *op. cit.*, p. 244; Wilbur-How, *op. cit.*, pp. 49–50.
5 Cf. Conrad Brandt, *The French Returned Elite in the CCP*, Hong Kong,
  1961, pp. 2–6; Chow, *op. cit.*, pp. 249–50.
6 Cf. Ch'en Kung-po, 'The Communist Movement in China' (MA thesis,
  Columbia University, 1924), Martin Wilbur (ed.), New York, 1960; cf.
  also Schram *op. cit.*, pp. 24–6; Wilbur-How, *op. cit.*, pp. 52–5, 80; Conrad
  Brandt, *Stalin's Failure in China*, Cambridge, Mass., 1958, pp. 22–4; Schwartz,
  op. cit., pp. 34–6.
7 Cf. Allen S. Whiting, *Soviet Policies in China, 1917–1924*, New York, 1954;
  Wilbur-How, *op. cit.*; Shao-chuan Leng and Norman D. Palmer, *Sun Yat-sen
  and Communism* (hereafter cited as Leng-Palmer), New York, 1960; Conrad
  Brandt, Benjamin Schwartz, John King Fairbank, *A Documentary History of
  Chinese Communism* (hereafter cited as BSF), Cambridge, Mass, 1952, also
  Domes, *Revolution, op. cit.*, pp. 62–89.
8 *Ko-ming wen-hsien* (*Revolutionary Documents*) (hereafter cited as KMWH),
  Vol. VIII, Taipei, 1955, pp. 97–8; *K'ai-kuo wu-shih-nien ta-shih nien-chi*
  (*Chronology of the Fifty Years after the Foundation of the Republic*) (hereafter
  cited as *KMT Chronology*), Taipei, 1962, Vol. I, pp. 246–7.
9 Wilbur-How, *op. cit.*, pp. 90, 495. Cf. also Teng Chung-hsia, *Chungkuo chih-
  kung yün-tung chien shih* (*Short History of the Chinese Labour Movement*), Yenan,
  1943, pp. 211–17; J. Heller, 'The Labour Movement in China', in *Communist
  International*, No. 17, November 1925, pp. 3–5.

10 On the faction struggles in the KMT after Sun's death cf. Domes, *Revolution*, *op. cit.*, pp. 150–6, 250–62, 265–301; T'ang Leang-li, *The Inner History of the Chinese Revolution*, London, 1930, pp. 269–71; Harold Isaacs, *The Tragedy of the Chinese Revolution*, Second ed., Stanford, Calif., 1951, pp. 74–82.

11 Cf. also T'ang, *op. cit.*, pp. 244–7; Wilbur-How, *op. cit.*, pp. 218–21; Isaacs, *op. cit.*, pp. 148–56; further source references in Isaacs, *op. cit.*

12 Isaacs, *op. cit.*, pp. 113–15; Conrad Brandt, *Stalin's Failure*, *op. cit.*, pp. 102–4.

13 KMWH, *op. cit.*, Vol. XXII, p. 208; *KMT Chronology*, *op. cit.*, pp. 426–7; *Min-kuo jih-pao (Republican Daily)*, Wuhan, March 8–22, 1927; cf. Wilbur-How, *op. cit.*, pp. 397–9, 533–4; T'ang Leang-li, *Wang Ching-wei (A Political Biography)*, Peking, 1931, pp. 144–6; Isaacs, *op. cit.*, pp. 127–9.

14 *Ibid.*, pp. 113–15; Cf. Schwartz, *op. cit.*, p. 73; also Brandt, *op. cit.*, pp. 100–2.

15 Cf. Schwartz, *op. cit.*, pp. 48–85; Wilbur-How, *op. cit.*, pp. 401–3, 460–5; Brandt, *op. cit.*, pp. 102–18, 154–78; Isaacs, *op. cit.*, pp. 143–5; Domes, *Revolution*, *op. cit.*, pp. 191–213.

16 *Inprecor*, No. 64, September 19, 1928; *Wu-chuang pao-tung (Armed Insurrections)*, collection of documents, Shanghai, 1929, p. 94; cf. Brandt, *op. cit.*, pp. 143–5, 162–4; Isaacs, *op. cit.*, pp. 280–2; T'ang, *op. cit.*, pp. 284–5; KMWH, *op. cit.*, Vol. XVIII, New York, 1945, p. 56; Schwartz, *op. cit.*, pp. 105–70.

17 Cf. Domes, *Revolution*, *op. cit.*, pp. 276–80.

18 *Ibid.*, p. 279.

19 Cf. Hsiao Tso-liang, *Power Relations Within the Chinese Communist Movement, 1930–1934, A Study of Documents*, Seattle, 1961.

20 Documents in *KMWH*, *op. cit.*, Vol. XXV, pp. 90–2, and Wu Hsiang-shuang (ed.), *Chung-kuo kung-ch'an-tang chih t'ou shih (Behind the Scenes of the CCP)*, Second ed., Taipei, 1962, pp. 156–8; cf. Charles B. McLane, *Soviet Policy and the Chinese Communists 1932–1946*, New York, 1958, pp. 54–6; Robert C. North, *Moscow and the Chinese Communists*, second ed., Stanford, Calif., 1968, pp. 166–8.

21 Descriptions of the 'Long March', in *Stories of the Long March*, Peking, 1959; Ch'en Chang-feng, *Mit dem Vorsitzenden Mao auf dem Langen Marsch*, Peking, 1960; *China – Eine Grossmacht im Wandel der Jahrhunderte*, (translation from the *Great Soviet Encyclopaedia*), Berlin (Ost), 1957, pp. 175–6; Wolf Schenke, *Neue Weltmacht China*, Hamburg, 1957, pp. 72–5. Schenke's account is essentially an uncritical reproduction of the standpoint of the CCP, with regard to this phase of Chinese history.

22 Dieter Heinzig, 'Mao Tse-tung's Weg zur Macht 1931 bis 1935 und die Otto-Braun-Memoiren', *Berichte des Bundesinstituts für Ostwissenschaftliche und Intrnationale Studien*, No. 52, 1970, pp. 28–33.

23 Cf. Domes, *Revolution*, *op. cit.*, pp. 674–6.

24 Cf. Lily Abegg, *Chinas Erneuerung – Der Raum als Waffe*, Frankfurt/Main, 1940; Freda Utley, *China at War*, London, 1939; Jack Belden, *China Shakes the World*, New York, 1949; Hollington K. Tong, *Chiang Kai-shek*, 2nd ed., Taipei, 1953, pp. 237–9; Gottfried-Karl Kindermann, *Der Ferne Osten in der Weltpolitik des industriellen Zeitalters* (dtv-Weltgeschichte des 20. Jahrhunderts, Bd. 6), München, 1970, pp. 384–6, 389–91.

25 Cf. Chalmers Johnson, *Peasant Nationalism and Communist Power – The Emergence of Revolutionary China 1937–1945*, Standord, Calif., 1962; Jacques

Guillermaz, *Histoire du parti communiste Chinois* (1921 to 1949), Paris, 1968, pp. 302–4.

26 Mao Tse-tung, 'Lun lien-ho-cheng-fu' (On Coalition Government), in *Chieh-fang jih-pao* (*Liberation Daily*), Yenan, May 2, 1945; reproduced in *Selected Works of Mao Tse-tung*, Peking, 1965, Vol. III, pp. 205–26.

27 *United States Relations with China, With Special Reference to the Period 1944–1949* (hereafter cited as *White Paper*), Washington 1949, pp. 127–255; Vidya Prakash Dutt, *East Asia – China, Korea, Japan 1947–1950*, Oxford University Press, 1958, pp. 197–201 (Wedemeyer Report); cf. Tang Tsou, *America's Failure in China, 1941–1950*, Chicago, 1963.

28 Carsun Chang, *Third Force in China*, New York, 1952, pp. 161–3; Tsou, *op. cit.*, p. 331.

29 *Ibid.*, p. 419.

30 Dutt, *op. cit.*, pp. 197–9.

31 Cf. Boyd Compton, *Mao's China – Party Reform Documents*, Seattle, 1952; also McLane, *op. cit.*, pp. 161–6.

32 Cf. Chang Kia-ngau, *The Inflationary Spiral – The Experience in China 1939–1950*, Cambridge, Mass., New York, London, 1958, p. 383.

33 Ho Ying-ch'in (Nationalist Minister of Military Affairs, 1929–46), in *Chung-yang jih-pao* (*Central Daily News*), Taipei, September 3, 1965.

34 Cf. Domes, *Revolution*, *op. cit.*, p. 685.

35 On the social and economic situation in China cf. Bernhard Grossmann, *Die wirtschaftliche Entwicklung der Volksrepublik China – Methoden und Probleme kommunistischer Entwicklungspolitik*, Stuttgart, 1960, pp. 40–4; Charles Bettelheim, Jacques Charrière, Hélène Marchisio, *La construction du socialisme en Chine*, Paris, 1965, pp. 12–13; Franz Schurmann, *Ideology and Organisation in Communist China*, second enlarged ed., Berkeley—Los Angeles, 1968, pp. 223–4; Richard Walker, *China unter dem Kommunismus – Die ersten fünf Jahre*, Stuttgart, 1956, pp. 127–8.

36 Jürgen Domes, *Politik und Herrschaft in Rotchina* (hereafter cited as Domes, *Rotchina*), Stuttgart, 1965, p. 31.

II. The Establishment of the Governmental System

During its first phase after coming to power the CCP aspired at co-operation with non-Communist parties and personalities; this was vindicated theoretically by Mao Tse-tung's essay of 1945, 'On Coalition Government'.[1] Pragamatic considerations, too, made such a co-operation seem at least temporarily inevitable. The Party needed former KMT members for the lower and middle levels of the administrative apparatus, and it still required the support of liberal and nationalist intellectuals to preserve or attract the following of intellectual youth. Above all, it needed the private entrepreneurs of the light industrial, coastal cities of East and North China to reconstruct the economy of the nation. In two speeches in May 1949, given before trade union representatives[2] and Party cadres in Tientsin,[3] Liu Shao-ch'i, Vice-Chairman of the CC, had stressed the importance of the 'national bour-geoisie' for national reconstruction. Guarantees of ownership and a disciplinary policy for industrial labour advocated by the Party aimed at winning the co-operation of entrepreneurs for the state. Even the structure of the provisional leadership organs of the state apparatus served to create the broadest possible political basis.

The Provisional Government of 1949

From the autumn of 1947 the CCP had gained the support of eight minor parties which were opposed to the KMT.[4]

1. The Revolutionary Committee of the KMT (*Chung-kuo Kuo-min-tang ko-ming wei-yüan-hui*: RKMT) was founded by leading op-ponents of Chiang Kai-shek within the ranks of the Nationalist Party during a congress held in Hong Kong from December 25, 1947, to January 1, 1948. It was presided over by the former regional warlord, General Li Chi-shen, and prominent members included Madame Sung Chi'ng-ling, the widow of Sun Yat-sen and Madame Ho Hsiang-ning, widow of the KMT leader Liao Chung-k'ai, assassinated in 1925. In 1949 more than fifty Nationalist generals who had gone over to the Communists during the last phase of the civil war had joined this group.

2. The China Democratic League (*Chung-kuo min-chu t'ung-meng-*

21

hui: DL) emerged from the 1941 'Alliance of Chinese Democratic Political Organisations' which was a combination of minor parties opposed to the one-party KMT state and its secret police. In 1944 the party changed its name to the Democratic League. Its president was Chang Lan, formerly the provincial governor of Szechwan. In 1946 the hardening conflict between the CCP and the KMT led to a shift to the left in the Party. The following year the Party was suppressed by the National Government. After a Party central had been re-established in Hong Kong in January 1948, the DL voted for co-operation with the CCP and active participation in the civil war.

3. The China Democratic National Construction Association (*Ch'üan-kuo min-chu chien-kuo hui:* DNCA) had been established on December 16, 1945, as a rallying point for KMT opponents among merchants and industrialists. Members of the industrial, technical intelligentsia soon began to join this party whose leaders, especially Huang Yen-p'ei, made overtures to the CCP after the spring of 1948.

4. The China Association for Promoting Democracy (*Min-chu ts'u-chin hui:* APD) was formed in Shanghai after the end of the war in 1945. It united teachers, lecturers and intellectuals engaged in adult education. Under the leadership of the former Nationalist Vice-Minister of Education, Ma Hsü-lun, it took up a stance of sharp opposition to the KMT, and in spring 1949 it declared its willingness to co-operate with the Communists.

Apart from these four more important groups of the non-Communist opposition, four minor associations were also in favour of an alliance with the Communists: the Chinese Peasants' and Workers' Democratic Party (*Nung-kung min-chu tang:* PWDP), a group of scientists led by Chang Po-chün; the China Chih Kung Tang (CKT) which had evolved from Overseas Chinese secret societies, led by Ch'en Ch'i-yü; the Chiu San Society (*Chiu-san hsüeh-hui:* CSS), originally a discussion circle of university teachers led by Professor Hsü Te-heng; and finally, the Taiwan Democratic Self-Government League (*T'ai-wan min-chu tzu-chih hui:* TDSL), established by left-wing participants in the uprising in Taiwan of February 28, 1947.[5] This was headed by Madame Hsieh Hsüeh-hung, who was at the same time a member of the CCP.

On May 1, 1948, the CC of the CCP had summoned these parties and groups, a number of professional organisations and leading non-Party personalities to send representatives to a 'Political Consultative Congress' to prepare the formation of a coalition government.[6] This summons was repeated and defined[7] by the Second Plenum of the Seventh CC which had met in Shihchiachuang (Hopei) from March 5 to March 13, 1949. Representatives of the CCP, the eight non-Communist parties, the PLA and a number of mass organisations as well as non-Party members convened a preparatory conference on June 15, 1949. It was decided to summon the First Plenary Session of the 'People's Political Consultative Conference' (*Chung-kuo jen-min cheng-chih hsieh-shang hui-i*) on September 21.[8] In this body the CCP was officially represented by only sixteen out of 584 delegates entitled to vote. The RKMT and DL each sent sixteen delegates, the DNCA and PWDP ten each, the APD eight, the CKT six and the CSS and TDSL five each.

Apart from these, 102 delegates came from the provisional regional governments already established, sixty from the PLA and 206 from sixteen different professional associations and mass organisations. Seventy-four 'specially-invited democratic personalities'[9] also took part in the conference. As most representatives of the regional governments and mass organisations as well as nearly all the PLA delegates were members of the CCP the Party had a conference majority in spite of its officially minor representation. On September 29, 1949 the 'People's Political Consultative Conference' adopted a 'Common Programme' which outlined the basic political guidelines of the new government's first phase.[10]

This programme defines the Chinese People's Republic as a state of the 'People's Democratic Dictatorship' which is described as the 'state power of the people's democratic united front' of workers, peasants, petty bourgeoisie and 'national bourgeoisie' under the leadership of the working class. This implies that the CCP regarded itself as the vanguard and the core of the working class and that it was to lead the new People's Republic. Nevertheless, the programme contained an explicit guarantee of the private ownership of the means of industrial production, and promised land reform to expand the peasants' private property through redistributing the land. On September 27 the conference passed a provisional constitution[11] which, according to its regulations, provided for the formation of the provisional government organs for the period of 'New Democracy'.[12]

The highest official decision-making body would be the Central People's Government Council in which Mao Tse-tung himself was Chairman. Designated as Vice-Chairmen were the Supreme Commander of the PLA, Marshal Chu Te, Liu Shao-ch'i and the Chairman of the People's Government of Tungpei, Kao Kang – all three members of the Poliburo of the CCP – Sun Yat-sen's widow and General Li Chi-shen of the RKMT as well as Chang Lan of the DL. Thirty-two of the Council's total of sixty-three members belonged to the CCP. Twenty-two were members of non-Communist United Front parties (thirteen from the RKMT) and nine were non-Party personalities. The Government Affairs Council under Chou En-lai was the central organisation of the administrative apparatus. The CCP provided ten out of the twenty-one members of its consultative and decision-making bodies, the non-Communist United Front Parties and non-Party personalities eleven. Sixteen of the thirty-one ministries were initially under Communists and fifteen under members of the other United Front parties. Shen Chün-ju, Vice-Chairman of the DL, became head of the Supreme Court, and the Communist General, Lo Jung-huan became the Procurator-General. In spite of a relatively strong representation of non-Communists in leading state organs, the CCP had already occupied the decisive positions. But in the Standing Committee of the People's Political Consultative Conference they remained, with eighteen out of fifty-one members, in a minority position. In this way they outwardly demonstrated the coalition character of the new leadership. However, they almost completely controlled the People's Revolutionary Military Council, which up to 1954 was, after the Party's Politburo, the most important decision-making centre and was also under Mao Tse-tung's chairmanship. Twenty-one of its twenty-eight members were Communists and seven were former Nationalist generals who had joined the RKMT. Until 1953–4 the military forces greatly participated in the country's regional administration, building up the governmental system. So the Military Council functioned simultaneously as a co-ordinating centre for regional leadership groups as well.

Regional Administration and the Influence of the PLA

At first the Communists had not enough personnel at their disposal to replace the residual officials at the provincial, district, and community levels by their own civil administration cadres. The five big PLA units of the last phase of the civil war, the 'Field Armies' (Yeh-chan-chün), were therefore entrusted with the building up of the regional administration in those regions which they had brought under the control of the CCP. Thus from 1948 to 1950 six large regions developed as intermediate administrative and control areas between the Central Government and the provincial administrations.

1. North China (Huapei), the provinces of which – Hopei, Shansi, Chahar, Pingyüan, and Suiyüan – as well as the autonomous cities of Peking and Tientsin had been placed under the direct control of the Central Government.[13]

2. North-east China (Tungpei), identical with former Manchuria, had already established a regional People's Government.

3. North-west China (Hsipei), with the provinces of Shensi, Kansu, Ninghsia, Tsinghai, and Sinkiang.

4. East China (Huatung), with the provinces of Shantung, Kiangsu, Anhui, Chekiang, Fukien, and the autonomous city of Shanghai.

5. Central-south China (Chung-nan), with the provinces of Honan, Hupei, Hunan, Kiangsi, Kwangtung, and Kwangsi.

6. South-west China (Hsinan), with the provinces of Szechuan, Kweichow, Yünnan, and Hsikang. The leadership of this region was entrusted with Chinese interests in Tibet as well.

The administrative committee of North China was headed by Liu Lan-t'ao who, since November 1949, had also been a member of the Government Affairs Council as Minister for North China affairs. Twenty-nine of the thirty-nine committee members belonged to the CCP. The North-east China People's Government in which the CCP held twenty-three of the thirty-five seats was headed by the Politburo member Kao Kang. The leadership of the other four regions was in the hands of 'Military and Administrative Committees' in which the influence of PLA members prevailed. The number of CCP members in these bodies diminished from the North to the South. This fact indicates that the influence of the Party south of the Yangtze was still relatively small. Here the CCP had gained military control in less than a year without having previously established its organisational bases in a long guerilla war. The leadership body of North-west China was headed by P'eng Te-huai, Commander-in-Chief of the First Field Army. Thirty-seven of its fifty-four members were Communists. Thirty-three of the sixty-four members of the East China 'Military and Administrative Committee' belonged to the CCP. The Chairman was the Political Commissar of the Third Field Army, Jao Shu-shih, and its Commander-in-Chief, Ch'en Yi, exercised considerable influence as Mayor of Shanghai. The Central-south region was headed by the Commander-in-Chief of the Fourth Field Army, Lin Piao, who was supported above all by the CC members Teng Tzu-hui, Yeh Chien-ying, and Li Hsien-nien. The CCP occupied forty-five of seventy-two seats on this committee. Finally, the South-west China 'Military and Administrative Committee' was placed under the chairmanship of the Commander-in-Chief of the Second Field Army, Liu Po-ch'eng, supported by his Chief of the General Staff, Ho Lung, and his Political Commissar, Teng Hsiao-p'ing. Forty-five of the seventy-eight members of this committee were Communists.[14]

The six regional administrations were largely autonomous in the areas of planning, economic organisation, education, and health service.[15] Considerable independence had been conceded in implementing the orders of the Central Government. During its early phase of rule, the new Chinese leadership thus basically compromised with the regional traditions of the country.

But the considerable independence of the regional administrations gave rise to certain dangers. Their leaders soon identified themselves with their respective regions more than with the Centre, and the re-

gions began to assume the character of semi-independent vice-king-
doms. Only gradually was the position of the Central Party and administrative apparatus strengthened in which Liu Shao-ch'i and Chou
En-lai, after Mao Tse-tung, steadily gained more influence. The initiation of truce negotiations in the Korean War, the growing stabilisation of the economy, and the successful settlement of the land reform
movement[16] provided the Centre from the autumn of 1952 onwards
with the opportunity to strengthen its position *vis-à-vis* the regional
leadership groups. Regional leaders were transferred to top-level
positions in Peking where they were deprived of their local power
bases and soon forced to identify themselves with the interests of the
Central apparatus. Thus Kao Kang was appointed Chairman of the
newly formed State Planning Commission in November 1952. This
measure initiated his later purge.[17] Teng Hsiao-p'ing had been nominated as Minister of Finance in September 1953; he was relieved in
June 1954 by Li Hsien-nien to take over a leading position in the
Central Party apparatus.

In summer 1954 the Centre had strengthened its influence to such a
degree that it could arrange the abolition of the six regions.[18] At the
same time the nine provinces of Tungpei were united to form three
major ones and the three provinces of Inner Mongolia formed an
autonomous region. The autonomous city of Tientsin was incorporated
in the province of Hopei. The twenty-one provinces, the five Autonomous Regions, and the two remaining autonomous cities of Peking
and Shanghai were now under the direct control of the Central Government. The building of a centralised administrative apparatus had been
completed, and the danger of a renewed dissolution of the country
into highly independent regions had for the time being been confined.
The general consolidation of the new governmental system 1953–4
created the preconditions for replacing the provisional government
organs by a long-term system of state control, the structure of which
was defined in the 1954 Constitution of the People's Republic of China.

The Constitution of 1954

Although the leadership bodies of the CCP from the very beginning
made the final decisions in Communist China, they endeavoured to
bring about at least the formal participation of the people in the
formation of the state apparatus and its leading organs at different
levels. In 1950 'People's Representative Conferences' had been convened in the communities (Hsiang) and counties (Hsien). At first
the representatives had been nominated, but since early 1952 they
had also been elected in open elections during the meetings. On December 8, 1950, the Central Government Administrative Council issued

statutes for these conferences which during that year had already been convened in 743 of the 2,185 counties.[19] In 1951 the numbers of counties having 'People's Representative Conferences' mounted to 2,143.[20] In 1952, 436 of the 2,185 counties already had leading organs elected by those conferences. So too did nineteen of the then thirty-six provinces of the country.[21]

The structure of the local and regional administrative machines was thus further consolidated, and at the same time the leadership prepared the convening of a National People's Congress (*Ch'üan-kuo jen-mint ai-pao ta-hui*; NPC). In December 1952 Prime Minister Chou En-lai announced that elections for the NPC would take place in summer 1953; the NPC would be convened in October of that year.[22] On January 13, 1953, the government formally proclaimed the election and nominated a committee to prepare the electoral law.[23] The electoral law of March 1, 1953,[24] provided for direct elections only to the People's Congresses of the communities (Hsiang). They were to be carried out in meetings where the candidates should be elected by 'show of hands or secretly' (paragraph fifty-five of the electoral law). The People's Congresses of the communities elected their own delegates to the People's Congresses of the counties, which in turn appointed the members of the provincial People's Congresses; out of the latter the NPC eventually emerged.

Single lists of candidates, which under CCP leadership encompassed representatives of the non-Communist, United-Front parties and mass organisations, as well as the system of indirect elections, facilitated Communist control over the election process. Furthermore, paragraph five of the electoral law denied *a priori* to former landlords and to all who had been denounced as 'Counter-revolutionaries' the right to vote and their eligibility for elections. Of the 1,226 delegates to the first NPC, 986 should represent the mainland provinces. In order to demonstrate the proletariat's leading role it was decided that in rural areas one delegate was to be elected for every 800,000 inhabitants, but in towns and industrial regions there would be one delegate for every 100,000 inhabitants. Apart from that, 150 delegates represented the national minorities, sixty the military forces, and thirty the Overseas Chinese communities.

Despite these regulations to secure control over the election process the election itself was not without difficulties; for in September 1953 the end of the election was postponed to March 1954,[25] and after further delays the first NPC could not be convened in Peking before September 15, 1954. It started its work by passing the constitution which came into force on September 20, 1954.[26] According to the preamble's wording the constitution was to be valid for the 'transitional period to socialism'. It describes the People's Republic of China as a 'people's democratic state led by the proletariat and based upon the alliance of workers and peasants'. In the People's Republic all 'power' was to belong to the 'people', and would be exercised according to the principle of democratic centralism.

The NPC is the 'highest organ of state power'. Representing the people, all power was theoretically to originate from it. The legislative, executive, judicial, controlling, and military organs of the state power did not possess any authority of their own. Their power was regarded as entrusted by the NPC. The NPC elects out of its members for a period of four years the head of state, the Chairman of the People's Republic of China (*Chung-hua jen-min kung-ho-kuo chu-hsi*), who simultaneously officiates as Chairman of the National Defence Council (*Kuo-fang wei-yüan-hui*). It further elects the Prime Minister of the State Council (*Kuo-wu yüan*), i.e. the Cabinet and the heads of the other state organs. Moreover, the NPC decides upon the economic plans, state budgets, and laws. However, as normally it is to be convened only once a year, its functions are exercised *de facto* by the Standing Committee of the NPC (*Ch'üan-kuo jen-min tai-piao ta-hui ch'ang-wu wei-yüan-hui*), composed of the heads of the Ministries and administrative committees in the centre of which the Prime Minister and his deputies form a kind of Inner Cabinet.

The People's Supreme Court (*Tsui-kao jen-min fa-yüan*) is also elected by the NPC according to the constitution. All courts of the country are subordinate to it. In 1955 it also acquired the exclusive right to confirm death sentences, but after 1957 this regulation was no longer observed. The highest prosecuting authority is the People's Supreme Procuratorate (*Tsui-kao jen-min chien-ch'a-yüan*). Its tasks include not only prosecution but the supervision of the courts and control of the administration. The constitution provides for all citizens the chance to put forward complaints to the Procuracy regarding irregularities in the administrative apparatus. It therefore resembles the 'Workers' and Peasants' Inspectorship' which in the Soviet Union had existed before the proclamation of the Stalin constitution in 1936. However, as inspection groups make tours throughout the country on behalf of the People's Supreme Procuracy, this organ also resembles the Censorate (*Tu-ch'a-yüan*) of Imperial China before 1911.

During the appointment of personnel to the new leading organs of the state apparatus, immediately after the proclamation of the constitution, the influence of the CCP was considerably reinforced in comparison with that in the provisional government organs.[27] The coalition character was relatively strongly preserved in the Standing Committee of the NPC. It was presided over by Liu Shao-ch'i-but among his thirteen deputies there were still eight non-Communists left. Among the total of seventy-nine members of this organ thirty,

nine Communists faced forty non-Communists. In contrast, Prime
Minister Chou En-lai and all ten vice-premiers of the State Council
belonged to the CCP. Among the total of forty-nine members of
this leading administrative organ, thirty-one were Communists and
only eighteen were non-Communists. The CCP dominated the National Defence Council too with sixty-eight out of ninety-five members. The office of Chairman of the People's Republic was occupied
by Mao Tse-tung for four years; Marshal Chu Te was elected as his
deputy. Mao's election as head of state and thereby *ex officio* Chairman
of the National Defence Council demonstrated that the three pillars
of the new government order – Party, state administration, and Army
– were merged into a unit at the top. Already the KMT government
system had been based upon the merging of these three pillars which in
China are described by the ideograms of the words *tang, cheng, chün*.[28]
However, in the KMT the importance of the Party organisation as a
leading political force had steadily decreased since about 1929. This
was evidenced by the fact that to a steadily growing degree promotions
within the hierarchies of Army and state administration preceded the
rise within the Party hierarchy of the Nationalist Party. Entry into
the leading organs of the Party in a way ratified the previous career
within the administration or the military forces.

However, from 1949 until the beginning of the crisis of the 'Cultural
Revolution' in autumn 1965, the Communists maintained the clear
dominance of their Party organisation over the administration and the
military. The central decision-making organ was the Politburo of the
Party which formally at least acted on behalf of the CC. Here the
channels of command of the state apparatus and of the PLA converged
personally too. For after appointments had been made to the new
state organs in autumn 1954, the Politburo included – apart from Mao
Tse-tung, who in addition to the office of head of state and Chairman
of the National Defence Council continued to be Chairman of the
CC and of the Military Affairs Committee – the deputy head of state,
Chu Te, the Chairman of the NPC, Liu Shao-ch'i, the Prime Minister,
Chou En-lai, the first vice-Premier, Ch'en Yün, P'eng Te-hai –
simultaneously the new Minister of Defence and Commander-in-Chief
of the PLA – and Teng Hsiao-p'ing.

Despite the centralised leadership of the three pillars of the political
system, the three parallel sub-systems were more and more evidently
separated after 1954 when the Communist régime was continuously
consolidated. The military withdrew from the regional leadership
organs and a process of professionalisation of the military top-level
leadership, which under the guidance of Marshal P'eng Te-huai was
concerned with military technical tasks, took place. At the same time
the systems of the civilian Party machine and the state administration

began to separate themselves from each other below their respective leadership levels. While the administration under the guidance of Chou and Ch'en Yün encompassed above all the experts in economic planning and the bureaucrats, the orthodox Leninist cadres under the influence of Liu, Teng, and P'eng Chen mainly gathered within the Party machine. The establishment of clearly defined parallel hierarchies did not yet lead to faction-building in the Party. But it caused the building of different kinds of careers and gradually led to a point where the Party's leading personalities evaluated differently the political processes because of their different organisational bases.

The CCP and the non-Communist United Front Parties, 1949-1957

Marxist theory as well as its Leninist version maintain that economic conditions, i.e. above all the means of production and the system of ownership, the so-called 'basis', determine social ideas and their corresponding institutions, the so-called 'superstructure'. Political theories, parties, state organs, laws, morals, art, philosophy, and religion reflect, according to Marxist–Leninist conceptions, the socio-economic conditions of the 'basis'. A political party therefore, strictly speaking, cannot but be the instrument of a class. By contrast, the CCP did, at least after the 'Cheng-feng Movement' of 1942, also theoretically regard itself as the political arm of the workers' and peasants' alliance, even if under the leadership of the proletariat.[29] However, as the new government order which resulted from the CCP's coming to power was understood as 'New Democracy', i.e. the 'united dictatorship of several revolutionary classes', the CCP represented the leading power – the industrial proletariat and the peasant masses. But formally at least the petty bourgeoisie and the 'national bourgeoisie' took part in the exercise of power as well.[30]

When the 1954 constitution came into force the phase of the 'national, bourgeois-democratic revolution' came to an end according to the Chinese Communist conception. The 'socialist transformation' of the country began in the socio-economic realm; it was characterised by agricultural collectivisation, the co-operativisation of trade and retail business, and the nationalisation of private industrial means of production. This transformation of the 'basis' would be reflected in the 'superstructure' by the re-education of the petty bourgeoisie and the 'national bourgeoisie' as members of socialist society. Until this re-education process had been completed they were not regarded as 'worthy' to be admitted to the Communist Party. The existence of non-Communist parties was therefore theoretically justified in the period of 'socialist transformation' as well. This followed from the task of these parties to contribute under the guidance of the CCP to the re-education of their adherents as members of socialist society. But a competitive relationship to the CCP was not permitted. The non-Communist United Front parties were clearly subordinate to the Communist leadership. So, in a joint resolution on the second Mayday celebration in 1950 they declared that:

> We, the democratic parties of China, are completely united under the leadership of the great Communist Party and its Chairman Mao Tse-tung to create an independent, free, democratic, united, and happy China.[31]

The detailed political programmes of all eight non-Communist parties were identical to the CCP programme until the spring of 1957. Some of their members were transferred to the CCP and they themselves had to accept Communists within their Party organisations. However, as the CCP even after 1949 feared the gathering of opposition forces in the United-Front parties, precautionary measures were taken which effectively prevented a strengthening of these groups. They were not allowed to enlist workers or peasants as members, whereas enlistment in the CCP was not restricted to specific social strata. Moreover, they were not permitted to establish youth and student organisations or cells in the military and state apparatus. The basic organisational unit was the municipality, and exceptionally the county. Every kind of merger was forbidden to them.[32] Only 9 per cent of the population remained to them for enlistment. Furthermore, specific social strata were allotted to the individual United-Front parties as enlistment domains. Thus the RKMT was restricted to former members of the KMT and to other non-Communist administrative officials. It further had the task to call upon KMT members in Taiwan to return to the 'socialist mother country'.[33] The DL turned to academicians, technicians, students of the petty bourgeoisie and the 'national bourgeoisie' as well as to Overseas Chinese. The DNCA enlisted merchants and industrialists and re-educated them. Members of the APD were teachers, lecturers, and artists. The PWDP encompassed engineers, technicians, and rural physicians. The CSS enlisted above all the natural scientists of the universities. The CKT worked among the Overseas Chinese communities, and the TDSL centred around CCP adherents who had escaped from Taiwan.

The strong restrictions on the work of non-Communist United Front parties, however, could not prevent internal criticisms of the Communist leadership becoming loud among their ranks after 1955. This criticism at first was not publicly evident. Only after Teng Hsiao-p'ing had proclaimed his thesis of 'long-term co-operation and mutual control of the parties'[34] in September 1956 at the first Plenum of the eighth Party Congress of the CCP, was it felt more strongly. Thus the non-Communist United-Front parties became, despite all kinds of restrictions, vehicles of a wave of opposition which initiated the first crisis of the Communist government system in China during the 'Hundred Flowers Movement'.[35]

References

1 Mao Tse-tung, *On Coalition Government, loc. cit.*

2 *I-chiu-ch'i-ling chung-kung nien-pao – 1970 Yearbook on Chinese Communism*, ed. by Institute for the Study of Chinese Communist Problems, Taipei, 1970, Vol. II, Ch. VII, pp. 72–9.

3 *Ibid.*, pp. 80–93, in particular pp. 81–3. These speeches were used as evidence for Liu Shao-ch'i's anti-Party behaviour in the Cultural Revolution. However, the decisions of the Second Plenum of the Seventh CC in Shihchiachuang in March 1949 make clear that Liu only advocated the official Party line in his two speeches of May 1949. With certainty Mao Tse-tung had also supported this 'line'.

4 For the history of the non-Communist United-Front parties cf. Lyman P. Van Slyke, *Enemies and Friends – The United Front in Chinese Communist History*, Stanford, Calif., 1967, pp. 208–10; also Helga Peppel, 'Die nichtkommunistischen Einheitsparteien', in Domes, *Rotchina, op. cit.*, pp. 75–8.

5 Cf. White Paper, *op. cit.*, pp. 307–9, 923–8.

6 *Chieh-fang jih-pao (Liberation Daily)*, Yenan, May 1, 1948.

7 *Jen-min jih-pao (People's Daily*, hereafter cited as *JMJP)*, September 15, 1956, cf. also Parris H. Chang, 'Research Notes on the Changing Loci of Decision in the CCP', in *The China Quarterly*, (hereafter cited as *CQ)*, No. 44, October–December 1970, p. 181; also Chin Ssu-k'ai, 'The Party', in Union Research Institute (hereafter cited as *URI)*, *Communist China 1949–1959*, Vol. I, Hong Kong, 1961, p. 11.

8 *JMJP*, June 15, 1949.

9 Peter S. H. Tang and Joan M. Maloney, *Communist China: The Domestic Scene, 1949–1967* (hereafter cited as Tang-Maloney), South Orange, N.J., 1967, p. 241; also Ch'in Ti, 'Political and Legal Work', in URI, *Communist China 1949–1959, op. cit.*, p. 59; also Max Perleberg, *Who's Who in Modern China*, Hong Kong, 1954, pp. 292–5.

10 *JMJP*, September 29, 1949, English translation in Theodore H. C. Chen, *The Chinese Communist Régime – Documents and Commentary*, London, and New York, 1967, document II, pp. 34–45.

11 *JMJP*, September 28, 1949, English translation in Chen, *op. cit.*, document III, pp. 46–51.

12 Lists of names in Perleberg, *op. cit.*, pp. 300–2, 327–32; also in URI, *Who's Who in Communist China*, Vol. II, Hong Kong, 1970, pp. 809–12.

13 *JMJP*, October 31, 1949.

14 List of members of the regional leadership groups in Perleberg, *op. cit.*, pp. 337–59.

15 *China Digest*, Hong Kong, December 14, 1949, cited in Tang-Maloney, *op. cit.*, p. 258.

16 See below pp. 36–8.

17 See below pp. 52–3.

18 *New China News Agency* (hereafter cited as *NCNA*), Peking, June 19, 1954.

19 Cf. *China News Analysis* (hereafter cited as *CNA*), Hong Kong, No. 8, October 16, 1953.

20 *JMJP*, October 2, 1951.

21 *JMJP*, September 22, 1952.

22 *JMJP*, December 24, 1952.

23 *JMJP*, January 14, 1953.

24 English translation in Chen, *op. cit.*, pp. 65–75; cf. also *CNA*, No. 1, August 25, 1953.

25 *JMJP*, September 19, 1953.

26 *Chung-hua jen-min kung-ho-kuo hsien-fa* (*The Constitution of the Chinese People's Republic*), Peking, 1954, English translation in Chen, *op. cit.*, pp. 75–92; cf. also Domes, *Rotchina*, *op. cit.*, pp. 46–57.

27 *JMJP*, September 27, 28, 29, 1954. Lists of names also in URI, *Who's Who*, *op. cit.*, pp. 813–17.

28 Domes, *Revolution*, *op. cit.*, pp. 476–89.

29 Cf. Mao Tse-tung, 'On Coalition Government', *loc. cit.*, also BSF, *op. cit.*, p. 353.

30 Cf. Mao Tse-tung, 'On New Democracy', in *Selected Works of Mao Tse-tung*, Peking, 1965, Vol. II, pp. 347–63; also BSF, *op. cit.*, pp. 199–201.

31 *Kuang-ming jih-pao* (hereafter cited as *KMJP*), May 1, 1950.

32 Peter S. H. Tang, *Communist China Today – Domestic and Foreign Policies*, New York, 1957, Vol. I, p. 147. On the limitation of membership also cf. *NCNA*, Peking, May 10, 1957.

33 Cf. Tang-Maloney, *op. cit.*, pp. 205–6.

34 Cf. Teng Hsiao-p'ing, 'Report on the Revision of the Constitution of the Communist Party of China', in *The Eighth National Congress of the Communist Party of China*, Vol. I, Documents, Peking, 1956, pp. 186–7.

35 See below, pp. 58–62.

III. The Road to a Socialist Society

In order to change Chinese society towards the Communist social order, which is understood by the Communists as the necessary goal of human development, Mao and his colleagues developed specific methods out of Leninist conceptions which henceforth determined the special character of Chinese Communism, its successes and failures. These methods – above all the system of mass movements – stress the change of social consciousness, i.e. the creation of new men for a 'New Society', more than the change of reality, i.e. the mode of production. The notion of the Great Number, the masses (*Ch'ün-chung*), which was relevant in Chinese political thought of the nineteenth and twentieth centuries for non-Communists too, played a role at least as decisive as that of élitist cadre (*Kan-pu*) formation.

The System of Mass Movements[1]

In comparison with other Communist countries, the 'mass movement' (*Ch'ün-chung yün-tung*) as an instrument of political communication from above to below is particularly representative of Chinese Communist rule. This phenomenon is of the utmost importance in understanding the nature and dynamics of the governmental system of the CCP. The theoretical foundation of the mass movement as a means of mediation between the will of the rulers and the people presupposes that nothing is impossible for the masses quantitatively understood as a collective subject, if their power is concentrated by a Party of 'correct' thought and action. This conception results out of Mao Tse-tungs' more romantic than 'scientific-socialist' conviction of the great strength which the masses are capable of developing in the interest of their supposed or actual happiness.[2]

If one is convinced that one belongs to an élite of socially critical and historically conscious prophets who have recognised the true needs of the masses, these needs have to be made inherent in the masses. Therefore, the theoretically underlying 'will of the masses' has to be projected for each single important action of the leadership group. The leaders need the legitimation from below. Where there is a lack of it, it has to be created. So the 'people's will' has to be articulated

34

by the masses and within the masses. That is what the Chinese Communists call the 'mass line' (*Ch'ün-chung lu-hsien*).

Mao's mass line theory required that the ruling élite is close to the people, that it is continuously informed about the people's will and that it transforms this will into concrete actions. These actions in turn require acclamation. They demand a positive attitudinal response:

> From the masses – back to the masses! This means: take the ideas of the masses (scattered and unsystematic ideas) and concentrate them (through study turn them into concentrated and systematic ideas), then go to the masses and propagate and explain these ideals until the masses embrace them as their own.[3]

However, this presented the Chinese leadership with a serious problem. What should be done if the 'will of the masses' did not articulate itself in the way that was demanded by the top level? How could they invoke before their own people and before the world the impression that the people consented to them and at the same time mobilise the people to realise their own conceptions? The CCP tried to resolve this problem by means of the system of mass movements. Certainly, the numerous, successive mass movements after 1950 did differ from each other in many respects, but common factors can be detected too which indicate a uniform, basic scheme. Mass movements were usually initiated by the top-level leadership.[4] The plan would be announced to reliable Party Cadres at Central and Regional Work Conferences, and was sometimes subjected to cadre criticisms and then modified. After that the first phase of the mass movement would start. The Party cadres and mass organisations were held to provoke the 'people's will'. Most important instruments of this phase were readers' letters, the contents of which agreed with the intentions of the leaders, and 'spontaneous' rallies at which the demands of the readers' letters to the newspapers would be repeated.[5]

When these demands had been repeated sufficiently in a number of provinces the leadership 'could not but take them into consideration'. What the inner leadership core had already decided upon in principle, was now (in the second phase of the movement) officially discussed by the leading organs of the Party and the state. It was clarified by detailed resolutions or acts of law, and the 'systematic people's will' was made public. Now followed the third and most important phase of the campaign. The 'mass movement' spread to the whole country. The Party leaders informed the CCP cadres through the organisational channels of the CC and the mass organisations through the channels of the United-Front committee of the CC about their intentions. All were used as 'transmission belts' between the leadership and the people. Newspapers, journals, broadcasting, films, theatre, and music groups served the campaign. Mass rallies, lasting many hours and sometimes even days, took place in the districts of the big cities, in small towns, market places, and in the hundreds of thousands of Chinese villages. Thousands of orators called upon the people to act according to the leaders' ideas. Any reluctance was softened by the presence of the security organs. But by the mid-1950s it was no longer necessary always to exert direct physical force. The threat to use it was often sufficient to break any resistance.

Until 1965 the leadership always transmitted its decisions to the people in this way. And so the domestic political history of Chinese Communism might be described as a history of mass movements. This is true particularly of all those measures which consolidated the government system after the seizure of power and which initiated the 'socialist transformation' of China.

The Land Reform Movement, 1950–1953[6]

The slogan 'The land to the Tiller' (*Keng-che yu ch'i t'ien*) (taken over from the first KMT leader Dr. Sun Yat-sen) proved an effective propaganda weapon of the CCP during the civil war. In the South Chinese Soviet by the early 1930s the Communists had started to resolve the problems of equal land distribution among the peasants. After 1947 they again began to rearrange the agricultural system of ownership in the areas they controlled. They dispossessed the land-lords and redistributed the acquired land to small peasants, tenants, and rural workers. The CCP thereby satisfied a large part of the land-hungry population in rural China and won their support. Thus the difficult, and in some regions catastrophic, situation of the small owners, tenants, and rural workers contributed considerably to the Communist victory in the civil war. Certainly, the statements of the CCP and of some of its protagonists in Western countries regarding the misery of the Chinese rural population before 1949 will have to be modified by careful research,[7] but the economic difficulties of the Chinese peasants, especially during the Sino-Japanese war and the civil war that followed, were undoubtedly considerable. Natural catastrophes, the effects of the war, and overtaxation often unbearably oppressed the small owners and tenants. Average rents amounted to 50 per cent of the main harvest,[8] and private loans were only obtainable at prohibitive interest – usually more than 50 per cent. After conquering the Chinese mainland the CCP immediately began conquering the Chinese mainland the CCP immediately began an all-embracing redistribution of the ownership of agricultural land. The Party pursued three aims:

1. The land of the landlords and richer peasants should be distributed among the poor peasants such that roughly equal shares of property would be created in the villages. Land reform was still regarded as part of the 'national, bourgeois-democratic revolution'. At first it was only concerned with achieving a more just distribution of private property.

2. In order to establish a more secure control over the villages, the potential forces of resistance had to be dispersed, and if necessary to be liquidated physically.

3. This movement served the mobilisation and organisation of the Chinese peasant masses.

The 'land reform law', decreed by the Central Government Administrative Council, provided the foundations for the movement.[9] By this law the rural population had been classified into five categories according to which differed from province to province and were not uniform at all: landlords, rich peasants, middle peasants, poor peasants, tenants, and rural workers.[10] This classification was introduced in every village at the beginning of the campaign, and often artificial inventions were arrived at because rigid distinctions of social groups only rarely existed within the Chinese villages before the Communists seized power. However, the classification fulfilled the purpose envisaged by the CCP leadership: potential forces of resistance could be isolated from the mass of the village population, ruined economically, and physically liquidated. General Teng Tzu-hui who had been commissioned with the task of land reform in the Central-South region openly announced this aim:

> The land reform is the most ruthless phase of struggle against the feudal system; involving as it does military, intellectual and political tactics. To set the land reform apart from the whole and simply to regard it as a technical affair, namely the distribution of land, would be a grave political mistake; for the feudal system can be removed only by the complete extermination of the landlord class through a number of military, intellectual, and economic confrontations.[11]

The 'struggle rally' (*Tou-cheng hui-i*)[12] served as the most essential mechanism for the land reform campaign as well as for most of the other mass movements following it. The Party sent specially trained agitators to the countryside to prepare the campaign in the villages: more than 270,000 were sent to the East China region alone.[13] At first the tenants and small peasants were called on to unite in 'Peasant Associations' (*Nung-hui*) for the struggle against the old rural upper strata, and were often provided with arms by the PLA to 'punish' the landlords and rich peasants. As soon as the desired mood had been achieved in a village the real 'struggle' began. The mobilised – and by now often fanatic – tenants and rural workers gathered together; their militia arrested those who were to be 'punished' and brought them before a 'People's Court' which was the 'struggle rally' itself. The landlords and rich peasants were tortured, and forced to surrender their property and repay the rents of past years, sometimes as far back as the year 1900. Finally, their whole landed property was confiscated. Many of them were put to death and others committed suicide. Cautious estimates put the dead at no less than five million in the course of the land reform movement.[14] The law of June 30, 1950, prohibited the use of force, but in the course of the campaign it was soon vindicated. The agricultural commissar of the province of Kwangtung declared:

> If we do not allow the peasants to beat and kill the landlords it is difficult to stir them up. Without mobilising them it is not possible to stamp out the exploitation of a thousand years by the landlords. Once the peasants have been stirred up the government cannot and should not check them.[15]

Doubtless bitterness and hatred against the landlords had mounted in the countryside, but in very many cases the peasants initially refused to take part in acts of violence and commandos from other villages had to start the terror.

By early 1953 the land reform movement – in all but a few areas inhabited by national minorities – had essentially come to an end. The landlords had been completely expropriated. The rich peasants had lost part of their property. The confiscated land was distributed equally among the small peasants, tenants, and rural workers as private property. 46·6 million hectares – nearly 40 per cent of the cultivated land changed ownership.[16] This is a high percentage, yet it still makes doubtful former Communist statements alleging that 80 per cent of the cultivated land was owned by landlords.

The land reform movement certainly achieved a redistribution of landed property, but it did not solve the problems of Chinese agriculture. The new owners tended to be content with what had been accomplished and to devote themselves exclusively to their own production in order to enhance their living conditions. Even increased land taxes and strong pressure from the control organs could not persuade them to decrease their consumption in the interest of acquiring investment capital for industrial construction.[17] Therefore soon after the end of the campaign the leadership was forced to initiate agricultural collectivisation in the interest of 'socialist transformation'. The necessary strengthening of Party control over the people was promoted by a basic reform of the family law as well.

Marriage Reform, 1950–1952

The clan system of the Chinese only very rarely functioned as a cohabitation unit among the mass of the population. It was more an organ for mutual aid, and the Communists could not but consider it as an important potential residual source of resistance, which would hinder their efforts at mobilising and changing the consciousness of the people. The Marriage Law of May 1, 1950, loosened family links.[18] It was intended not only to secure the emancipation of women, but to give the state the opportunity of intervening directly in the family. It prohibited marriages arranged by parents, thereby contributing considerably to the liberation of the younger generation. The dissolution of forced marriages already in existence was facilitated by generous divorce regulations. The civil law proclaimed by the KMT in the early 1930s had forbidden polygamy, and now it was decided that second wives and concubines, who under Nationalist law had been permitted to remain, were to leave their husbands' houses. The Marriage Reform, like the Land Reform, was combined with a mass movement.[19] A regulation of the Government Affairs council of September 26, 1951, provided 'people's courts' for 'tyrannical husbands' and decided to use the same technique for Marriage Reform as had been used for Land Reform.[20] Initially the campaign led to a remarkable increase in the number of divorces: in 1950 there were 186,000; in 1951 409,000; and in the first half of 1952 alone 396,000. But the campaign also caused a good deal of injustice and suffering. In many cases older concubines driven out of their husbands' homes became destitute, and local Party cadres often used the new law to acquire wives, who, because they were already married, were forced into divorces with the help of 'struggle rallies'. This led to a mounting number of suicides among women. In the first half of 1952 in the province of Chekiang alone there were 438 such suicides; in Fukien in 1950–1 there was a monthly average of fifty, and in 1952 a monthly average of eighty-eight. In Shantung the press recorded 1,245 cases of suicide for 1950 and in the Central-South region there were more than 10,000 in the same year.[21] In some places women forced into divorce from their erstwhile husbands and into marriage with Party cadres fled and returned to their former husbands. Such behaviour was then condemned as 'adulterous' by the 'People's Courts'.[22]

In spite of some success in the emancipation of women, the mass of the population participated only hesitantly in the campaign. As late as the summer of 1952 the Minister of Justice, Mme. Shih Liang (DL), announced that up to then the Marriage Reform had been carried out in only three of the then 2,086 counties.[23] In the autumn of 1953 the Secretary-General of the Committee for the Implementation of the Marriage Reform, Liu Ching-fan, reported that only 15 per cent of the population had accepted the Marriage Law and family reform, 60 per cent hesitated and 25 per cent had not been touched at all by the campaign.[24]

Malpractices which occurred in the course of the campaign were strongly criticised by the leadership, and after the spring of 1953 the implementation of the new Marriage Law ceased to be emphasised. This was the first time that the top-level leadership was undercut by passive opposition from the people to the implementation of new policies. This therefore became the first campaign which achieved only partial success.

Collectivisation and Nationalisation

The successes of the Land Reform movement and a number of rectification campaigns conducted from 1951 to 1953,[25] and the partial success of the Marriage Reform movement, encouraged Mao and his colleagues in the summer of 1953 to initiate the next phase of the revolutionary process: the transformation of the 'national, bourgeois democratic revolution' to the 'proletarian, socialist revolution'. From June to September 1953 the guidelines of the impending political turning-point were discussed at two 'National Work Conferences' (*Ch'üan-kuo kung-tso hui-i*) on economic and organisational questions,[26] and on October 1, 1953, the Party leader announced the new 'General Line of Socialist Transformation'.[27] From now on private enterprise in agriculture as well as in industry and commerce was to be curbed step by step and replaced by collective and state ownership. Simultaneously in the political sphere there was a further limitation on the room for manoeuvre which the non-Communist, United-Front parties had retained, and the influence of the Party leaders on the state apparatus grew. Liu Shao-ch'i removed any doubts which might have existed regarding China's declared course. At the fourth plenum of the seventh CC in February 1954 in Peking, he declared that the end of the 'New Democratic Revolution' had come. Now the 'struggle for socialist transformation'[28] would begin.

Only a few weeks after the proclamation of the new general line, the collectivisation of agriculture began.[29] It had been preceded by lengthy disputes within the Party leadership during which Liu Shao-ch'i had put himself in opposition to Mao. As early as May 7, 1951, at a work conference on propaganda he had taken up a position against 'agrarian socialism' which demanded agricultural collectivisation before its mechanisation.[30] During the summer of 1953 it became clear that the land reform could neither guarantee food supplies to the cities nor provide sufficient investment capital for industrial reconstruction. Several provinces were deficient in vegetables, tea and food oil.[31] The peasants preferred to sell their harvest surplus not to the state's new purchasing organs, but to private firms, which the leadership regarded as 'speculators'. Tax evasion was widespread in the villages.[32] Thus the initiation of collectivisation appeared advisable to the CCP not only for theoretical reasons, but also for pragmatic reasons, as was recognised by the entire leadership in the late summer of 1953. In spite of Maoist accusations made during the Cultural Revolution, all the available evidence shows that at this point Liu too had abandoned his resistance to the initiation of collectivisation prior to the successful mechanisation of agriculture and supported Mao's drive for collectivisation.[33]

'Mutual aid teams' (Hu-chu tsu), whose members cultivated the fields jointly and acquired agricultural tools and machines jointly, had created the preliminary preconditions for establishing collectives. By December 1951, 43 per cent of peasant households had already been merged into these teams. That year, on the basis of the teams, the first 'Agricultural Production Co-operatives' (Nung-yeh sheng-ch'an ho-tso-she: APC) had also been established; tools and machines became collective property, but agricultural land remained private property. In March 1953 there were already more than 14,000 such 'lower-type' APCs whose experimental introduction had been emphatically recommended by the CCP Politburo on December 15, 1951, in a 'Resolution on Mutual Aid and Co-operatives for Agricultural Production'.[34] At the same time, 58 per cent of all peasant households had been merged in 'Mutual aid teams'. On the basis of these forms of agricultural organisation the massive collectivisation campaign began in the whole country on December 16, 1953, once again taking the form of a mass movement.[35] It was implemented in two stages in the course of three and a half years.

At first the establishment of 'lower-type' APCs continued, members receiving their shares according to a mixed system which took into account on the one hand the landed property brought in and on the other the work rate of the individual. There then followed the second stage, the establishment of 'fully socialist APCs', in which the members were paid only according to their work rate and retained nothing but their houses and vegetable gardens. All tools, machines and fields were transferred to collective ownership.

The quantitive development of the collectivisation campaign from 1950 to 1957 is demonstrated in Table III/1 below. It shows clearly the change which occurred in the course of the collectivisation campaign in the year 1955. At a conference of provincial Party leaders which opened on July 31 of that year in Peking, Mao pressed with great

Table III/1

DEVELOPMENT OF APCs IN THE
PEOPLE'S REPUBLIC OF CHINA, 1950-1957[36]

	APCs 'lower-type'		'Fully socialist APCs'		Total	
Year	Number	Households	Number	Households	Number	Households
1950	18	178	1	32	19	210
1952	3,634	57,000	10	1,800	3,644	58,800
1953	15,053	273,000	15	2,100	15,068	275,100
1954	114,165	285,000	201	12,000	114,366	297,000
1955	633,213	16,881,000	529	40,000	633,742	16,921,000
1956	210,000	10,407,000	540,000	107,422,000	750,000	117,829,000
1957	84,032	4,520,000	668,081	114,360,000	762,113	118,800,000

energy for the acceleration of the campaign and demanded that by spring 1957 four-fifths of all peasant households be merged into 'lower type' APCs.[37] The massive use of the entire organisational and propaganda apparatus of the Party and of the mass organisations led to a 'socialist high tide' in Chinese agriculture after the autumn of 1955.[38] In October the Sixth Plenum of the Seventh CC decided to transform the residual 'lower-type' APCs into 'fully socialist' collectives and to accelerate the establishment of new co-operatives of both types.[39] Although there was peasant resistance in some places, the campaign as a whole proceeded faster and more smoothly than had the collectivisation of agriculture in the Soviet Union in 1929–30. This was due above all to the skill with which the CCP adapted to the campaign its method of mass movements, combining persuasion and coercion.[40] Certainly considerable organisational and financial problems arose in the new collectives,[41] but the quantitive progress of the movement was not impaired thereby. Thus in spring 1957, after three and a half years, not less than 93·3 per cent of the Chinese rural population had been organised in 'fully socialist APCs';[42] the rest followed in the autumn of the same year. Initially, in 1956, collectivisation resulted in a noticeable decrease in agricultural production. However, this was balanced in 1957 by the grain and potato harvest of 185 million tons, which for the first time exceeded the average production of the years 1931 to 1937 which had been recorded as 171 million tons,[43] and thereby reached the highest ever recorded production level in this century. Thus in less than four years the CCP had successfully completed the collectivisation of Chinese agriculture.

Parallel to collectivisation, a campaign in 1955–6 transformed private ownership of the industrial means of production at first into joint state–private property and later into state property. As early as 1949 to 1952 production by enterprises in private hands and by private handicraft firms fell from 62·7 per cent to 42 per cent of China's total commercial production. In 1954 not less than 71 per cent of commercial production originated from state, co-operative and joint state–private firms and only 29 per cent from private enterprise.[44] Joint state–private firms had come into existence through the participation of the Government in firms with 49–50 per cent, according to its own estimates, of the private investment and through the appointment of of a reliable cadre as director with the same rights as the former owner. At the end of 1955 these semi-state enterprises were ready for the 'transition to socialism'. At a conference of the executive committees of the All-Chinese Association of Chambers of Industry and Commerce on October 29 of that year, Mao himself gave the signal for a movement to transfer joint enterprises to state ownership.[45] In the following months groups of agitators induced entrepreneurs to cede their property to the state in return for compensation which was to be paid within five years and which was, on the whole, generously calculated. If only because their expertise could not be forgone, most of the entrepreneurs were appointed directors in their former firms, and until 1962 they were to receive, apart from their compensation, shares from the dividends of the respective companies. By November or December 1955 the movement, which was also extended to include retail shops, restaurants and handicraft firms, had already made rapid progress.[46] In the realm of industry, the process of nationalisation was completed in January 1956.[47] The private entrepreneurs, who as early as 1952–3 had been intimidated by heavy pressure and severe punishment in the 'Five Anti Movement' (*Wu-fan yün-tung*) – directed against 'tax evasion, fraud, bribery, production espionage, theft of state property' – offered hardly any resistance to the nationalisation of their firms. The combining of the last retailers and craftsmen in state controlled co-operatives, which had been implemented in 1956–7, was achieved without great difficulties.

The following data give information about the development of the 'socialist transformation' of industry from 1949 to 1956.

Table III/2

THE PRODUCTION OF INDUSTRIAL SECTORS AS A PERCENTAGE OF THE VALUE OF INDUSTRIAL PRODUCTION, 1949–1956[48]

Year	State	Joint state–private	Private
1949	34·7	9·5	55·8
1950	45·3	17·8	36·9
1953	57·5	28·5	14·0
1956	67·5	32·5	—

Thus, in only a few years, the CCP had achieved the transition of agriculture, industry, commerce and handicraft to collective or state ownership. Despite recurrent resistance and even setbacks, the process of 'socialist transformation' as a whole came about rather smoothly up to 1957. The preconditions required by Marxist–Leninist theory to reach a socialist social order were established. An evaluation within the confines of this theory must regard this fact as a remarkable success.

References

1 On the theory and practice of the mass movements cf. James R. Townsend *Political Participation in Communist China*, Berkeley and Los Angeles, 1967 pp. 65–102; John Wilson Lewis (ed.), *Major Doctrines of Communist China* New York, 1964, pp. 182–5; Schurmann, *op. cit.*, pp. 111–13, 125–8; Tang-Maloney, *op. cit.*, pp. 483–4, 489–95; also Domes, *Rotchina, op. cit.*, pp. 110–17.

2 Cf. Mao Tse-tung, 'Hunan nung-min yün-tung k'ao-ch'a pao-kao' (Report on an Investigation of the Peasant Movement in Hunan), original version in *Hsiang-tao chou-pao*, March 20, 1927, also in *Kung-fei huo-kuo shih-liao hui-pien* (*Collection of Historical Materials on the Communist Attack on Our Country*), Documents of the Nationalist Information Service, Vol. I, Taipei, no date; cf. also *Hung-ch'i* (*Red Flag*, hereafter cited as *HC*), No. 10, 1958; also cited in Stuart R. Schram, *The Political Thought of Mao Tse-tung*, New York, 1963, p. 253.

3 Mao Tse-tung, 'Some Questions Concerning Methods of Leadership', *Selected Readings from the Works of Mao Tse-tung*, Peking, 1967, pp. 234–9; cf. also the preamble of the Party constitution in P. S. H. Tang, *Communist China Today, op. cit.*, Vol. II, p. 114.

4 For the decisions of the conferences of the CCP leadership concerning new campaigns cf. Table of Conferences, in Chang, *loc. cit.*, pp. 181–4.

5 Lee Wen-yi, *The Press in China*, Hong Kong, no date, p. 7.

6 Cf. also Schurmann, *op. cit.*, pp. 431–7; Walker, *op. cit.*, pp. 153–79; Chao Kuo-chün, *Agrarian Policy of the Chinese Communist Party, 1921–1959*, Bombay, Calcutta, London, 1960, pp. 147–281; Jean Monsterleet, *L'Empire de Mao Tze-toung*, Lille, 1955, pp. 8–45; Yang Mo-wen, 'Socialist Transformation of Agriculture in Communist China', in URI, *Communist China, op. cit.*, pp. 149–52; Ezra Vogel, 'Land Reform in Kwangtung, 1951–1963, Central Control and Localism', in *CQ*, No. 38, April–June 1969, pp. 27–62.

7 Cf. in particular John L. Buck, *Chinese Farm Economy*, Chicago, 1930; also Ch'en Han-sheng, *Landlord and Peasant in China*, Shanghai, 1936, and Ch'en, *Agrarian Problems in Southernmost China*, Shanghai, 1936; Chuikai Ming, 'Agriculture', in McNair, *China*, Los Angeles, 1951, pp. 473–4; Wolfgang Wilmanns, *Die Landwirtschaft Chinas*, Berlin, 1938; Gottfried-Karl Kindermann, *Kulturen im Umbruch*, Freiburg, 1962, pp. 84–91; cf. also Domes, *Revolution, op. cit.*, pp. 46–7.

8 Cf. Kindermann, *Kulturen, op. cit.,* pp. 90–1; also Jean Monsterleet, *Wird der gelbe Mann rot?,* Freiburg, 1956, p. 22; also Ch'en Po-ta, *A Study of Land Rent in Pre-Liberation China,* 2nd. ed. Peking, 1958.

9 'The Agrarian Reform Law of the People's Republic of China', in Chen, *op. cit.,* document XX, pp. 196–303; cf. also P. Destombes, 'La réforme agraire en Chine', in *Bulletin de la Société des Missions Etrangères de Paris,* Hong Kong, July 1952, pp. 439–56; Werner Klatt, 'Chinese Agriculture as a Model for Asian Countries', in C. F. Szcepanik (ed.), *Symposion on Economic and Social Problems of the Far East,* Hong Kong, 1963.

10 'How to Analyse Class Status in the Countryside', in Chen, *op. cit.,* document twenty-one, pp. 204–5; cf. also Perleberg, *op. cit.,* pp. 379–80.

11 *JMJP,* December 28, 1950.

12 An extremely impressive description of such a meeting is given by Hsiao Ch'ien, *How the Tillers Win Back Their Land,* Peking, 1951, pp. 72–80; also Chen, *op. cit.,* document XXIV, pp. 210–15.

13 Chieh-fang jih-pao, Shanghai, January 17, 1950.

14 Cf. Kim, 'La réforme agraire en Chine', in *Quatrième Internationale,* No. 6, October 1953, pp. 30–2; also Henry J. Lethbridge, *The Peasant and the Communes,* Hong Kong, 1963, p. 198.

15 Cited in Kim, *loc. cit.,* p. 35.

16 *JMJP,* September 28, 1953, cf. also Yang, *loc. cit.,* p. 151; also Werner Klatt (ed.), *The Chinese Model,* Hong Kong, 1965, p. 98.

17 Cf. Thomas P. Bernstein, 'Problem of Village Leadership after Land Reform', in *CQ,* No. 36, October–December 1968, pp. 1–22.

18 *JMJP,* May 1, 1950; English translation in Chen, *op. cit.,* document thirty-three, pp. 270–4.

19 Cf. *CNA,* No. 5, September 25, 1953; Tang-Maloney, *op. cit.,* pp. 499–501; Christopher Lucs, *Women of China,* Hong Kong, 1965, pp. 43–87.

20 *JMJP,* September 29, 1951.

21 *JMJP,* March 20, 1953.

22 40,000 people took part in the accusation meetings in Chungking in August 1952. Cf. *Hsin-hua jih-pao (New China Daily),* Chungking, August 14, 1952.

23 *JMJP,* July 4, 1952.

24 *JMJP,* November 19, 1953.

25 See above pp. 36–8.

26 *I-chiu-wu-ch'i nien jen-min shou-ts'e (People's Handbook 1957),* (hereafter cited as *JMST),* Peking, 1957, pp. 31, 33.

27 *JMJP,* October 2, 1953.

28 *CNA,* No. 26, March 5, 1954.

29 Cf. Schurmann, *op. cit.,* pp. 442–64; also Tang-Maloney, *op. cit.,* pp. 341–53; also Yang, *loc. cit.,* pp. 152–76; also Klatt, *op. cit.,* pp. 99–100, also *CNA,* No. 7, October 9, 1953, No. 23, December 12, 1954.

30 *Nung-yeh chi-hsieh chi-shu (Agricultural Mechanics),* Peking, No. 9, 1968; English translation, in *Selections from China Mainland Magazines,* (hereafter cited as *SCMM),* Hong Kong, No. 633, November 4, 1968.

31 *Ta-kung pao* (hereafter cited as *TKP),* Tientsin, July 30, 1953, August 6, 1953, August 10, 1953,

32 *TKP,* November 13, 1953; *JMJP,* November 20, 1953.

33 *JMJP*, March 26, 1953; *JMST*, 1955, p. 477.

34 *Ibid.*

35 *JMJP*, January 9, 1954.

36 Yang, *loc. cit.*, p. 156.

37 *Hsin-hua yüeh-k'an* (*New China Monthly*), (hereafter cited as *HHYK*), Peking, Vol. 73, No. 11, 1955, pp. 1–18.

38 Cf. Kenneth R. Walker, 'Collectivisation in Retrospect; The Socialist High Tide of Autumn 1955–Spring 1956, in *CQ.*, No. 26, April–June 1966, pp. 1–43.

39 *JMST*, 1956, p. 87.

40 An interesting comparative study on the collectivisation of the Soviet Union in 1929–30 and of Communist China in 1955–6 has been done by Thomas P. Bernstein, 'Leadership and Mass Mobilisation in the Soviet and Chinese Collectivisation Campaign of 1929–1930 and 1955–1956: A Comparison', in *CQ*, No. 31, July–September 1967, pp. 1–47.

41 Cf. Yang, *loc. cit.*, pp. 157–72.

42 *TKP*, April 8, 1957.

43 *CNA*, No. 27, March 12, 1954.

44 For data cf. Tang-Maloney, *op. cit.*, p. 331.

45 *JMJP*, January 20, 1956.

46 Data in *TKP*, December 14, 1955.

47 *JMJP*, January 20, 1956.

48 Data in Chao I-neng, *Industries*, in *URI, Communist China 1949–1959, op. cit.*, p. 157.

IV.   Control and Opposition
1949–1957

The partly genuine, partly synthetic spontaneity of the mass campaigns
from 1950 to 1956 endowed the system with dynamics of modernisation which evoked surprise and admiration even among its opponents
and critics. However, the efficiency of these campaigns cannot completely explain the great initial success of the Chinese Communists.
It has to be stated that they were reinforced by a strict system of control thanks to which strong psychological and physical coercion could
be developed. Thus this coercion became the second constituent element in the process of 'socialist transformation'.

Instruments of Control

The Party organisation was the most important channel for conveying the will of the leadership to the people. Simultaneously it served
to effect at all levels of political organisation an attitudinal response that
was positive for the top leadership. Party members held privileged
positions in the system of rewards and deprivations. Party membership meant an advantageous starting-point for professional careers,
but on the other hand it demanded intense personal dedication and individual views which conformed to those of the leadership. As a Party
member one belonged to an élite obliged to dedicate itself to the
concepts of the 'transition to socialism' developed by the leadership, to
make propaganda for them and to mobilise the mass of the population
in their favour. The number of CCP members increased slowly at first
up to 1953 and then grew very rapidly. Thus, in the summer of 1950
the CCP had only 4·5 million members,[1] and in July 1953 6·1 million.[2]
In June 1956, at the time of the election of representatives to the eighth
Party Congress, this number had already risen to 10·73 million,[3]
and in the autumn of 1957 to 12·72 million.[4] However, in spite of
this rapid growth in membership, the CCP remained a small group
which in 1953 scarcely comprised 1 per cent of the population. This
percentage grew by 1956 to nearly 2 per cent and by 1957 to somewhat
more than 2 per cent. That there was only one Party member for more
than fifty inhabitants shows clearly the high degree to which this
élite was under stress while implementing the will of the leadership.

47

Furthermore, since the year 1951 the leadership had begun to appoint trustworthy Party members as 'propagandists' (*Hsüan-ch'uan yüan*) specifically responsible for conveying the Party line to the population. As a rule it was assumed that every such 'propagandist' should be responsible for a hundred peasants and ten industrial workers. Their numbers rapidly increased: in December 1951 there were 1,920,000, in September 1952, 2,900,000 and in January 1953, 3,790,000. The goal had not yet been achieved but the system of communication from the top down to the population already had so many ramifications that directives from the leadership quickly spread to the vast majority in the country. While the network of 'propagandists' served the transmission of impulses from the Centre, a parallel system of 'informants' (*Pao-kao yüan*) was to supervise the activities of the propagandists and to report to the leadership on the mood of the population. In December 1951 more than 50,000 such 'informants' were already active, and by January 1953 their number had increased to 75,000.[5]

Moreover, in the cities the Party put especially reliable members into operation as street secretaries who, being in permanent contact with the population, fulfilled the function of conveying the will as well as of informing.[6] In 1955 there came into being under their control 'street offices' which served as the agencies of the most important organs of state and local administration,[7] and above all 'residents' committees' as well which supervised from 100 to 600 households.[8] These committees, which at first had been conceived only for cities with more than 100,000 inhabitants, were to 'reinforce the work of the government among urban residents' and to 'mobilise the inhabitants to support the government and to obey the law'. Under their guidance 'residents' groups', comprising fifteen to forty families, co-operated in transmitting the directives of the committee to all households. With the help of this system the leadership could not only rapidly reach the entire urban population but could also receive information about the political and social behaviour of individuals.

While the regular Party apparatus, the 'propagandists', the 'informants', as well as the control institutions of the 'street offices' and 'residents' committees' fulfilled the function of general social control, the security police and the domestic secret service served the function of direct force.[9] All branches of the police were administratively subordinate to the Ministry of Public Security, which in 1949 had been founded under General Lo Jui-ch'ing as part of the state and administrative machine, and which since 1954 had been attached to the State Council. While the regular police were subordinate at all levels to the Security Bureaux, militarily organised units of the 'security forces' (*Kung-an pu-tui*) had been formed soon after the coming to power of the CCP. They had their own command structure at the headquarters of the PLA under the personal leadership of the Minister of Security. The security forces had the task of defending the border and of overcoming militarily more substantial acts of resistance. Tendencies towards opposition among the population were suppressed by a network of civil security organs which from December 1954 even had the authority to make arrests without the consent of the People's Procuratorates and to impose penalties in secret trials.[10] Early in 1955 'branch offices for the security of the people', whose members had to supervise the population at grass-roots, had been established in urban districts and in the villages.[11] They co-ordinated the activities of the 'security committees', which had been founded as early as 1952 and which undertook the permanent supervision of the populace in factories, commercial firms, schools, administrative services and residential districts.[12] In this way the security apparatus had been structured on the lowest level according to the principles of a mass organisation in order to combine the operation of the political police with struggle meetings and mass courts. There is but little documentary material on the operational results of this system, and only rarely do the Chinese public media report its operation. Thus, for example, it had been reported that the 'security committees' in Peking alone had dealt with more than 26,000 'counter-revolutionary and criminal actions' in 1952–3.[13] However, even the extensive security apparatus itself needed supervision. This task was fulfilled by the 'Department of Social Affairs' of the CC of the CCP which had an independent structure of command at its disposal; however, little is known about its operation.[14]

Thus an efficient system of political police was established during the first years after assuming power. Yet it never achieved the strong position initially held by OGPU and later by the NKVD in the Stalinist Soviet Union. The independence of the security organs was checked on the one hand by interweaving them with the state apparatus and by integrating their military units into the structure of command of the PLA, and on the other hand by their intimate connection to the administrative organs at the lowest level and by their being supervised by a special department of the Party leadership. Therefore they could not appear as an independent pillar of the political system apart from or in opposition to the Party machine and the military.

Methods of Control

In order to implement their decisions and to reinforce their mass campaigns, the Chinese Communists used a catalogue of psychological and physical sanctions at the heart of which was the idea that opposition was not only to be suppressed but that the actor was to be re-educated as well. Thus 'thought reform' (*ssu-hsiang kai-tsao*) became the most important method of controlling the population.[15] Its spectrum ranged from permanent re-education through meetings to 'labour reform' (*lao-tung kai-tsao*) in forced labour camps and, to change completely the consciousness of prisoners, a process which the Chinese have often called 'brain washing' (*hsi-nao*). The principle of preferring to change the consciousness of political opponents instead of physically liquidating them led to the use of every available psychological technique to change the personality of the individual.

Thought reform begins with an attack on the identity of the subject. In labour camps and prisons it is impressed on him that he is not what he supposes himself to be. Binding in chains and acts of torture serve as means of education.[16] During this first phase the physical needs of the prisoner may not be satisfied. Physical violence is the punishment for obduracy. He is treated as if he were mentally ill to show him that the view he has up to then held about himself and about the world is wrong. Next, the prisoner is imbued with deep feelings of guilt, and is repeatedly called upon to confess his actual or alleged crimes. After each 'confession' recorded in written form his physical suffering is relieved somewhat, but each relapse leads to a renewed aggravation of his conditions of imprisonment. This treatment usually causes the prisoner to develop a fear psychosis: he loses all personal perspectives on the future. However, in this situation for which there appears to be no remedy new possibilities open up. Minor, personal wishes will be gratified and a seemingly benevolent and helpful cadre takes charge of further treatment. The pressure will be diminished to a degree such that the prisoner can adjust himself to the new principles of life offered to him. In this situation his urge grows to make confessions and to exhibit the kind of behaviour that the apparatus requires him to show. Only thereafter is the sentence passed, which in some cases is pronounced as a death dentence but which will not be executed if he qualifies himself as a 'useful member of society' through forced labour. Up to 1965 sentences of forced labour were pronounced in most cases for periods of five to ten years. Usually they had to be served in corvée labour under harsh conditions in the remote areas of the north and north-west. It is impossible to determine the exact number of forced labour workers in the early years of the Communist Government. In October 1952 the Minister of Water Works, General Fu Tso-yi (RKMT), stated in his report that since autumn 1950 '10,370,000 forced labour workers had been engaged in water works under the supervision of 320,000 police.'[17] American reports for autumn 1953 spoke of 18 million forced labour workers in more than 5,000 labour camps.[18] Nationalist reports in the spring of 1954 referring to Party documents of the CCP, spoke, of 24 million such forced labourers.

If thought reform and forced labour do not fulfil their purpose, the system may, as a last resort, also effect the physical liquidation of its opponents. Certainly executions for political reasons became rare exceptions from 1955 up to the 'Cultural Revolution', but in the first years after the coming to power of the Communists they essentially dominated the struggle of the new leadership élite against alleged and actual 'counter-revolutionaries'.[19]

The 'Campaign against Counter-revolutionaries', 1951–1952[20]

Late in 1949 there were still units of the Nationalist Army in many places which tried to resist the new leadership through guerilla warfare, as well as other opponents of the Communists who were not willing to co-operate. Already in the first years after coming to power the PLA had taken measures against these forces. One tool was a system of 'mass courts', i.e. struggle meetings at which death sentences were carried out at once. The leaders of four of the six great regions reported that from October 1949 to October 1950 altogether 1,176,000 people had been executed in their administrative areas.[21] Teng Tzu-hui spoke of 322,000 executions for the Central-South region from January 1950 to November 1951.[22]

However, only after the 'Guide-lines for the Suppression of Counter-revolutionaries' had been promulgated by the Central People's Council on February 20, 1951, did the struggle to exterminate centres of political resistance achieve the systematic character of a mass movement.[23] This directive envisaged the death penalty or long-term imprisonment for a great number of crimes that were usually vaguely defined and which could be brought to trial retrospectively. Included in these were, for example, participation in 'counter-revolutionary acts' or in 'espionage' and membership in 'feudalistic sects and societies' as far back as prior to the coming to power of the CCP. Immediately after the proclamation of this directive there were mass meetings to try the accused and to execute them at once.[24] Soon the movement spread over the whole country. One hundred and sixty-five executions were reported for three days in July 1953 from Shanghai alone;[25] 277 for one day from Peking;[26] from the province of Kwangtung the Vice-Governor, Ku Ta-ts'un, reported altogether 28,332 executions for the period from October 10, 1950, to August 10, 1951.[27] In the capital alone, 29,626 'struggle meetings' took place in the first nine months of 1951, and in Tientsin there were 21,000 from March to July 1951.[28] There are no definite statistics about the sum total of the victims of this campaign. The Minister of Public Security, Lo Jui-ch'ing, spoke of 800,000 executions at the eighth Party Congress of the CCP in September 1956. The Minister of Finance, Po I-po, however,

C

spoke of more than two million in a work report published in Peking in autumn 1952.[30]

However, if one makes a compilation of the detailed reports of the official publication media, only a few of which could be quoted here, and projects them for the whole country one comes to a figure which must greatly exceed three million. But the exact number of victims in this campaign is not of particular relevance. Rather it is the effect which is important. A great number of executions in all cities and in many villages of the country clearly demonstrated to the population the consequences of withholding support. The campaign thereby fulfilled its function of tightening control over the populace. Two further movements served to discipline officials and the urban bourgeoisie: in autumn 1951 the 'Three Anti Movement' (*San-fan yün-tung*) began in Tungpei. It was directed against 'corruption, waste and bureaucracy' and led to a purge of elements among officials whose loyalty appeared doubtful.[31] This campaign, extended to the whole country in December 1951, was followed early in 1952 by the 'Five Anti Movement' in the course of which about 500 business men were executed and 34,000 sentenced to long-term imprisonment.[32]

Although by spring 1953 the leadership had consolidated its control over the people with the aid of mass mobilisation, terror and persuasion, and had created the preconditions for the thoroughgoing social changes of the years 1953 and 1956, in the spring of 1954, the first major conflict within the Party leadership occurred.

The Case of Kao Kang and Jao Shu-shih

On March 31, 1955, a 'National Delegates Conference' of the CCP was convened in Peking, which adopted a resolution expelling the chairman of the State Planning Commission, Kao Kang (a member of the Politburo) and the head of the Organisation Department of the CC, Jao Shu-shih, from the Party.[33] Seven other leading cadres were reprimanded. Most of them had worked earlier with Kao in Tungpei.[34] When the Fifth plenum of the Seventh CC of the CCP approved this purge on April 4, 1955, it announced at the same time that Kao had committed suicide as an 'extreme expression of his betrayal of the Party'.[35] Jao was imprisoned.[36]

The reasons for the purge have remained unclear up to this day. Some observers are convinced that the two Party leaders had attempted to build a new leadership group in Peking which would have been more compliant in its relations with the Soviet Union. Kao and Jao had therefore been supported by Moscow. There is no doubt that Kao had had rather intimate relations with the Soviet authorities when he was in charge of the administration of Tungpei from 1946 to

1952. But that is not true of Jao. On the other hand, some of Kao's colleagues in Tungpei who had had relations at least as close with the Russians – for example, Li Fu-ch'un – had been promoted at the time that Kao became a victim of the purge. Although the possibility of a Soviet attempt to gain greater influence on the leadership group of Communist China through Kao's help cannot be excluded, there are at least three discernible areas of domestic politics in which differences of opinion existed between Kao and Jao on the one hand and leading personalities in the centre on the other.

First, there were disputes over the speed of agricultural collectivisation in which Jao Shu-shih had evidently interceded for a more gradual advance.

Secondly, there were disputes over the regional allocation of investments during the first five-year plan, and it appears that Kao Kang – contrary to the wishes of other regional leaders – interceded for the priority of a further industrial development of Tungpei.

Finally, it was maintained that Kao, who did not belong to the core of the leadership which had developed in the course of the Long March, had attempted to take over Liu Shao-ch'i's position as number two in the leadership group,[37] while Jao had aimed at Chou En-lai's position as prime minister.

However, this leadership crisis remained limited. The purge concerned only two of the forty-three full members of the CC, and although these two held influential positions they were marginal figures compared with the members of the inner leadership group who had come to the top during the Long March. Thus the basic outcome of this purge was a stricter co-ordination of centralised control of the Party organisation and a strengthening of the positions of Liu Shao-ch'i and Chou En-lai. Yet during the next major crisis, the 'Hundred Flowers Movement' of 1957, these two evidently developed differences of opinion.

The Purge of the Intellectuals

Since the early 1930s, many Chinese intellectuals, especially scholars of the humanities, writers and artists, had turned to the Communist movement. Their aversion to the authoritarian system of government of the KMT contributed to this development, as did the consistent anti-Japanese attitude of Communist propaganda and the devotion of the Nationalists to a state brand of Neo-confucianism in the form of the New Life[38] movement, which the intellectuals regarded as a threat to their intellectual freedom. Thus a great number of the Chinese intelligentsia gathered in several Communist-influenced organisations, especially the 'League of Left-wing Writers', and made an important contribution in terms of propaganda to the CCP's victory.[39] But many of these intellectuals had not subscribed to the overall programme of the Party. They had regarded it rather as a force which would regain for China an honoured place in the world. Some of them may have hoped that under a Communist-led coalition government a more pronounced democratic political system might be developed. However, this hope was soon destroyed, for when the CCP came to power, the Party made the intellectuals the object of the first 'thought reform' campaign which began in the summer of 1950 shortly after the outbreak of the Korean war and lasted to the end of 1951. University teachers, writers, artists and architects who had studied in western countries were induced to confess their 'ideological faults' in a great number of 'self-confessions' and to recognise the leadership of the CCP as their own.[40] In the context of this campaign, libraries and bookshops were 'purged' of 'counter-revolutionary literature', especially works by Western authors and a number of classical Chinese novels. In Canton alone, 16,000 books were sized and burnt in autumn 1951.[41] Then the leadership's concentration on several campaigns to change the socio-economic structure led to an ephemeral relaxation in 1952-3. The number of 'struggle meetings' in the universities and among intellectual circles tailed off remarkably. Only after the internal Party disputes, in particular the Kao-Jao case, had been decided substantially in favour of the central leadership group, did the Party feel sufficiently confident again to push energetically the indoctrination and disciplining of the Chinese intelligentsia.[42]

The principle which had been formulated by Mao in 1942, that the only reason for the existence of literature is to serve the interests of the workers, peasants and soldiers,[43] was placed at the heart of the re-education endeavours. The campaign began with the expulsion of proponents of nonconformist ideas from the leading literary organ *Wen-yi pao* in December 1954: the editor-in-chief, Feng Hsüeh-feng, was demoted and the editor, Ch'en Ch'i-hsia, was dismissed.[44] Prior to this, with the support of the Propaganda Department of the CC, two young Party intellectuals had already made severe attacks on the literary historian, Yü P'ing-po; they denounced his works on the classical novel *Dream of the Red Chamber* (*Hung-lou meng*) as 'individualistic, romanticist and uncritical towards the feudal system'.[45] Out of this debate there originated a grave conflict. The writer Hu Feng, a follower of the Communist movement since the 1930s, in an elaborate memorandum turned sharply against the policy of repressing intellectuals. He declared that the demands to study Marxism, to live with the workers, peasants and soldiers, to overcome 'bourgeois ideology', to 'preserve and promote national traditions only selectively', and to serve politics actively 'stuck like five daggers

in the backs of writers' and considerably impaired their work. Only if
the Party removed these 'five daggers' and revived the complete freedom of artistic expression could artists become creative.[46] The protest
of the Communist veteran Hu Feng against the regimentation of
writers and artists provoked an extremely sharp reaction from the
leadership.[47] He was forced to undertake a 'self criticism' in May 1955;
but this did not gain the approval of the Party and was rejected.[48]
The leadership decided to take more severe action. Hu's case was
handed over to the security forces and it was soon discovered that he
'had instigated a reactionary conspiracy' which was to be shattered.
Now Hu was removed from all his positions in the writers' organisations,[49] and finally, in July, he was apprehended as a 'counter-revolutionary'.[50] In 1967, Red Guard papers reported that he had committed
suicide in 1958 in the psychiatric section of a Peking prison.[51] The
arrest of Hu Feng initiated a comprehensive new campaign of purges
among intellectuals which developed fully as the 'Movement for the
Suppression of Counter-revolutionaries' (Su-fan yün-tung) from the
middle of 1955. Again there were 'struggle meetings' in the universities, schools and cultural organisations. A great number of non-
Communist intellectuals as well as long-standing members of the CCP
were accused of counter-revolutionary activities, subjected to humiliations, arrested or sent to forced-labour camps.[52] In the province of
Hupei alone, 2,784 'counter-revolutionaries' were 'punished' during the
first two months of the campaign,[53] and thirty-three scientists from
the universities of Wuhan were arrested.[54] According to reports
from JMJP the number of 'counter-revolutionaries' who had been
unmasked and sentenced during the campaign amounted to
81,000. Furthermore, more than 300,000 Chinese were denounced as
'politically unreliable' and were deprived of their civil rights.[55]
Terror and insecurity reigned among the leading intellectual forces
of the country in the second half of 1955. Around the turn of 1955-6
it had spread so much that the universities and research institutions of
the country were partially paralysed. China's intelligentsia was now
scarcely in a position to perform the work the leadership expected it
to do in the interests of economic and educational development.

Détente – The Eighth Party Congress of the CCP, 1956

The paralysis of the intelligentsia must have given the leaders of the
CCP considerable cause for anxiety; for they soon felt forced to
make concessions. At the turn of 1955-6 future policy towards the
intellectuals was reconsidered at a session of the Politburo.[56] Chou En-
lai and other leading functionaries of the state apparatus evidently favoured an ending of the purification campaign, a general decrease in

pressure on the intellectuals and more freedom of expression in the realm of art and literature. They pressed their arguments successfully, and on January 14, 1956, with a demand for a more cautious treatment of intellectuals, proclaimed the beginning of a change of direction in the Party's politics at a Party conference in Peking.[57] Festivals of modern drama in Peking in March 1956 pointed to a distinct relaxation in the demands made on writers,[58] and this tendency was reinforced under the impact of Soviet de-Stalinisation which Kruschev had initiated at the Twentieth Party Congress of the CPSU in February 1956. In the first Chinese comment on the new Soviet Policy, in his article 'On the Historical Exprerience of the Dictatorship of the Proletariat', Mao referred to the fact that the Chinese Party had always avoided the politics of repression and the personality cult of the Stalinist period.[59] Further substantial decisions were made at an enlarged session of the Politburo on April 25.[60] Mao now led those who pressed for a moderation of the domestic political course. In a speech on the 'Ten Great Relationships', which anticipated the essential elements of his 'Hundred Flowers' speech of February 1957,[61] the Party leader declared that contradictions would continue in socialist society; they would have to be resolved by discussion and mutual persuasion. The Party should make a fresh effort so that no gap would appear between it and the rest of the population.[62] The head of the Propaganda Department of the CC, Lu Ting-i, could be sure of the support of the Party leader when, referring to Mao, he launched the slogan 'Let a Hundred Flowers Bloom, Let a Hundred Schools of Thought Contend' (*Pai-hua ch'i-fang, pai-chia cheng-ming!*) in his speech before cadres and intellectuals on May 26. Lu called on intellectuals and artists not to restrict themselves slavishly to one style, but to claim complete freedom of artistic expression and freedom of opinion.[63]

Thus the Party initiated an extensive campaign of domestic political relaxation. Above all it proceeded from the conviction that after the decisive social changes and the waves of purges of 1950-5 the time had come to reunite the country and to enter into a phase of consolidation. However, we now know that the methods of relaxation were a cause of controversy among the leadership. Chou En-lai and his colleagues in the state apparatus as well as leading personalities in the propaganda department of the Party interceded for a more pronounced freedom of discussion inside the CCP and between Communists and non-Communists. Leading representatives of the Party organisation centring around Liu Shao-ch'i, however, continued to emphasise particularly the leadership role of the CCP as well as internal Party discipline, and they held rather that their fundamental interest lay in the unity of the Party as a means of moderation. Mao himself had stated his particular interest in resolving existing conflicts through free discussion at a session of the Politburo in April, and in a speech on May 2, the text of which has not yet been published. Thus he initially gave his support to the group around Chou. However, in the second half of 1956 he restrained himself, and the Eighth Party Congress of the CCP, which took place in Peking from September 15 to September 27, 1956, was dominated largely by the men of the Party machine around Liu Shao-chi'i and Teng Hsiao-p'ing.[64] For the first time since the First Party Congress in 1921 the delegates (1,026 altogether) were elected by the members of the Party. At the six previous Party Congresses they had been nominated by the leadership.[65] Unity and consolidation became the main topics of the Congress. At the election of the new CC, the membership of which had been extended from forty-three to ninety-seven full members, old enemies of Mao were also shown consideration. Among them were the former Party leaders Li Li-san and Ch'en Shao-yü. The new Party constitution of September 26, 1956,[66] provided for institutional safeguards for a more open process of internal Party decision-making. In order to reaffirm the assertion that a personality cult had never existed in the CCP, the preamble of the new Party constitution no longer referred to the 'thought of Mao Tse-tung' which could be found in the 1945 version. In the work report of the Secretariat, Teng Hsiao-p'ing announced an 'extensive movement for improving the working style of the Party and the administration'.[67] The election of the new Politburo at the first plenum of the eighth CC on September 28 made clear the interest in broadening the basis of politics. While K'ang Sheng, a former full member of the Politburo, who as head of the security services had played a leading role in the rectification campaigns, was demoted to alternate membership of the Politburo, economic bureaucrats such as Li Fu-ch'un and Li Hsien-nien, and the Marshals of the PLA, Liu Po-ch'eng, Ho Ling, Lo Jung-huan and Ch'en Yi became new members of the leading organ of the Party. The enlargement of the Politburo to seventeen full members and six candidate members, however, was accompanied by the establishment of a new inner leadership which, as the Standing Committee of the Politburo (Cheng-chih-chü ch'ang-wu wei-yüan-hui), comprised the Party leader Mao, his four deputies, Liu, Chou, Marshal Chu Te and Ch'en Yün, as well as the newly appointed Secretary General of the CC, Teng Hsiao-p'ing.[68] Thus the leading group in the civil Party apparatus under Liu had prevailed for the time being at the Party Congress with its policy of preserving external discipline, at the same time broadening the political basis of the Party. However, events in Poland and Hungary in autumn 1956, and the serious difficulties in supply resulting from a bad harvest caused Mao to resurrect the topic of a more open debate, even with non-Communists, in the winter of

1956–7. He had come to the conclusion that the unity of the people should be emphasised more strongly than 'struggle', having regard to the great successes in reconstructing the economy after the civil war and in attempting to change the social order as well as in generally improving the standard of living; and this despite acute bottle-necks. At the same time, Mao assumed that there was continuous discontent among considerable sections of the population due to the arrogance of many Party cadres and the bureaucratic obduracy of the machine structures. Such considerations caused him to call for a campaign of open criticism at the beginning of 1957, with the support of the men around Chou and the group of Lu Ting-i as well as the head of the Department of the CC of United Front work, Li Wei-han. Mao and his colleagues evidently expected that critiques by members of the non-Communist United Front parties, non-Party intellectuals and other circles among the population would be mainly directed against low and medium level Party cadres. The fact that Liu, Teng and the mayor of Peking, P'eng Chen, as well as other leaders of the civilian Party machine kept silent for a long time about the new 'rectification campaign' indicates a certain scepticism among orthodox circles in the leadership. Developments in spring 1957 confirmed their views; for the criticism which Mao had called for did not confine itself to particular deficiencies, but was soon directed against the system, the top leadership and the ideology itself.

The 'Hundred Flowers Movement', 1957[69]

The decision to broaden the scope of the movement to criticise the Party machine had apparently already been made at a session of the Politburo during the last days of December 1956; for as early as December 29 an editorial in *JMJP* entitled, 'More on the Historical Experience of the Dictatorship of the Proletariat', called on CCP members to seek 'closer relations with and more active support from the masses'.[70] Only a few days later, on January 9, 1957, the First Secretary of the Shanghai Party Committee, K'o Ch'ing-shih, spoke for the first time of 'contradictions' (*mao-tun*) in the socialist society which had to be resolved by discussion and persuasion.[71] But the real beginning of the new movement was signalled by Mao himself, who, at an enlarged session of the 'Supreme State Conference' on February 27, gave his four-hour speech 'On the Correct Handling of Contradictions among the People'[72] before 1,800 leading cadres of the CCP, the non-Communist United Front parties and non-Party intellectuals.

First, Mao stated that 'our country has never before been as united' as it is now and that an 'even more brilliant future' lay ahead. Yet there remained a great number of contradictions even during the building of socialist society and after its completion. These were not 'contradictions between the enemy and ourselves' (*ti-wo mao-tun*) but 'contradictions among the people' (*jen-min nei-pu mao-tun*). They were not therefore of an antagonistic nature and should not be resolved by a dictatorship, i.e. physical force, but by open discussion with criticism and counter-criticism. The Party leader called on non-Communist especially to criticise openly the working style of Party cadres. But the original draft of his speech contained no definite criteria setting the limits for criticism. After the experience of 1955 the reaction of his audience was at first extremely hesitant. At the conference itself the leaders of the non-Communist United Front parties responded to Mao only with general praise, and even a confirmation of this call in another speech by Mao at a national work conference of the CCP for propaganda work on March 12 could not penetrate the reluctance of potential critics.[73] As late as March 24, the sociologist Fei Hsiao-t'ung wrote in *JMJP* that the Chairman's speech resembled 'early spring weather' which is very capricious, 'sometimes cold and sometimes warm', and therefore even 'blooming flowers could easily perish from the frost'.[74] The hesitance and reluctance of the non-Communists caused the CCP in a directive of the CC of April 30, to call for the establishment of forums in which members of minority parties and non-Party individuals should state their opinions in 'complete freedom'.[75] Although the people called upon to make criticisms still demanded unequivocal guarantees against sanctions which might follow the stating of their opinions;[76] but then the Department for United Front work of the CC sent out invitations to a series of discussions, of which eleven took place in Peking from May 8 to June 3.[77]

At these forums comprehensive criticism set in, which soon spread to other cities, especially Shanghai and Tientsin.[78] Again there were 'struggle meetings' in the universities, cultural circles and administrative authorities; this time, however, they were not directed against opponents but against the Party and their members. The wave of criticism did not stop at administrative deficiencies; day by day it took on a more fundamental aspect. Journalists complained about press censorship, university teachers about tutelage by Party cadres, and artists about the limitation of their freedom of expression. Non-Communist ministers were frustrated by their impotence in the state apparatus. Criticism grew steadily sharper, finally concentrating, at the end of May and the beginning of June, on a number of substantial demands for changes in the policies of the CCP:

1. The diminution if not the extinction of the CCP's influence on literature, art and science,

2. The abolition of the regulations for the United Front parties

which confined their propaganda to certain strata of the population,

3. The appointment of at least one or two non-Communist vice-premiers,

4. The transformation of the People's Political Consultative Conference, in which non-Communists were more strongly represented than the CCP, from a purely consultative body to a second decision-making body besides the National People's Congress, i.e. into a Political Planning Board (*Cheng-chih she-chi yüan*),

5. The abolition of one-party rule and free competitive elections,

6. The resignation of Mao Tse-tung and of the Communist leadership groups.

To elucidate the form and intensity of the attack on the Party, four characteristic examples will be chosen from the mass of existing material.

1. Ch'u An-p'ing (RKMT), editor-in-chief of the KMJP:

After Liberation the intellectuals at first warmly supported the Party, and recognised its leadership. But during the last few years relations between the Party and the masses have not been good; they have rather become a problem in our political life and must be adjusted urgently. Where is the key to this problem? In my opinion the key lies in the idea that now 'the world belongs to the Party'. I believe a party that guides a people is not the same as a party that possesses a people; the public supports the Party but the members of the public have not forgotten that they and not the Party are the masters of the nation.[79]

2. Huang Chen-lu, editor of the student newspaper of the Shenyang Teacher Training college:

The CCP has twelve million members. That is less than 2 per cent of the entire population. 600 million people have become the docile subjects of this 2 per cent. What principle is this? The absolute leadership of the Party must be abolished and the privileges of the Party members must be abolished.[80]

3. Chang Po-sheng, member of the CCP and head of the propaganda section of the Communist Youth Corps at the Shenyang Teacher Training College:

In the years after Liberation there did not exist a socialist democracy. What did exist in democracy was simply formalistic. There is not even the pseudo-democracy of capitalist countries. The constitution is a scrap of paper, and the Party need not take it into consideration. We give the impression that there are democratic elections, United Front politics and even non-Party individuals in the leadership. In reality, however, a Party dictatorship reigns and a handful of people in the Politburo of the Party exercise absolute power.[81]

4. Ko P'ei-ch'i, lecturer in industrial economics at the People's University of Peking:

When the CCP occupied the city in 1949 the people welcomed it as a benefactor. Today, however, the common people keep away from the CCP as if its members were demons or devils. . . . The Party members behave like secret police and supervise the masses. But they cannot be blamed for that; for the Party organisation demands that they gather information. . . . If the Communist Party mistrusts me then this mistrust is mutual. China belongs to 600 million people, even to the counter-revolutionaries. It does not belong to the Party alone. . . . If you continue to our satisfaction, O.K.! If not then it might happen that the masses will strike you down, kill the Communists and overthrow you. This would not be unpatriotic for the Communists do not serve the people. The downfall of the CCP does not mean the downfall of China![82]

Not only the intelligentsia rebelled. Soon the movement spread among the workers and peasants as well. In Kwangtung a movement of withdrawal from the APCs developed. In Szechwan and Kwangsi there were acts of sabotage, and in the provinces of Shensi, Hupei and Kiangsu unrest flared up in a number of villages.[83] The Party leadership must have thought it extremely dangerous that the movement had spread with growing vehemence from mid-May to include the students as well, for they had received the greater part of their education under the new system.[84] As during the 'May Fourth Movement' of 1919, to which the now developing student opposition explicitly referred, the National Peking University, *Peita*, became again, in 1957, the stronghold of resistance. Here there appeared the first Big Character Posters on May 19, which were removed by Party cadres. However, only one day later new placards appeared, and their tone had become sharper.[85] From May 23 onward daily mass meetings of the students took place on campus, and their resistance organised itself in a number of *ad hoc* units among which the 'Hundred Flowers Society' held a leading position, but which combined themselves on May 29.[86] At the head of the movement in Peking stood the twenty-one-year-old girl student Lin Hsi-ling. With the help of a committee under her leadership she effected the incorporation into this movement of other Peking universities and, from June 2, universities from Tientsin too.[87] The wave of student protest reached its zenith in the central

Chinese industrial metropolis of Wuhan on June 12-13, 1957. Thousands of high school pupils and students, led by the teachers Wang Chien-kuo and Yang Sung-tao, as well as by the students Chang Yü-wen and Yang Huan-yao, demonstrated in the streets of the city. The slogan 'Welcome KMT! Welcome Chiang Kai-shek!' spread during the demonstrations. Communist Party offices were raided, and Party cadres physically attacked. Counter-demonstrations of workers, organised by the CCP, were at first ineffective, and only the use of the police could suppress the unrest.[88] Similar student demonstrations were reported from Nanking, Chengtu, Tsingtao, Chinan, Kweilin, Suchou and Nanchang during the first half of June 1957.[89]

Thus, out of Mao's call for criticism of specific deficiencies there developed an extensive movement of opposition and resistance which threatened to jeopardise the foundations of the political system of the PR of China. Those Party leaders who from the beginning had warned against the toleration of free expression of opinions saw their views confirmed. Mao had to admit that he had overestimated the political support of the Chinese people, and in order to save the system the campaign was halted. What had at first been regarded as a non-antagonistic contradiction had now become an antagonistic contradiction whose solution lay in the hands of the 'organs of the dictatorship of the proletariat'. The Party's counter-offensive began.

References

1 *JMJP*, September 14, 1956.
2 *JMJP*, July 2, 1953.
3 *JMJP*, September 14, 1956.
4 *JMJP*, October 19, 1956.
5 *CNA*, No. 6, October 2, 1953.
6 Cf. Schurmann, *op. cit.*, pp. 115-16; also Tang-Maloney, *op. cit.*, pp. 267-8.
7 'Regulations for Urban Street Offices', in *JMJP*, January 1, 1955, English translation, in Chen, *op. cit.*, document XIII, pp. 112-13.
8 'Regulations for Urban Residents' Committees', in *JMJP*, January 1, 1955, English translation, in Chen, *op. cit.*, document XII, pp. 109-12.
9 Cf. Tang-Maloney, *op. cit.*, pp. 302-7; also Walker, *op. cit.*, pp. 62-3; also Wang Hai-po, 'An Analysis of the Intelligence Organisations of the Chinese Communists, in *Tzu-yu chen-hsien (Freedom Front)*, Hong Kong, No. 1, July 17, 1953.
10 *JMJP*, January 8, 1955.
11 'Regulations for Branch Offices of Public Security', in *JMJP*, January 1, 1955, English translation, in Chen, *op. cit.*, document XIV, pp. 113-14.

12 'Provisional Guide Lines for the Organisation of Security Committees', passed by the Ministry of Public Security on August 10, 1952, cited in Tang-Maloney, *op. cit.*, p. 306.

13 *JMJP*, September 30, 1954.

14 Tang-Maloney, *op. cit.*, p. 303.

15 Cf. in particular Robert J. Lifton, *Thought Reform and the Psychology of Totalism*, New York, 1961; Walker, *op. cit.*, pp. 234–35; Schurmann, *op. cit.*, pp. 514, 516, 518; Tang-Maloney, *op. cit.*, pp. 522–3; Mu Fu-sheng, *The Wilting of the Hundred Flowers: Free Thought in China Today*, London, pp. 208–47; Theodore H. E. Chen, *Thought Reform of the Chinese Intellectuals*, (hereafter cited as *Intellectuals*), Hong Kong, 1960, pp. 72–3.

16 Cf. Dries van Coillie, *Der begeisterte Selbstmord*, Donauwörth, 1961, p. 94.

17 *Far Eastern Economic Review* (hereafter cited as *FEER*), Hong Kong, Vol. XIII, No. 18, October 30, 1952; cf. also Jerome A. Chen, *The Criminal Process in the People's Republic of China, 1949–1963*, Cambridge, Mass., 1968, pp. 238–40.

18 *New York Times*, November 26, 1953.

19 *New York Times*, April 24, 1954.

20 Cf. also Tang-Maloney, *op. cit.*, pp. 312–17; Walker, *op. cit.*, pp. 244–51.

21 *Current Background* (hereafter cited as *CB*), Hong Kong, No. 39, December 3, 1950.

22 *Ch'ang-chiang jih-pao (Yang Tze Daily)*, Wuhan, December 13, 1951.

23 'Guide-lines for the Suppression of Counter-revolutionaries', in *JMJP*, February 21, 1951, English translation in Chen, *op. cit.*, document XXXVI, pp. 293–6.

24 *JMJP*, March 25, 1951.

25 Cited in Walker, *op. cit.*, p. 247.

26 *JMJP*, July 12, 1951.

27 *Nan-fang jih pao* (hereafter cited as *NFJP*), Canton, September 18, 1951.

28 Data in a report by Lo Jui-ch'ing, in *JMJP*, October 11, 1951.

29 *NCNA*, Peking, September 19, 1956.

30 Cited in Georg Paloczi-Horvath, *Der Herr der blauen Ameisen – Mao Tse-tung*, Frankfurt/Main, 1962, p. 249.

31 Cf. also Tang-Maloney, *op. cit.*, pp. 491–2.

32 *Ibid.*, p. 493.

33 *JMJP*, April 5, 1955; *CNA*, No. 80, April 22, 1955; *HHYK*, December 1952, p. 4.

34 Hsiang Ming, Vice-Governor of the province of Shantung, follower of Kao; Chiang Hsiu-shan, member of North-east China People's Government and Chairman of the latter's Control Commission; Chang Ming-yüan, Third Secretary of the North-east China Bureau of the CC of the CCP and Vice-Chairman of the North-east China People's Government; Chao Te-ts'un, Director of the Department of Agriculture of the North-east China Bureau and Governor of the province of Heilungkiang; Ma Hung, Director of the Secretariat of the North-east China Bureau and member of the State Planning Commission; Kuo Teng, Vice-Director of the Organisation Department of the North-east China Bureau; Ch'en Po-ts'un, Director of the Organisation Department of the North-east China Bureau and Vice-Director of the

Personnel Department of the North-east China People's Government. (*CNA*, *ibid*.).

35 *JMJP*, April 5, 1955.

36 According to a Red Guard source Jao had been discharged from custody in the early 1960's, but had been rearrested in 1967. Cf. Kuangchou jih-pao hung-ch'i, Canton, July 11, 1967.

37 *JMJP*, October 2, 1953.

38 Cf. Domes, *Revolution*, *op. cit.*, pp. 550–9.

39 For a survey of modern Chinese literature and its political orientation cf. C. T. Hsia, *A History of Modern Chinese Fiction 1917–1957*, New Haven, 1961; cf. also C. T. Hsia, 'Literature and Art under Mao Tse-tung', in Frank N. Trager and William Henderson (ed'), *Communist China, 1949–1969, A Twenty-Year Appraisal*, New York, 1970, (hereafter cited as Trager-Henderson), pp. 199–202.

40 Eleven of these confessions have been collected, in Feng Yu-lan, Fei Hsiao-t'ung, *Wo-te ssu-hsiang shih tsen-yang chuan-pien kuo-lai-te?* (*In what way did my thought change?*), Peking, 1951, *passim*.

41 *Hua-ch'iao jih-pao* (*Wat-kiu yat-po*) (*Overseas Chinese Daily*), Hong Kong, November 9, 1951; cf. *CNA*, No. 2, September 4, 1953.

42 Cf. also Douwe W. Fokkema, *Literary Doctrine in China and Soviet Influence, 1956–60*, The Hague, Paris, 1965.

43 Cf. also Mao Tse-tung, 'Talks at the Yehnan Forum on Literature and Art', in *Selected Readings from the Works of Mao Tse-tung*, Peking, 1967, pp. 204–33; also Fokkema, *op. cit.*, pp. 3–11.

44 *Wen-yi pao*, (hereafter cited as *WYP*), Peking, No. 23–4, 1954, p. 46.

45 Li Hsi-fan and Lan Ling, 'Kuan-yü "Hung-lou meng chien lun" chi ch'i-t'a', in *WYP*, No. 18–19, 1954, pp. 31–7; *KMJP*, October 10, 1954; *JMJP*, October 24, 1954; cf. Fokkema, *op. cit.*, pp. 43–8.

46 *WYP Supplement*, No. 1–2, 1955. The supplement has not been distributed outside China, extracts in *Hu Feng wen-yi ssu-hsiang p'i-p'an lun-wen hui-chi* (*Critique of Hu Feng's Literary and Artistic Thought*), Peking, 1955; also *JMJP*, May 13, 24, 1955 and July 3, 1955.

47 Cf. also Merle Goldman, 'Hu Feng's Conflict with the Communist Literary Authorities', in *CQ*, No. 12, October–December 1962, pp. 102–37; Fokkema, *op. cit.*, pp. 21–7, 49–55; Chen, *Thought Reform*, *op. cit.*, pp. 88–90; Tang-Maloney, *op. cit.*, p. 524.

48 *JMJP*, May 13, 1955.

49 *JMJP*, May 24, June 10, 1955.

50 *JMJP*, July 18, 1955.

51 *Kuei-i-chtng feng-lei* (*Spring Storm of the First High School of Kueichou*), Kweilin, June 17, 1967.

52 Professor Yang Chih-chan's letter to Mao Tse-tung, in *Ch'angchiang jih-pao* (*Yang Tze Daily*), Wuhan, July 13, 1957, English translation in Roderick MacFarquhar, *The Hundred Flowers Campaign*, Paris, 1960, pp. 94–6; also *KMJP*, May 12, November 6, 1957.

53 *JMJP*, March 23, 1957.

54 *JMJP*, March 26, 1957.

55 *JMJP*, July 18, 1957.

56 Chang, *loc. cit.*, p. 184; *JMJP*, January 30, 1956.
57 Cf. Chou En-lai, *Report on the Question of Intellectuals*, Peking, 1956, English translation, in Robert R. Bowie and John K. Fairbank, *Communist China 1955–1959, Policy Documents with Analysis*, (hereafter cited as Bowie-Fairbank), Cambridge, Mass., 1962, pp. 128–44; cf. also Fokkema, *op. cit.*, pp. 57–8.
58 *JMJP*, March 2, 1956; cf. Fokkema, *op. cit.*, pp. 67–70.
59 *JMJP*, April 5, 1956.
60 *Hsin chien-she*, Peking, No. 6, 1960, p. 4.
61 See below, pp. 58–9.
62 Mao Tse-tung, 'Lun shih-ta kuan-hsi' (On Ten Great Relationships), in *1970 Yearbook on Chinese Communism*, T'aipeii, 1970, Vol. II, Ch. VII, pp. 36–43; English translation, in *CB*, No. 892, October 21, 1969.
63 Text of Lu Ting-i's speech, in *JMJP*, June 13, 1956, English translation, in Bowie-Fairbank, *op. cit.*, pp. 151–64.
64 Cf. Liu Shao-ch'i, 'The Political Report of the Central Committee of the Communist Party of China to the Eighth National Congress of the Party', in *Eighth National Congress of the Communist Party of China*, Vol. I, pp. 13–111; cf. also Teng Hsiao-p'ing, *Report on the Revision of the Constitution of the Communist Party of China*, ibid., 169–228.
65 Speech of the Minister of Public Security, Hsieh Fu-chih, in Peking on October 26, 1967, in *Wen-ko t'ung-hsün* (*Cultural Revolution Bulletin*), Canton, December 11, 1967, English translation in *Survey of the China Mainland Press* (hereafter cited as *SCMP*), Hong Kong, No. 4097, January 11, 1968.
66 English text of the Party constitution, in Chen, *op. cit.*, document XV, pp. 127–48.
67 Teng Hsiao-p'ing, *Report on the Revision of the Constitution of the Communist Party of China*, *loc. cit.*, pp. 185–7.
68 *JMST*, 1957, p. 69.
69 For the following paragraph cf. MacFarquhar, *op. cit., passim;* Chen, *Intellectuals, op. cit.*, pp. 127–201; Merle Goldman, *Literary Dissent in Communist China*, Cambridge, Mass., 1967, pp. 158–202; Mu Fu-sheng, *op. cit.*; Fokkema, *op. cit.*, pp. 82–146; René Goldman, 'The Rectification Campaign at Peking University: May–June 1957', in *CO*, No. 12, October–December 1962, pp. 138–153; also Vincent Y. G. Shih, *The State of the Intellectuals*, in Trager-Henderson, *op. cit.*, pp. 229–32; *CNA*, No. 185, 187, 189, 195, June 21, July 5, 19, September 6, 1957.
70 *JMJP*, December 29, 1956.
71 *Chieh-fang jih-pao*, Shanghai, January 9, 1957.
72 Extracts of Mao's speech, in *JMJP*, April 13, 1957. On June 13, 1957 the *New York Times* reproduced a version of the speech transmitted by the newspaper's Warsaw correspondent Sidney Gruson. On June 18, 1957 the *NCNA* published the officially authorised and revised version. A comparison of the most relevant parts of the two versions in English, in MacFarquhar, *op. cit.*, pp. 265–77.
73 *NCNA*, Peking, September 1, 1968.
74 *JMJP*, March 24, 1957.
75 *JMJP*, March 30, 1957.

76 For example Professor Wang Shao-shih, in *KMJP*, May 1, 1957.

77 Reports on these forums in *NCNA*, Peking, May 8, 9, 10, 11, 13, 15, 16, 17, 21, 22, 30 and June 1, 3, 1957; *JMJP*, June 2, 4, 1957; *TKP*, May 12, 1957; *KMJP*, May 19, June 4, 7, 1957; cf. MacFarquhar, *op. cit.*, pp. 38–58, 77–124.

78 *NCNA*, Shanghai, May 19, 1957; *NVNA*, Tientsin, June 6, 1957.

79 *JMJP*, June 2, 1957, English translation, in MacFarquhar, *op. cit.*, pp. 51–2.

80 *Shenyang jih-pao*, June 11, 1957, English translation, in MacFarquhar, *op. cit.*, p. 106.

81 *Ibid.*, p. 107.

82 *JMJP*, May 31, 1957, June 8, 1957, English translation, *ibid.*, pp. 87–8.

83 *NCNA*, Kwangtung, May 14, 1957; *NCNA*. London, July 25, 1957; *JMJP*, July 29, 1957; *NCNA*, Ch'engtu, August 6, 1957; *Kuangsi jih-pao*, Kweilin, August 24, 1957.

84 Cf. MacFarquhar, *op. cit.*, pp. 130–73; René Goldman, *loc. cit.*

85 MacFarquhar, *op. cit.*, p. 131.

86 *KMJP*, May 26, 1957; *Wen-hui pao* (hereafter cited as *WHP*), May 27, 1957; *NCNA*, Peking, July 12, 1957; *JMJP*, July 24, 1957.

87 *JMJP*, June 29, July 24, 1957.

88 *JMJP*, August 8, 17, 1957; cf. MacFarquhar, *op. cit.*, pp. 145–52.

89 *JMJP*, July 12, 1957; *Hsin-hua jih-pao*, Nanking, June 28, July 6, 1957; *WHP*, June 29, 1957; *Ch'engtu jih-pao*, July 9, 1957; Ch'ingtao jih-pao, July 18, 1957; *NCNA*, Peking, July 28, 1957; Kuangsi jih-pao, Kueilin, October 3, 1957; *Chung-kuo ch'ing-nien pao*, (hereafter cited as *CKCNP*), Peking, August 15, 1957; *Kiangsi jih-pao*, Nanchang, September 6, 1957.

V. The CCP at the Crossroads 1957

The rebellion of the intellectuals in the spring of 1957 must be regarded as the first decisive turning-point in the internal politics of the PR of China. Up to then, the policies of Mao and of the CCP had achieved considerable success. Land reform had been carried out without any interruption. The struggle for women's emancipation had made progress. In spite of some setbacks, collectivisation and nationalisation had, in the opinion of the Communists, prepared the way for a socialist society. The campaigns of suppression and thought reform had reinforced Party control over society. Through its participation in the conferences at Geneva in 1954 and Bandung in 1955, the PR of China had become an active factor in international politics with which other powers had to reckon. As we shall see, economic development policies were extraordinarily successful, and in spite of some difficulties the general standard of living was undoubtedly higher than at any time since the outbreak of the Sino-Japanese War in 1937. Thus the degree of opposition which had become evident during the 'Hundred Flowers Movement' must have been a shock to the Party leadership and must have cast doubts on the political line which had been pursued up to then.

The Party Hits Back

By the second half of May 1957 there were already signs that the CCP leadership was alarmed by the spread of intellectual criticism and that it was preparing a counter-attack. On May 25, at a session of the Standing Committee of the Politburo Mao expressed his anxiety about these developments and apparently gave his approval, for the first time, to those who had warned against too much liberty.[1] Later on the same day the Party leader said at a conference of Communist Youth League cadres that 'all words and deeds which deviate from socialism are basically wrong'.[2] At the same time the session of the National People's Congress, originally convened for June 3, was postponed to June 20 and then, on June 19, to June 26;[3] the Party evidently wanted to regain control over the situation in the country first. Student unrest at the beginning of June brought about an irrevocable change of direction. On June 6, a non-Communist member of the RKMT, Lu Yü-wen, declared that he had received an anonymous threatening letter because of his counter-criticism of intellectual opposition. This incident caused *JMJP* to announce officially, on June 8, the counter-attack of the Party in an editorial entitled 'What is That Good for?' The critics had had their say: now the CCP would start to make its criticism of the critics. On the same day, Ch'u An-p'ing was dismissed from his post as editor-in-chief of *KMJP*.[4] Ten days later, on June 18, the news agency *NCNA* published the revised text of Mao's speech of February 27. In contrast to the original draft this version contained clear criteria for the limits of criticism. Mao inserted the following section in his text:

> We consider that, broadly speaking, the criteria should be as follows:
> 1. Words and actions should help to unite, and not divide, the people of our various nationalities.
> 2. They should be beneficial, and not harmful, to socialist transformation and socialist construction.
> 3. They should help to consolidate, and not undermine or weaken, the people's democratic dictatorship.
> 4. They should help to consolidate, and not undermine or weaken, democractic centralism.
> 5. They should help to strengthen, and not discard or weaken, the leadership of the Communist Party.
> 6. They should be beneficial, and not harmful, to international socialist unity and the unity of the peace-loving people of the world.
> Of these six criteria, the most important are the socialist path and the leadership of the Party.[5]

The Party leader made it clear that any criticism of the past few weeks which did not correspond to these criteria would be regarded as antagonistic, i.e. 'contradictions between the enemy and ourselves'. In a further editorial of June 22, entitled 'An Extraordinary Spring', *JMJP* intensified its criticism still further. The Party leadership declared that the 'bourgeois rightist opportunists had been warned before' and that now the class struggle would be turned against them. At the opening session of the National People's Congress on June 26 Chou En-lai initiated the counter-criticism (*Fan-p'i-p'ing*).[6] Thus the premier who had contributed to the initiation of the 'Hundred Flowers Movement' publicly placed himself on the side of those who were now calling the critics to account. The session of the People's Congress became the first tribunal to sit in judgement over the leaders of the opposition. Ch'u An-p'ing, the Minister of Forestry, Lo Lung-chi

(DL), the Minister of Transport, Chang Po-chün (PWDP), and the Minister of Food, Chang Nai-ch'i (DNCA), as well as a number of leading non-Communist intellectuals, were forced to make humiliating self-accusations before the Congress.[7] This was the beginning of the 'First Campaign against Rightists' (*I-tz'u fan-yu yün-tung*), which was to continue as an extensive purge up to April 1958.[8]

The turning-point in the summer of 1957 has received different interpretations from observers of Chinese politics. Even now some people say that the 'Hundred Flowers Movement' was nothing but a gigantic hoax by means of which the forces of opposition were exposed and destroyed. Indeed, this assertion was made by the CCP itself in July 1957, in an editorial in *JMJP*, which declared that the period of freedom of expression had seen the growth of 'fragrant flowers' (*hsiang-hua*) as well as of 'poisonous weeds' (*tu-ts'ao*) which could now be uprooted.[9]

This *ex post facto* explanation is not convincing. Roderick MacFarquhar's arguments have proved that the 'Hundred Flowers Movement' was not projected as a trap by the Party leader.[10] The history of the CCP offers additional evidence. Whatever the Party's tactical skill, only rarely did Mao and his colleagues hide their actual intentions. Just as before coming to power Mao had always referred to the fact that his ultimate aim was the establishment of a Communist social order and that all political decisions served this aim, so also had he made clear his real intentions in his speech of February 27. A primitive hoax by the Party leader cannot be substantiated. This judgement is supported by the fact that the new leadership of the CCP after the Cultural Revolution in 1969 no longer spoke of a trap for the opposition, but rather reproached Liu Shao-ch'i for having turned the rectification campaign into 'an attack on the Party by the forces of opposition'.[11]

Therefore we must assume that Mao's call for open criticism was meant seriously, and that the discussion he had conceived of as a safety-valve reached a degree of intensity he had not anticipated. Mao overestimated the stability of his political system when he initiated the 'Hundred Flowers Movement'. The experiences of spring 1957 could not but bring about an incisive reconsideration of CCP policy. Mao, together with the Party, stood at the crossroads; and a substantial domestic political change in direction resulted from the discussions among the leadership group in the summer and autumn of 1957.

Reconstruction and Development of the National Economy[12]

These discussions within the leadership group were conducted against a background of an economic development policy which, since 1950, had led not only to a rapid recovery of the national economy from war damage, but also to a remarkable expansion of production in almost every sector of the economy, and considerable improvements in the infrastructure. From the mass of available data on the economic development of China from 1950 to 1957, we shall select only those which elucidate general trends in development. In the realm of agricultural production, cultivated land, which during the 1930s already amounted to more than 102 million hectares, had increased 11 per cent, from 100 million hectares in 1950 to 111 million in 1957. Moreover, a systematic reforestation of about 10 million hectares of land, especially in North-west China, curbed further erosion.[13] By means of large water conservancy projects, especially projects on the Hwang-ho and Huai-ho, attempts were made to reduce the effects of flood and drought. Thus a considerable increase in the harvest yield was effected:

Table V/1

HARVESTS IN THE PEOPLE'S REPUBLIC OF CHINA, 1949–1957[14]

Year	Official estimates Amount (1,000,000 tons)	Per capita (kilos.)	Estimates by O. L. Dawson Amount (1,000,000 tons)	Per capita (kilos.)
1949	108·1	199·4	150	276·8
1952	154·4	268·5	175	304·3
1953	156·9	266·8	166	282·3
1957	185·0	285·9	185	285·9

Having regard to the vagueness of the actual size of the Chinese population, data on *per capita* production must be evaluated with great caution. If we follow official data supplied by the Chinese Communists, then the production of grain and potatoes increased 42·8 per cent during the years of reconstruction from 1949 to 1952 and increased again by 17·3 per cent during the first five-year plan from 1953 to 1957. Dawson, who is probably justified in estimating the harvest of the last year of the civil war as considerably higher, arrives at increases of 16·6 per cent for the phase of reconstruction, and 11·4 per cent for the period of the plan. But whichever column of estimates one considers, there was in any case more food available for the population than at the time of the Communist take-over.

Successes in the realms of industry and mining were even greater than for agriculture. There the extensive political endeavours for development of the CCP became particularly evident (see Table V/2). The Sino-American economist Wu Yüan-li calculated from these data the following average rates of growth per annum for the periods 1949–52 and 1952–7 (see Table V/3).

Table V/2

PRODUCTION OF IMPORTANT INDUSTRIAL AND MINING PRODUCTS, 1949–1957[15]

Year	Coal (mil. tons)	Electricity (1,000 mil. kWh)	Crude oil (mil. tons)	Crude steel (mil. tons)	Cotton cloth (1,000 mil. m)
1949	30·98	4·31	0·121	0·158	1·89
1952	63·53	7·26	0·436	1·349	3·83
1953	66·57	9·20	0·622	1·774	4·69
1957	123·23	19·34	1·458	5·350	5·05

Table V/3

AVERAGE RATE OF GROWTH PER ANNUM, 1949–1952, 1952–1957[16]

Item	1949–52 %	1952–57 %
Coal	27·00	14·10
Electricity	18·95	21·66
Crude oil	53·30	27·30
Crude steel	104·40	24·30
Cotton cloth	26·55	5·70

Official Chinese Communist data suggest that the average rate of growth for industrial production as a whole was 34·8 per cent for the period of reconstruction and 17·95 per cent for the period of the first five-year plan. Wu, however, even arrives at an average growth rate of 18·5 per cent per annum for the period of the first plan.[17] In foreign trade the PR of China succeeded in turning what until 1950 had been a chronic deficit in the balance of trade[18] into a surplus, although at first this was undoubtedly achieved only by means of a decisive cut-back in consumption. The volume was increased 240 per cent. During the phase of reconstruction from 1949 to 1952 the increase therefore amounted to 56 per cent, and during the period of the first plan to 53·8 per cent. In 1957 the volume of foreign trade reached US $3,025 million, and the export surplus came to US $165 million.[19] The most important trade partners at first were the Soviet Union and Eastern Europe; trade with these countries accounted for two-thirds of the total percentage of Chinese trade.

Overall economic development cannot be determined for the phase of reconstruction with the data available because reliable estimates of the gross national product do not exist for 1949 and 1950. According to official reports, however, it increased by 53·5 per cent from 1952 to 1957. Wu calculated an increase of 32·3 per cent for the same period, and the Sino-American economists Liu Ta-chung and Yeh Kung-chia opt for an increase of 35 per cent.[20] Liu and Yeh in their comprehensive study came to the conclusion that the average growth rate per annum of the gross national product during the period of the first five-year plan was about 6 per cent. This is a figure which Dwight H. Perkins has also adopted.[21] Official CCP reports, however, suggest a growth rate of 9 per cent.

The development of communications in the country made great progress during the years of reconstruction and during the first five-year plan. There is an absence of reliable data for the year 1957, but from 1950 to 1958, altogether 5,453 kilometres of railways and 94,000 kilometres of new roads were constructed.[22] Among these were first and foremost the railway link between Peking and Ulan Bator which provided a connection with the Trans-Siberian Railway as well as the Sinkiang railway which was later to be connected with the Soviet 'Turksib' network, and a motor road from Szechwan to the Tibetan capital of Lhasa. Furthermore, a number of railway lines already in existence were converted to double-track. During the years 1950 to 1957 the Chinese Communists set themselves the task of mobilising and training new labour for industrial expansion. This they did with great energy and considerable success. The number of industrial workers increased from 5 to 18 million, and among them the number of skilled workers increased from 2·5 to 6 million.[23]

From the beginning the leadership laid particular stress on the building up of the educational system. In the main they inherited the school system developed by the KMT since 1928, and concentrated their efforts on quantitative expansion. They introduced political education in the interests of Party doctrine and replaced Western school books by those of Soviet origin. Otherwise the system of strict competition and intensive specialised learning was retained. The successes obtained in the field of regular educational institutions are elucidated by the following data:

Table V/4

NUMBER OF STUDENTS AND PUPILS IN THE
PEOPLE'S REPUBLIC OF CHINA, 1949-1957[24]

Year	University students	Secondary pupils	Primary pupils
1949	130,058	1,271,342	24,391,032
1952	219,750	3,078,826	49,034,081
1953	212,000	3,601,000	51,664,000
1957	441,000	7,059,000	64,279,000

The number of pupils and students showed an overall increase of 170 per cent during the first eight years of Communist rule in China, and the struggle against illiteracy was considerably advanced. Evening courses to familiarise illiterate adults with the fundamentals of reading and writing also served this purpose. In 1953, 2·9 million people undertook such courses, and in 1957, 7·2 million.[25] These endeavours, together with an expansion of the school system and a simplification of written Chinese in 1955, led to a 25 per cent decrease in the number of illiterates in the population and to a remarkable increase in the percentage of those undergoing compulsory education and of those who could actually attend school. Nevertheless, the problems which arose in this field were so difficult that in spring 1957, 40 per cent of the children who were due for compulsory education still could not enter classes.[26]

Finally, considerable improvements were made in the health service, especially in the cities. But even in the countryside the first steps had been taken. Health service centres were established in many villages and vaccinations resulted in a decrease of contagious diseases.

However, the impressive achievements in the field of development policy which may be deduced from these data led to an imbalance in the different sectors of the economy. The first five-year plan was officially applicable to the period 1953-7, but it had not been formally adopted before the second session of the National People's Congress on July 30, 1955. Following the example of the first two five-year plans of the Soviet Union it clearly emphasised the development of 40.9 per cent of all basic and heavy industrial investment, and 58.2 per cent of capital-forming investment in the plan was allocated to this sector, whereas only 8 per cent and 7·6 per cent respectively was made available for the development of agriculture.[27] Heavy industry as a proportion of capital-forming investment in the industrial sector fluctuated between 82·4 per cent in 1953 and 87·7 per cent in 1955, so that the average ratio between capital-forming investment in heavy industry and in light and consumer goods industry was 5·7 : 1.[28] In spite of all its successes, the priority accorded to heavy industry and raw materials at the expense of agriculture and the production of consumer goods created the danger that the gap between the urban and rural sectors of the national economy might increase further, and that dependency on expansion in capital-intensive branches of the economy for economic growth might be reinforced. If the CCP leadership wished to check this trend it had to formulate new concepts in development policy better adjusted to Chinese conditions. But this implied, if not a dissociation from the Soviet development model, at least a limited divergence.

Soviet Model or 'Independent Path'

The economic and social development of China, since the end of the period of reconstruction, was determined mainly by three factors:

1. The effort to build up heavy industry and the raw materials

industry at the expense of agriculture in order to achieve national autonomy in this sphere as fast as possible.

2. The establishment of an extensive system of individual incentives by means of which productive forces could be developed. Basically it stemmed from the conviction that the superiority of socialist modes of production would be made evident by a visible rise in the standard of living.

3. The acceleration of the 'socialist transformation' of society in order to create the preconditions required by the Party for establishing a socialist social order.

The clear successes of the concept of development policy which had been defined by these considerations and which, as we have seen, had determined the norms of the first five-year plan, could be traced not least to the consistency with which the CCP leadership itself subscribed to it. It clearly followed the model practised by the Soviet leadership during the period of early and fully-fledged Stalinism, with the forcible collectivisation of agriculture, the order of preference of the first two Soviet five-year plans and by the instruments of work norms and the Stakhanovite system. The transference of Soviet principles of development to China was considerably reinforced by the strong participation of the Soviet Union in building up Chinese heavy industry. As early as 1950 the Soviet government had given its support to the establishment of 141 industrial projects. In 1954 another fifteen were added and in April 1956 a further fifty-five. A number of these projects were merged and others were not realized; yet 166 industrial projects remained which were completed with Soviet assistance. Most were completed before the end of the first plan period.[29] These new enterprises formed the core of the industrial establishment in China, and according to Soviet reports, they soon produced 30 per cent of the pig-iron, 39 per cent of the lorries, 30 per cent of the synthetic ammoniac and 35 per cent of the electricity of the nation. But the Soviet Union's technical assistance to the PR of China considerably exceeded this. China received more than 24,000 collections of scientific and technical data from the Soviet Union, including 1,400 blueprints of complete factories. About 10,000 Chinese engineers, technicians and skilled workers were trained in the Soviet Union, and more than 10,000 Soviet technicians supported economic reconstruction in China through their labour.[30] Thus national economic dependence on the Soviet Union increased from year to year from the beginning of the first five-year plan. Under these conditions, in 1957 there developed a disparity between a capital-intensive and rapidly developing heavy industry and a severely underdeveloped light industry as well as an extremely backward agriculture.

The system of production incentives put into practice by the CCP during the first plan, and the emphasis on specialised technology necessary for heavy industrial development, caused a widening gap to develop between the living standard of technicians and skilled workers on the one hand and the rural masses on the other hand.[31] This was further reinforced by the introduction of a new wage system in June 1956. At that time eight clearly differentiated industrial wage levels were established in accordance with different levels of education.[32]

New kinds of problems accompanied the achievements made in reconstruction during the first plan. The range of tools used till then in development policy, which were largely Soviet in origin, were no longer adequate. It was necessary rather to set a course for the balanced development of industry and agriculture. Two different paths were open to the CCP leadership:

(a) to refrain from further substantial changes in the economic structure and to initiate a *phase of consolidation* during which a sustained expansion of production in all sectors would gradually enhance the living standards of the population and thereby prove the superiority of the socialist system; or

(b) to rely upon the impressive achievements of the campaigns for social change and to trust in the efficiency of the government mechanism to accomplish innovations and thus push forward towards a *permanent* completion of the socialist social order and the transition to Communism.

The latter method would be dependent primarily upon the tool of the mass movement, and hence specifically representative of the Chinese Communists' system. The liberalisation tendencies which had grown within the Eastern Bloc since the spring of 1956 provided the framework in which the concept of such an 'independent path' for the PR of China was made possible.

A potential theoretical concept for such an 'independent path' had been outlined since 1956. Mao had already demanded a greater equilibrium between the development of the several economic sectors and the different economic regions in his speech of April 25, 1956. The 'National Programme for the Development of Agriculture, 1956–67',[33] put forward under his guidance, accorded a higher degree of priority than hitherto to the expansion of agricultural production within the general order of economic development. However, it also made it clear that even in the future the agricultural sector could not be provided with much more capital investment from the state. Agricultural development would be advanced through self-reliance.

It was the opinion of Mao and of those members of the Party leadership who supported his concept that with the ending of the first five-year plan the time had come to replace the clear priority accorded to the capital-intensive reconstruction of heavy industry by the simultaneous development of industry and agriculture. In order to harness all national technological resources to this conception one could not, so the Party leader thought, rely solely upon modern technology; both modern and traditional techniques would have to be used to the same extent.

Yet even under these conditions a simultaneous development of industry and agriculture, predominantly advanced by capital investment, would have necessitated a financial backing which, in view of the lack of capital in China, as in most other developing countries, could not be provided. Mao and his colleagues were convinced that this stumbling block could be overcome by substituting a comprehensive mobilisation of China's vast labour reservoir for the absent investment capital. They thought it possible to switch to a labour-intensive concept of development since a capital-intensive policy of development could not be undertaken.[34] In this situation the tool of the mass movement, successfully employed from 1950 to 1956 in the sphere of economic transformation, presented itself. If political campaigns were connected with production campaigns, quantitive and qualititative *leaps* could replace the linear type of development. Seasonal unemployment among a population of which more than four-fifths were peasants could be overcome, and the abolition of the division of labour which Party theory anticipated for Communist society could be initiated.

The combining of mass movements of a predominantly political nature with comprehensive production campaigns offered, according to Mao's understanding, the further opportunity of overcoming the substantially anti-egalitarian system of incentives. If it were possible to awaken the enthusiasm of the masses in the interests of a 'just and equal' future society, then their consciousness, still attuned to the profit motive, could be transformed as well. Their productive forces could be awakened and the preconditions in the sphere of consciousness for the transformation of modes of production and of society could be created thereby. 'New Men' would place themselves in the service of the establishment of a 'New Society' and they would be willing to suffer temporary hardships.

Out of such convictions grew a Chinese concept which prevailed during the second half of 1957 as an alternative to the Soviet model of development.

Mao Tse-tung's Decision

This alternative concept may with justification be called 'Maoist';

for its principles had been created by Mao, and it could become politically effective only through his decision. The change in the general concept of development policy is not only contemporaneous with the interruption of the 'Hundred Flowers Movement' and with the beginning of the 'Anti-rightist Campaign', but rather its content was decisively moulded by the events of June and July 1957. Mao had initiated far-reaching liberalisation measures during the first months of the year because he was convinced that China 'had never before been so united'. Great economic achievements led to sustained improvements in the standard of living, to such an extent that the leader of the Chinese Communists had expected a substantially positive response from the population. Permitting criticism within the system of the administrative deficiencies and work style of low- and medium-level functionaries seemed to be possible without jeopardising the whole system. However, Mao's optimism was disappointed. Orthodox Leninists within the Party apparatus who had warned against internal political liberalisation and who had repeatedly emphasised the necessity of greater discipline were justified. The failure of the 'Hundred Flowers Movement' must have convinced Mao that it was impossible to create a socialist, even less a Communist, consciousness through enhancing material living conditions. In spite of all the economic achievements the opposition of the intelligentsia and of other strata of society as well became massively apparent, for a short time rocking the foundations of the political system in the early summer of 1957. To substantiate the full effects of this traumatic experience on Mao we should need far more comprehensive material and the methods of political psychology. However, from the available material we can ascertain that the failure of his experiment in liberalisation forced Mao to conclude that the transformation of consciousness would not necessarily follow that of reality, but that consciousness and reality had to be changed simultaneously and in conjunction through gigantic new efforts at mobilisation. Mao veered to the left: to a combination of methods of rule founded substantially on force and favoured by the orthodox leaders of the Party apparatus and a system of mobilisation for permanent campaigns to effect changes. The alternative of a gradual enhancement of national living conditions during a period of consolidation was rejected. With this decision, however, Mao Tse-tung made his own political future dependent on the success of the policy of permanent mobilisation.

References

1 *NCNA*, Peking, September 1, 1968.
2 MacFarquhar, *op. cit.*, p. 261.
3 *NCNA*, Peking, May 26, June 19, 1957.
4 *JMJP*, June 8, 1957.
5 *NCNA*, Peking, June 18, 1957: *JMJP*, June 19, 1957,
6 *NCNA*, Peking, June 26, 1957.
7 *JMJP*, July 15, 16, 1957; *NCNA*, Peking, August 10, 1957; cf. MacFarquhar, *op. cit.*, pp. 285-91.
8 See below, pp. 84-6.
9 *JMJP*, July 22, 1957.
10 MacFarquhar, *op. cit.*, p. 12.
11 'Chiu-ta' wen-chien ming-ts'e chieh-shih (*Definitions of Terms in the Documents of the Ninth Party Congress*), Hong Kong ed. of an anonymous pamphlet published in Canton, Hong Kong, 1969, p. 19.
12 Cf. also John Lossing Buck, Owen L. Dawson, Yuan-li Wu, *Food and Agriculture in Communist China*, New York, 1966, pp. 3-72; Werner Handke, *Die Wirtschaft Chinas*, Frankfurt/Main, 1959, pp. 143-284; Grossmann, *op. cit.*, pp. 44-82; also Audrey Donnithorne, *China's Economic System*, London, 1967, *passim*; Ta-chung Liu, Kung-chia Yen, *The Economy of the Chinese Mainland – National Income and Economic Development*, Princeton, 1965, pp. 39-67, 83-124, 126-70; Werner Klatt, *op. cit.*, pp. 94-111; Wu Yüan-li (Liyuan Wu), 'The Economy after Twenty Years', in Trager-Henderson, *op. cit.*, pp. 123-51; Chao I-neng, *Industries*, in URI, *Communist China 1949-1959*, *op. cit.*, Vol. II, pp. 145-219; Kung Nien-jen, 'Agricultural Production in Communist China', *ibid.*, Vol. I, pp. 91-115; Shih Ch'ing-shih, *The Economic Tangles in Communist China*, *ibid.*, Vol. I, pp. 117-47.
13 *Wei-ta-te shih nien* (*The Great Decade*), Peking, 1959; Buck-Dawson-Wu, *op. cit.*, p. 53.
14 Data in Wu, Trager-Henderson, *loc. cit.*, p. 150; other source references *ibid*.
15 Data ibid.
16 Calculated by Wu, *ibid.*, p. 138.
17 *Ibid.*, p. 139.
19 Dwight H. Perkins, 'Mao Tse-tung's Goals and China's Economic Performance', in *Current Scene*, (hereafter cited as *CS*), Hong Kong, Vol. IX, No. 1, January 7, 1971, p. 3.
18 Cf. Domes, *Revolution*, *op. cit.*, p. 599.
20 Wu, *loc. cit.*, p. 150; also Liu-Yeh, *loc. cit.*, p. 213.
21 Perkins, *ibid*.
22 *CNA*, No. 543, December 4, 1964.
23 Cf. Jürgen Domes, *Von der Volkskommune zur Krise in China*, (hereafter cited as Domes, *Volkskommune*), Duisdorf, 1964, p. 13.
24 Data in I Wo-sheng, 'Education in Communist China', in URI, *Communist China 1949-1959*, *op. cit.*, Vol. III, p. 101.

25 *Ibid.*

26 According to the 'Warsaw version' of Mao's speech of February 27, 1957, in *New York Times*, June 13, 1957.

27 *First Five-Year Plan for Development of the National Economy of the People's Republic of China, 1953–1957*, Peking, 1956, pp. 28–9.

28 Chao, *loc. cit.*, p. 174.

29 Chao, *loc. cit.*, pp. 169–71; also Wu, *Economy, op. cit.*, pp. 185–90; Institut für Asienkunde, *Die wirtschaftliche Verflechtung der Volksrepublik China mit der Sowietunion*, Bd, III, Schriften des Instituts für Asienkunde in Hamburg, Frankfurt/Main, Berlin, 1959, p. 58.

30 M. Kapitsa, 'Ein bedeutendes Datum im Leben zweiger Völker', in *Krasnaja Swjesda*, Moscow, February 14, 1964, cited in Wu, *ibid.*, p. 187.

31 Cf. Wu, *ibid.*, pp. 81–4.

32 *Ibid.*, pp. 82–3, cited from Charles Hoffmann, *Work Incentives in Communist China*, Berkeley, Calif., 1964.

33 *National Programme for Agricultural Development, 1956–1967*, Peking, 1960; cf. Schurmann, *op. cit.*, pp. 199–202.

34 Joachim Glaubitz, *Opposition gegen Mao – Abendgespräche am Yenshan und andere politische Dokumente*, Olten-Freiburg Brsg., 1969, p. 22.

Part Two
Experiment 1957-1965

VI.   The 'Anti-rightist Campaign' 1957–1958

The CCP's counter-attack against the critics of the spring of 1957 was by no means restricted to the extraction of public confessions from leading personalities in the non-Communist United Front parties at the plenary session of the National People's Congress in late June 1957. These actions were simply the beginning of a systematic and extensive campaign to discipline the opposition. Influenced by the spread of the wave of criticism to students and secondary pupils, the leadership declared that contradictions which at first had been called 'non-antagonistic' had turned into 'antagonistic' ones. Accordingly, they would have to be resolved by the organs of the 'dictatorship of the proletariat', i.e. by means of physical force. At the end of August, three leaders of the student movement in Wuhan, Wang Chien-kuo, Chang Yü-wen and Yang Huan-yao, were sentenced to death by a 'mass court', and the sentence was executed immediately without the approval of the People's Supreme Court.[1] The physical liquidation of critics was, however, limited to special cases. Altogether some 400 executions were reported in the course of four months from the middle of July,[2] so that even if we project these data from most of the cities and from a few rural areas to the whole of the country, then certainly less than a thousand opponents of the Party were executed. The new purge employed the so-called 'education through labour' which the leadership had initiated by means of a resolution of the State Council of August 1, 1957.[3] The authorities now sent 'vagabonds, loafers' and persons who offended against police regulations as well as 'counter-revolutionaries' and 'reactionaries', even if they had not committed any crime in law, to forced labour camps for an indefinite time. The new camps for 'education through labour' were subordinate to the Ministry of Justice and the Ministry of Public Security. In accusation meetings, administrative offices, mass organisations, economic enterprises and schools opponents were branded as 'bad elements' (*Huai fen-tzu*) and 'rightist deviationists' (*Yu-ch'ing fen-tzu*), and were handed over to the security authorities to be sent to labour camps. Simultaneously they lost, for at least the period of their internment, their civil and political rights. In this way the organisations and institutions to which the critics belonged were given the authority to deal with them.

The Disciplining of the non-Communist United Front Parties

Although the non-Communist United Front parties had played a leading role in the 'Hundred Flowers Movement', and although the extension of the criticism of the CCP from particular deficiencies to the ideology and the system themselves had originated from within their ranks, nevertheless there were a number of personalities among them who had remained loyal to the CCP even during the high tide of criticism. Among them were not only those Communists who had dual membership of the minority parties, but also those politicians who in their anxiety about their personal future existence had kept themselves back in the dispute with the CCP. These circles now became the tools of the Communist counter-attack. During a new series of forums in August and September 1957 they directed their criticism against the leading dissidents and handed over the 'right deviationists' to the security authorities.[4] The non-Communist United Front parties never recovered from the struggles of the summer and autumn of 1957. The areas for recruiting members were further limited, and the purges weakened their personnel to such an extent that thenceforth they were irrelevant to the political process in the PR of China. Altogether more than 2,000 members of the RKMT were labelled as 'rightist deviationists'. The DL lost more than one-third of the members of its CC, and 4,300 more party followers. The DNCA lost 3,400, the APD 452 and the CSH 700.[5] The party chairman of the PWDP, the Minister of Transport, Chang Po-chün, and the chairman of the TDSL, Mme Hsieh Hsüeh-hung, were dismissed from their posts. Being labelled as 'rightist deviationists' meant for most of those reprimanded that they lost their government positions as well. Thus the Minister of Forestry, Lo Lung-chi (DL), the Minister of Transport, Chang (PWDP) and the Minister of Food, Chang Nai-ch'i (DNCA) were dismissed at the fifth session of the first National People's Congress in February 1958, and together with them ten members of the Standing Committee of the National People's Congress and fifty-four other members.[6]

However, the purge was not limited to the smaller parties, but rather rapidly extended to scientists and artists as well. Even members of the CCP were not exempted, although the number of purges among the ranks of the Party was restricted.

Purges among the Intellectuals and in the CCP

Among the intellectuals the purges affected primarily the older scientists who, like the sociologist Fei Hsiao-t'ung,[7] had protested against the overwhelming influence of the Communist Party cadres in the universities and schools, as well as a number of left-wing writers who in the spring of 1957 had propounded the independence of literature from any kind of tutelage. In this case the campaign was initiated in July and August after preliminary attacks on the critics by the Third Plenum of the Eighth CC which convened in Peking from September 21 to October 9. Teng Hsiao-p'ing declared in his speech 'On the Rectification Campaign' that the principle 'Let a Hundred Flowers Bloom' was still valid, but he now related it to the 'comprehensive participation of workers and peasants as writers', announcing that from now on the Party, in its counter-attack, would deal the opposition 'decisive blows'.[8] Four weeks later the journal *Wen-yi hsüeh-hsi* (Literary Studies), which had provided an opportunity for many young writers to publish their works since 1954, was closed down. The poet Hsiao Ch'ien, editor of the journal *Wen-yi Pao*, and five other members of its editorial board were dismissed from their posts and replaced by reliable cadres from the Propaganda Department of the CC.[9] Attacks by the CCP in November and December concentrated on the vice-chairman of the Writers' League, Mme Ting Ling (holder of the Stalin Prize and a long-standing Party member), and Feng Hsüeh-feng as well as the writer Ch'en Ch'i-hsia, who had already been seriously criticised in December 1954.[10] They were expelled from the Party and the Writers' League and were interned in camps for 'education through labour'. Since then they have not been mentioned again officially. Only one Red Guard source reported in 1967 that Ting Ling had been released from the camp in 1962 and that she was working as a charwoman in the Ministry of Foreign Affairs.[11] As early as August 1957 the president of the Central Academy of Arts, Chiang Feng, had been expelled from the Party and been dismissed;[12] and up to February 1958 more and more writers and artists were subjected to endless accusations at 'struggle meetings'. Finally they were branded as 'rightist deviationists', handed over to the security authorities and sent to labour camps.

In spite of extensive purges in the field of science, literature and art, which were mainly directed by the deputy head of the Propaganda Department of the CC, Chou Yang, the head of this department, Lu Ting-yi, evaded criticism. Although Lu had contributed substantially to the initiation of the domestic political relaxation by his speech of May 26, 1956, and was regarded as one of the main advocates of permitting criticism, his high rank as a candidate member of the Politburo and the evident identification of his actions in 1956-7 with Mao's own decisions saved him from suffering the fate of some lower-ranking intellectuals in the Party.

Although a great number of Party members and many members of the non-Communist United Front parties had been denounced as 'rightist deviationists', been reprimanded and some even arrested, the leadership had nevertheless attempted to preserve the appearance of unity during the first months of the 'Anti-rightist campaign', at least among full members of the CC. The purges were restricted to the lower and middle levels of the Party organisation and to some provincial leadership cadres and leading officials of the Central administrative apparatus. Two candidate members of the CC were dismissed from their posts: the Vice-Minister of State Control, Wang Han, who has not appeared in public since then,[13] and the First Secretary of the provincial Party committee of Honan, P'an Fu-sheng,[14] who was rehabilitated in 1962, only to be purged again in 1970. The president of the criminal court of the People's Supreme Court, Chia Ch'ien, his deputy, Chu Yao-t'ang,[15] the Governor of Chekiang, Sha Wen-han,[16] the Governor of Tsinghai, Sun Tso-pin,[17] the Vice-Governor of Anhui, Li Shih-nung,[18] as well as the Vice-Governors of Kansu, Sun Tien-ts'ai and Ch'en Ch'eng-yi,[19] were expelled from the Party and sent to 'education through labour' camps. No reliable data exist concerning the extent of the campaign. Up to the end of August 1957, however, more than 1,000 cadres of the CCP had been denounced as 'right deviationists'.[20] In the winter of 1957–8 Chinese Communist sources mentioned figures of between 300,000 and 550,000 'rightist deviationists' who had been sent to labour camps.[21]

The Party leadership succeeded in reconsolidating its control over the whole country and in shattering the combination of opposition forces. After experiencing 'struggle meetings' in the autumn and winter of 1957, nonconformist intellectuals and dissidents within the Party scarcely dared state their opinions openly. Nevertheless, the events of spring 1957 had proved that the leadership could no longer count on the consent of essential sectors of the population. It had to rely upon the apparatus of control to the same extent as during the first years after its coming to power if it intended to bring about a substantial change in the internal political course. But this rendered necessary an agreement upon the new course within the leading organs of the Party, in which new disputes had developed parallel to the campaign against the 'rightist deviationists'.

Disputes over a New General Line

Discussions concerning the order of preferences and investment directives for the second five-year plan which was to have commenced in 1958 had already begun in January 1957. Apparently there were two opinions which stood in mutual opposition. One group within the Party leadership pressed, even if not yet in concrete terms, for a sustained acceleration in general economic development. It is certain that this group comprised Mao's long-standing secretary, Ch'en Po-ta, and probably Marshal Lin Piao. There are signs which suggest that Liu Shao-ch'i too was already willing at that time to favour an intensification of the pace of development. Those members of the leadership directly responsible for economic policy, notably the First Vice-Premier, Ch'en Yün, the Chairman of the State Planning Commission, Li Fu-ch'un, and the Chairman of the National Economic Commission, Po I-po, appear to have favoured the continued application of the principles of the period of the first plan which were determined by a cautious evaluation of economic reality.[22] A number of public statements made by Chou En-lai in 1957 lead one to deduce that even the Premier himself supported this group which proposed the principle of gradual growth. At a conference of provincial secretaries of the CCP during the second half of January 1957 the two groups of opinion had their first confrontation. Ch'en Yün made severe attacks on 'those people who demanded a ruthless and rash advance'.[23]

It appears that at first the group of economic politicians prevailed, for the plan report, which Li Fu-ch'un put forward at the fourth plenum of the First National People's Congress in June did not contain any views that were essentially new. But in under a month the situation had changed. Under the influence of the failure and interruption of the 'Hundred Flowers Movement', Mao Tse-tung placed himself on the side of those radical forces within the Party leadership who favoured the mass mobilisation of human labour and the speeding up of the pace of development. In his speech at an enlarged conference of CCP provincial secretaries in Tsingtao, the Party leader called for a development policy which would bring 'faster, better and more economical results'. The influence of Mao's experience with the opposition of the intellectuals became particularly evident in his demand that the 'working class' should produce 'its own technical cadres, its own professors, teachers, scientists, journalists, writers, artists and theoreticians of Marxism–Leninism' and if possible a 'great contingent of them'. He laid down a period of ten to fifteen years to create this new proletarian élite.[24] However, the dispute continued after the expression of Mao's opinion. The radical group specified its conceptions: the APCs should be reorganised and merged into bigger units. The development of agriculture and of small rural industry should be financed in the main by means of the APCs in order to relieve the state budget. But the leading men in the administrative apparatus, particularly those responsible for economic administration, continued to emphasise a policy of capital-intensive development. The radicals were not yet able to prevail at the State

Conference on Agriculture in early September; their proposals to merge the APCs into bigger units of production were not taken into account in the guide lines adopted by the Party centre on September 14 for the reorganisation of agricultural collectives.[25] But during the Third Plenum of the Eighth CC the tendency leading to a turning-point in internal politics became more distinct. Up to then it had been stressed that economic development and social transformation should be advanced simultaneously and according to the 'objective conditions', but now the leadership began to stress the 'revolutionary enthusiasm of the Party' and correct ideological thinking. Thanks to the documents which reached the outside world during the course of the Cultural Revolution it is now possible to obtain some evidence regarding the composition of the various groups of opinion during this conflict.[26] Ch'en Yün, Li Fu-ch'un, the Minister of Metallurgical Industry, Wang Ho-shou, the Minister of Coal and Industry, Chang Lin-chih and the Minister of Agriculture, Liao Lu-yen, apparently supported by Po I-po and Chou En-lai, turned against the transition to a labour-intensive development policy, while Lin Piao, Ch'en Po-ta as well as the First Secretary of the Shanghai City Committee of the CCP, K'o Ch'ing-shih and the newly appointed First Secretary of the Provincial Committee of Honan, Wu Chih-p'u, supported Mao.

From early December 1957 a number of articles in *JMJP*, which called unequivocally for a combination of mass movement and development policy,[27] confirmed that the radicals had increased their influence in the Politburo and in the CC. Once control over the population had been reimposed, a change of direction manifested itself which aspired to transform society with a qualitative leap and which simultaneously aimed at maximising the intensity of the organisation of human labour in order to awaken completely those powers in the Chinese people which were allegedly or actually still un-mobilised. In spring 1958 Mao succeeded in winning over the majority of the Party leadership.

*Mao Tse-tung Prevails : The Second Plenum of the
Eighth Party Congress*

During the first months of 1958 the leader of the CCP attempted to by-pass the central leadership organ by trying to gain the support of the provincial Party secretaries at a series of regional conferences.[28] At the beginning of January the leading provincial cadres of East China met in Hangchow and at the end of January those of South China met in Nanking. At both conferences they consented to the *Sixty Articles on Work Methods* which Mao had expounded and in which the Party leader had formulated the principles of mass mobilisation, the relationship between cadres and the population and mutual control in the Party apparatus.[29] After thus securing the backing of the leadership of two important regions, in March Mao again demanded, at a third regional conference in Chengtu, that the APCs be merged into larger units and that agricultural planning be decentralised to a greater degree.[30] There, however, he was confronted by another critic, who being a revolutionary veteran and a successful general of the civil war enjoyed great esteem: the Minister of Defence, Marshal P'eng Te-huai, declared that the Chairman talked about 'greater, faster, better and more economical results' as if he were 'chanting liturgies'. He warned against Mao's theory of qualitative and quantitive leaps.[31] However, Mao gained the support of the provincial cadres gathered in Chengtu. Several weeks later, Wu Chih-p'u, without waiting for the fundamental decision of the Central organs, began to merge APCs in Honan and to establish public dining-halls in the villages in order to release human labour for mass campaigns in production and public works.[32] At the beginning of May the provincial leadership of Shantung followed suit.[33]

At the same time, K'o Ch'ing-shih ordered the construction of small furnaces in the villages and backyards of towns in the region of Shanghai, thereby aiming at a considerable increase in steel production. With respect to this initiative Mao himself later took responsibility.[34] In collaboration with some provincial Party leaders he had succeeded in creating a *fait accompli*. Thus the impending fundamental decisions of the Central organs could not but be taken in accordance with his views.

Nevertheless, Mao's policy could hardly have prevailed at the time had it not gained the approval of the leading men in the civil Party apparatus around Liu Shao-ch'i and Teng Hsiao-p'ing. Although the Maoists alleged that Liu, in connection with a general condemnation of him during the Cultural Revolution, had argued against the policy of the Party leader in the spring of 1958 as well, this was without doubt an *ex post facto* accusation.[35] For Liu, in his speech on the fortieth anniversary of the October Revolution on November 6, 1957, at last, had placed himself on the side of the radicals in the dispute, which was by no means settled by then. He took up Mao's theory of contradictions during the phase of socialist society and declared that the 'class struggle between the bourgeoisie and the working class' had by no means ended yet, but would continue for a 'long time'.[36] Simultaneously he called, like Mao, for 'better and faster' results in economic production.[37]

At the Second Plenum of the Eighth Party Congress, held from May 5 to 23, 1958,[38] Liu's support substantially contributed to the fact that this nominally supreme decision-making body of the CCP adopted Mao's concept of development. When Liu read the CC's work report he outlined the programme of collectivisation, mass mobilisation and the intensified formation of consciousness. Like Mao he predicted a new tide of enthusiasm which would rapidly create a Communist social order in China:

> The broad masses of the working people have realised more fully
> . . . that the happiness of the individual lies in the realisation of the
> lofty socialist ideals of all the people. That is why they have dis-
> played an heroic Communist spirit of self-sacrifice in the work.
> Their slogan is: 'Hard work for a few years, happiness for a thous-
> and.' This mighty torrent of Communist ideas has swept away
> many stumbling blocks – individualism, departmentalism, localism,
> and nationalism [of the national minorities – J.D.] . . . All this is,
> as Lenin said, 'the actual beginning of Communism', 'the beginning
> of a change which is of world historic significance'.[39]

After severe attacks on those comrades who prefer 'to advance slowly and not quickly' Liu launched a call to 'build our country, in the shortest possible time, into a great socialist country'.[40] This, however, could only be achieved through revolutionary means in the course of 'uninterrupted' or 'permanent revolution' (*Pu-tuan ko-ming*):

> Marx, Engels and Lenin often pointed out that the watchword of
> the working class should be 'uninterrupted revolution'. In putting
> forward new revolutionary tasks in good time, so that there is no
> halfway halt in the revolutionary advance of the people, the revolu-
> tionary fervour of the masses will not subside with interruptions of
> the revolution, and Party and state functionaries will not rest content
> with the success won and grow arrogant or apathetic, the Central
> Committee of the Communist Party and Comrade Mao Tse-tung
> have always guided the Chinese revolution by this Marxist–Leninist
> theory of uninterrupted revolution.[41]

This belief of Mao's, that only a series of quantitative and qualitative leaps could stimulate a Communist consciousness among the population, was combined with Liu's concern for the disciplining of the mobilised and controlled masses – a homogeneous concept of development against which sceptics in the state and economic administration could no longer prevail. The policy of the 'Three Red Banners' (*San-mien hung-ch'i*) carried its point.

This also became evident in the personnel decisions of the Fifth Plenum of the Eighth CC on May 25[42] Marshal Lin Piao, one of the earliest followers of the Maoist line, joined the Standing Committee of the Politburo as the fifth vice-chairman. T'an Chen-lin, who had taken over responsibility for establishing bigger agricultural units of production,[43] as well as Li Ching-ch'üan ,and K'o Ch'ing-shih, who, with the provincial CCP organisations of Szechwan and Shanghai, had energetically supported Mao's policy during the disputes of the winter of 1957–8, were elected by the CC as new full members of the Politburo, while the six alternate members of the Politburo were passed over.

At an enlarged conference of the Politburo in Peitaiho from August 17 to 30, 1958, a new collectivisation campaign which aimed at the establishment of agricultural super-collectives, the people's communes, was proclaimed the obligatory political line of the whole Party.[44]

From the behaviour of the members of the Politburo during the time between the Second Plenum of the Party Congress and the Peitaiho conference we may draw conclusions regarding the composition of opinion groups within the leadership. It was a period during which the leadership was not yet obliged to back the new course. In part, the evidence consists of materials from the Cultural Revolution. While a number of Party leaders explicitly favoured the new course publicly, others remained quiet until they were bound by the decisions of Peitaiho, or, like P'eng Te-huai they even made criticisms against Mao's policy.[45] Thus it can be stated that there were at least three clearly articulated groups in the summer of 1958 who had tried to influence the political decision-making process:

1. The group of those around Mao himself who supported the new course in principle, Marshal Lin Piao, K'o Ch'ing-shih, Ch'en Po-ta and K'ang Sheng.

2. The leading men of the Party machine (Liu Shao-ch'i, Teng Hsiao-p'ing, P'eng Chen, T'an Chen-lin and Li Ching-ch'üan, perhaps Ulanfu as well) who had placed themselves on the side of the Chairman after the interruption of the 'Hundred Flowers Movement'.

3. The group of moderates, sceptical or resistant to the new course, comprising Chou En-lai, Ch'en Yün, Li Fu-ch'un, Lin Po-ch'ü, Tung Pi-wu, Marshal P'eng Te-huai, Po I-po as well as probably Li Hsien-nien and Chang Wen-t'ien.[46]

The attitude of Marshals Chu Te, Liu Po-ch'eng, Ch'en Yi and Lo Jung-huan, however, remains unclear. But if we assume that Mao gained a majority for his concept in the Politburo at the Peitaiho conference, then he must have won over not only the group around Liu but also the leading representatives of the PLA. They apparently expected a faster expansion of the industrial and technological foundations of national defence from the Maoist line, just as Liu and his group hoped that the mobilisation of human labour would contribute to the completion of the socialist social order and to the accomplishment of the material basis for the transition to Communism without jeopardising the structures of control of the Party and state apparatus. Mao could count on the consent of both these groups as long as their expectations were fulfilled. If their expectations were disappointed the new course would have to be reversed, which would hardly be in accordance with the views of the Party leader.

References

1 *NCNA*, Wuhan, September 2, 1957; cf. MacFarquhar, *op. cit.*, p. 264.

2 Compiled from reports of *JMJP*, *TKP*, *KMJP*, *WHP* and Hong Kong newspapers July 15 to November 30, 1957; also *Chekiang jih-pao*, October 25, 1957; *Ch'inghai jih-pao*, December 12, 1957; *Kansu jih-pao*, February 2, 1958; *Shensi jih-pao*, March 11, 1958; cf. Fokkema, *op. cit.*, p. 147.

3 'Decision on the Question Concerning Education Through Labour', in *JMJP*, August 2 and 3, 1957. Cf. *CNA*, No. 194, August 23, 1957.

4 For the DL, *NCNA*, Peking, August 10, 1957, English translation in extracts, in MacFarquhar, *op. cit.*, pp. 288-91.

5 Data in Liu Ta-yüan, 'Persecution of all Political Parties by Chinese Communists', in *A Decade of Chinese Communist Tyranny*, T'aipei, 1960, pp. 109-11. This study contains no list of source references. However, JD checked the collection of source materials in T'aipei in summer 1965. The data are reliable.

6 *NCNA*, Peking, December 30, 1957, January 19, 31 and February 1, 1958; cf. MacFarquhar, *op. cit.*, p. 263; also Fokkema, *op. cit.*, p. 151.

7 *NCNA*, Peking, January 19, 1957.

8 *JMJP*, October 19, 1957; *JMST*, 1958, p. 182.

9 Fokkema, *op. cit.*, p. 155.

10 *WYP*, No. 19, 21, 22, 23, 25, 1957; cf. also Shih, *loc. cit.*, pp. 232-4.

11 *Pei-yi tung-fang-hung* (*Peking Art School 'The East is Red'*), Peking, February 17, 1967.

12 *JMJP*, August 3, 1957.

13 *Hsin-hua pan-yüeh-k'an*, Peking, January 10, 1958.

14 *JMJP*, May 25, 1958.

15 *KMJP*, December 12, 1957.

16 *Hsin-hua jih-pao*, Nanking, December 4, 1957; also *WHP*, December 22, 1957; cf. also Frederick C. Teiwes, 'The Purge of Provincial Leaders 1957-1958', in *CQ*, No. 27, July-September 1966, pp. 14-32.

17 *Ch'inghai jih-pao*, Hsining, March 11, 1958.

18 *JMJP*, March 10, 1958.

19 *JMJP*, September 17, 1958.

20 *TKP*, September 1, 1957.

21 *JMJP*, December 5, 1957, March 7, 1958; *KMJP*, May 24, 1958; *Chieh-fang jih-pao*, Shanghai, February 16 and March 14, 1958.

22 See above, pp. 73-6.

23 'Ch'en Yün – A Man Full of Wickedness', in *Peking kung-she* (*Peking Commune*), No. 5, January 29, 1967.

24 First reports on this conference, in *JMJP*, October 19, 1957; also in *Chung-kuo shui-li* (*China's Water Conservancy*), Peking, No. 1, January 1958, p. 7; extracts of Mao's speech, in *Wen-yi hung-ch'i* (*Red Flag of Literature and Art*), Peking, May 30, 1967, English translation, in *SCMP*, No. 4000, August 14, 1967.

25 *JMST*, 1958, p. 520.

26 In particular, Mao's speech before the eighth Plenum of the eighth CC of the CCP, probably on July 23, 1959: extracts from Red Guard publications (Chinese language), in *URI*, *The Case of P'eng Te-huai*, Hong Kong, 1968, pp. 405-12, English translation, *ibid.*, pp. 15-26, (hereafter cited as *Mao's first Lushan speech*). For an early discussion of these group buildings cf. Roderick MacFarquhar, 'Communist China's Intra-Party Disputes', in *Pacific Affairs*, Vol. XXXI, No. 4, December 1958, pp. 323-5.

27 *JMJP*, December 12, 1957.

28 Cf. Chang, *loc. cit.*, pp. 174-5.

29 'Sixty Points on Working Methods, A Draft Resolution from the Office of the Centre of the CCP', February 19, 1958, in Jerome Chen (ed.), *Mao Papers – Anthology and Bibliography*, London, 1970, pp. 57-76.

30 *JMJP*, August 29, 1959; *Hsin chien-she* (*New Construction*), Peking, No. 6, 1960, p. 4; *JMST*, 1959, p. 25.

31 *URI*, *P'eng Te-huai*, *op. cit.*, 203, 479.

32 Mao, first Lushan speech. *loc. cit.*, p. 23, 410.

33 Domes, *Volkskommune*, *op. cit.*

34 Mao, first Lushan speech, *loc. cit.*, pp. 25, 411.

35 Cf. also Dieter Heinzig, 'Mao contra Liu', *Berichte des Bundes-instituts für Ostwissenschaftliche und Internationale Studien*, No. 48, 1967, pp. 23-4.

36 *NCNA*, Peking, November 6, 1957, English translation, in *URI*, *Collected Works of Liu Shao-ch'i, 1945-1957*, Hong Kong, 1969, pp. 445-58, in particular pp. 449-50; also *Shansi jih-pao*, T'aiyüan, October 1, 1958.

37 *Ibid.*, pp. 454-5.

38 *JMST*, 1959, p. 16.

39 *NCNA*, Peking, May 26, 1958; English translation, in *Collected Works of Liu Shao-ch'i 1958-1967*, Hong Kong, 1968, pp. 1-40, in particular p. 10.

40 *Ibid.*, pp. 14-15, p. 20.

41 *Ibid.*, p. 19.

42 *JMST*, 1959, p. 32.

43 *JMJP*, August 11, 1958.

44 *JMJP*, September 10, 1958; *JMST*, 1959, p. 32.

45 *URI*, *Peng Te-huai*, *op. cit.*, pp. 203, 479.

46 Cf. also MacFarquhar, *loc. cit.*, p. 328.

VII. 'Three Red Banners'

The so-called policy of the 'Three Red Banners' – a slogan summarising the fundamental political decisions of the CCP in the spring of 1958 – was to initiate the simultaneous development of industry and agriculture through the use of both modern and traditional methods of production under the 'General Line for Building Socialism' (*She-hui chu-i tsung-chien tsung lu-hsien*). It was to carry through a concept of a labour-intensive development policy by a 'Great Leap Forward' (*Ta-yao-chin*) and to prepare a comprehensive collectivisation of life by the establishing of 'People's Communes' (*Jen-min king-she*). An intricate tissue of ideological and practical political considerations had urged this turn to the left upon the Party leaders. Their statements that China was now in the phase of the 'transition to Communism' suggested *inter alia* an ideological offensive against the Soviet Union. In the eyes of the Chinese Communists, Moscow showed that it was more and more determined to neglect the global revolutionary aims of the Communist movement, to avoid the international tensions caused by the interests of its allies, and to regard itself as a *socialist* state for a long time in order to strengthen its own economy and to increase its political and material capacity to compete with the USA. Mao now prepared the creation of a *communist* social order, and for the first time announced his claim to the leadership of the international Communist movement.

Three of the practical domestic political motives for switching to the policy of the 'Three Red Banners' must be mentioned above all.

1. In spring 1958 Mao and his colleagues were convinced that by collectivising every aspect of life they could break the backbone of one of the most tenacious centres of resistance against the dictatorship of the Party, the traditional Chinese family system.

2. The combination of mass movement and the mobilisation of labour seemed to guarantee a tighter control of the individual and thus to provide better facilities for changing the consciousness of the population.

3. Finally they believed, in the light of the clear diminution in Soviet economic aid since 1956, that they were obliged to accomplish their declared aim of leading China into the ranks of the great industrial powers by themselves, straining all their material and human reserves to the uttermost limits.

The 'General Line'

The Marxist–Leninist concept of history predicts the inevitable progress of mankind in stages, from 'primitive communist society' to 'feudal' society under the rule of a rural upper class, to 'capitalist' urban society and to the final stage of the Communist social order. The essential criteria of the first post-capitalist stage of development, the socialist one, are the co-operative organisation of agriculture, trade and handicraft, nationalised industry, central planning and a system of distribution of goods which rewards the individual according to his work, usually in money.

As the PR of China encountered social and economic problems, particularly in the realm of agriculture, the 'fully socialist' APC in which almost the entire rural population had been organised up to the end of 1957, was regarded as the most important institution of the socialist social order. It generally comprised a village or a hamlet in a comprehensive village unit. The members and their families lived in their houses which still remained private property. Machines, work tools, animals, and cultivated land were under collective administration. Members of the collectives were paid according to their work, and there were individual bonuses for special success in production. With the new change in direction Mao believed it possible to initiate the phase of the 'transition to communist society' and thereby approach the second post-capitalist stage, the final stage of social development. As units of production, however, the APCs appeared to him to be too small for this stage and, moreover, they were too strongly influenced by the principle of private ownership. Bigger collectives were to serve as the means of production of the future. As yet, however, there were no people's communes; for the amalgamations of APCs which first came into being did not go through any drastic changes in the system of ownership. They were essentially determined by productive rationality.

The establishment of big units of agricultural production already suggested a turn towards those priorities in development policy which became the core of the new 'General Line'. Although heavy industry retained its pre-eminence in the field of industry, agriculture and industry were in future to receive the same amount of attention within the framework of the general economy. But as national means of investment did not suffice for the simultaneous development of both economic sectors, the 'General Line' provided that a stronger use of traditional techniques in handicrafts and agriculture was to supplement modern technology in order to expand production. Small local industries were to meet the needs of the villages for simple tools outside the framework of central planning and administration and

Agricultural Production Cooperatives.

would thereby relieve the modern industrial sector. Moreover, campaigns were started to mobilise agricultural labour to construct roads, water conservancy and irrigation projects on which 90 million Chinese worked without pay from March to December 1958.[1] Thus there came into being, especially in the north China plain, extensive dike and irrigation systems without the use of central means of investment.[2] While the economic administration and planning of the modern industrial sector remained with the Central machine, the responsibility for small, local industries, public works and the food supply of the rural population was at first transferred to the districts and communities and later, after August 1958, to the people's communes. Thus a considerable part of the general economic administration was decentralised. The Chinese Communists called the new system the 'Two Decentralisations, Three Centralisations, One Responsibility' (*Liang-fang san-t'ung i-pao*).[3] By this they understood the decentralised use of labour and local investment, central control over political decisions, planning and administration of national investment capital. They saw it as the duty of the basic units to account for themselves to their superior units.

Such a mixed system of centralised and decentralised economic administration could, if at all, only function if the CCP was able to communicate the will of the leadership to the basic units through its own structures of command. The 'General Line' therefore stressed not least the pre-eminence of politics over economic considerations, and linked the campaign for the expansion of production to the idea of reinforcing the indoctrination of the people.

The 'Great Leap'

Through a 'Great Leap Forward' the PR of China wanted to 'catch up with and overtake'[4] the *per capita* production of heavy industry in Great Britain within fifteen years, i.e. by 1972. Steel production thus occupied a key position. To achieve the greatest possible expansion in a short time, not only was investment in steel mills – a number of which had been built with Soviet assistance and had started production in 1958 – considerably increased but attempts were also made to construct a great number of small and miniscule enterprises. Following the example of Shanghai, primitive, clay 'small furnaces' (*Hsiao kuo-lu*) were constructed to produce steel in 'production battles'. As early as September, Li Fu-ch'un reported that steel production would increase from somewhat more than five million to over eleven million (metric) tons,[5] and in April 1959 the Statistical Office of the State Council reported an increase of steel production to 11·8 million tons, i.e. an increase of 107 per cent, reflected by an overall growth rate of 31 per cent in industrial production for 1958.[6]

The steel campaign had made quantitative progress which overshadowed every single achievement made hitherto. This also held good for the production of coal, for which a growth rate of 108 per cent was reported, for crude oil, for which one of 55 per cent was recorded, and for electricity, for which a growth of 42 per cent was reported.[7] But as early as October 1958 it had become clear that the quality of steel produced in small furnaces was extremely low. Po I-po stated on December 7 that it proved to be 'bad or useless'.[8]

The 'production battles' not infrequently impaired the health of the population.[9] Some people's communes took emergency measures which jeopardized the economy in general in order to fulfil the required production norms. For example, cadres ordered their work units to dismantle rails at night and to smelt them down in their small furnaces.[10] During the autumn harvest of 1958 in many regions only 40 per cent of the peasants worked in the fields, and finally many small furnaces had to be closed down to release sufficient labour for the harvest.[11]

Even more dangerous, however, was the long-term damage to the central planning and administration of the economy which resulted from the fast and furious production drive of the summer and autumn of 1958. The misallocation of material, bad preparation for investment and a scarcely tolerable strain on transport communications had aggravated the work of the planning authorities to such an extent that they ceased work for several months after the Peitaiho conference, either to express their opposition to the Maoist development policy or because of an objective inability to survey the situation as a whole.[12]

The successes and failures of the new course, however, were determined in the final analysis not by the events of the 'Great Leap' in production, but by the development of the people's communes.

The People's Communes Movement[13]

We have seen that, as early as April 1958, some regions of the province of Honan – initially the counties of Suip'ing and P'ingyü – started to put into practice the plans of Mao and his followers to merge the APCs.[14] From the end of May this movement spread to other provinces. On July 1, Ch'en Po-ta used the term *commune* for the big collectives for the first time in an article in the new Party theoretical journal, *Hung-ch'i*, and from the beginning of August this term was generally adopted.[15] By mid-July there were only a few regions in which there had not been at least a few people's communes established, and soon such big collectives were set up in the cities as well.[16]

However, the rapid expansion of the new form of organisation caused considerable differences in the character of the collectives. By the end of September four basic types came into being:

1. The most common type of rural commune which on average comprised some 5,000 households and was frequently identical to a community (*Hsiang*).

2. The urban commune based on a residence district.

3. The urban commune based on a big factory.

4. The big agricultural commune which comprised an entire county.[17]

The CCP used the adjectives 'big' (*ta*) and 'common' (*kung*) to describe the people's communes.

'Big' meant that the communes united all kinds of vocational groups and that all economic sectors (agriculture, local industry, fishing and forestry) were placed under a co-ordinated command.

'Common' meant the establishment of co-ordinated public administration and management of the commune, the extension of collective ownership from cultivated land and tools to houses, household tools, small animals and vegetable gardens as well as the comprehensive regulation of the life of individual members by the collective. Working hours in most communes amounted to twelve hours a day during the first phase of the movement, and during harvest time to sixteen and even eighteen hours in exceptional circumstances. Apart from breakfast, meals were taken – officially voluntarily – in canteens. Children and babies often stayed for the whole week in nurseries or crèches. The old were occupied in light work in old people's homes. In a number of communes, which were apparently conceived as models for future overall development, houses were redistributed among the members, or they were demolished and people were accommodated in separate barracks according to their sex.[18] Most communes, however, did not follow this example, not even in the autumn of 1958.

The notion that communes should serve as the basic units for the 'transition to Communism' was widespread, however, and therefore that there should be experiment with the system of wage distribution 'to each according to his needs'. According to this principle about 70 per cent of one's pay was usually provided in kind and 30 per cent in cash.[19]

In most of the communes labour was organised according to military principles in 'labour regiments', 'labour companies' and 'labour platoons'.[20] Their leaders had the same power of command over the members as officers over soldiers, and frequently people were lined up in military formations in the morning to set off for field work.[21]

But it was not only work which was militarily organised. Under the influence of the armed conflict in the Formosa Strait, which culminated in the shelling of Quemoy and Matsu from August 23 to October 5, 1958, commune members between the ages of fifteen and fifty-five years began to be recruited into the militia (*Min-ping* – sometimes also *Jen-min wu-chuang pu-tui: Jen-wu-pu*) and to be trained with weapons.[22] However, ammunition was only distributed in a very few cases, and the essential character of the militia was that of a mass organisation rather than of combat units. Nevertheless, their creation further reinforced the considerable degree of organisational density which had been achieved previously.

The Party leadership attempted to compensate for the disproportions which had been the inevitable result of the rapid development of the people's communes through publicising and recommending for general imitation the draft statutes of the model commune 'Sputnik' (*Wei-hsing*) in Suip'ing, Honan, on September 4, 1958.[23]

According to this document, supreme decision-making power lay, in theory, in the hands of the 'Representatives' Conference' (*Tai-piao ta-hui*) which was elected by all members (except 'landlords, rich peasants, counter-revolutionaries, bad elements and rightist deviationists') and which replaced the existing People's Congresses in all communes which were identical with a community (*Hsiang*). The conference elected its own leadership committee and transferred executive authority to it. According to the directives of this standing committee there operated an administrative head office, a planning committee, the command of the commune militia, the administrative sections for agriculture, water conservancy, industry, transport, domestic work, finance, food supply, trade, culture and health as well as a political department controlled by the local Party committee which in turn became in most cases identical with the standing committee.

The vertical structure of the people's communes consisted of production brigades (*Sheng-ch'an ta-tui*) which received their directives from the commune leadership. But they soon obtained a certain degree of independence in the administration of the canteens and in organising work in the fields. The brigade was usually the equivalent of a former APC. So, as a rule, it united 120 to 150 households and was itself subdivided into production groups (*Sheng-ch'an hsiao-tsu or hsiao-tui*) of ten to fifteen families which, however, had no independent authority to make decisions.

Relations between the communes and state organisations for storing and supplying food were governed by the system of production guarantees (*Pao-ch'an*). This guarantee was given by the commune before each harvest. If it was not fulfilled the commune had to curtail supply for its own members in order to reach the amount of food which it had to deliver. This system inevitably transferred to the commune leadership responsibility for planning in the whole of agricultural production. Further, it was supposed to counteract the tendency to regard the new, big collectives simply as loose federations of APCs and thus to evade intensified collectivisation. When the Peitaiho conference was convened on August 17, 1958, the people's communes movement was already in full swing in almost every province. But it was only then that the Politburo decided to proclaim the creation of the communes as the 'basic policy of the Party' and to declare it to be obligatory. The resolution adopted by the Peitaiho conference on August 22 gave further directives regarding the organisational structure of the collectives and decided on an average size of about 2,000 households.[24] However, investigations made in eighteen provinces at the end of September which took into consideration 5,500 communes, arrived at an average of 4,797 households per commune.[25] Thus the trend was towards bigger units than the leadership had anticipated.

Using enthusiastic slogans the Peitaiho resolution enthused about a 'Great Leap' in food production which was to be caused by the new tide of collectivisation:

> By overcoming reactionary conservatism and by breaking down old conventions in agricultural technology, agricultural production takes a Great Leap Forward. Harvest yields increase 100 per cent, several hundred per cent, more than 1,000 per cent, several thousand per cent. Thus the ideological liberation of the people will be advanced further.[26]

In fact, in 1958, the PR of China, under extraordinarily favourable weather conditions, enjoyed one of its highest, if not the highest hitherto, harvest yields. But the assertion of the Party press that altogether more than 375 million tons of grain and potatoes had been harvested[27] soon proved to be extremely exaggerated. A harvest of between 205 and 215 million tons might be regarded as realistic.[28] But the CCP was in need of high production data in order to convince the people of the success of the collectivisation campaign which since the Peitaiho conference was increasingly regarded as the beginning of the 'transition to Communism'.

The decisions reached at Peitaiho provoked an accelerated, almost uncontrollable, tide of collectivisation which reached almost every village in September. While no more than 20 per cent of rural households had been incorporated into people's communes by mid-August, Peking reported that by September 90·4 per cent of Chinese peasant families had been formed into 23,390 communes.[29] On November 15, JMJP reported that 99 per cent of the rural population were combined in 26,578 people's communes with an average size of 4,637 households.[30]

At the same time the period announced by the publication media of the CCP for the establishment of Communist social order grew shorter and shorter. At the beginning of September some newspapers wrote that the 'transition to Communism' would be completed within twenty years.[31] But at the end of September it was not to need more than ten or fifteen years.[32] The journal of the Communist Youth League reported in the beginning of October that in some people's communes there were 'septuagenerians and octogenerians' who were delighted that 'they would certainly experience the completion of Communist society',[33] and on October 1 the central organ of the CCP promised the Chinese people 'a life in abundance of food and clothing in two or three years'[34] i.e. 1960 or 1961! From mid-October, however, the situation turned against Mao and his followers. It became evident that the CCP leaders had been over-confident.

The Road to Economic Crisis

The hectic period of the People's Communes Movement in August and September 1958 was not without grave consequences. Although leading functionaries had continued to issue warnings and to advise a cautious approach,[35] the majority of the Party leadership, thanks to Mao's influence, had accelerated the pace of collectivisation. Indeed, the people's communes had been established, although almost everywhere the fundamental preconditions for their establishment were absent. Only in rare cases were they provided with sufficient public offices. Canteens, nurseries and old peoples' homes had inadequate accommodation. Accountancy was frequently deficient. In other places the leadership of the communes took the proclamations of the impending 'transition to Communism' at their face value and began to sever all connections with superior organs, because concomitant with the establishment of the Communist social order 'the state would wither away' and they would no longer be obliged to follow any directives.[36]

In some provinces disorder grew into chaos. The Chinese Communist press lamented that the delivery of grain to the state organisation in autumn 1958 was proceeding considerably more slowly than during the preceding year.[37] The lack of tools and experience among personnel led to catastrophic situations in the canteens,[38] and it was not much better in the nurseries.[39] A report of October 1958 may serve as an example:

In the district of Yüling, Shansi, more than 6,000 nurseries and

crèches were established in seventeen days. In the district of
Lingtung 2,000 nurseries were constructed hastily in a week. Winter
came and snow storms set in early. The children in the nurseries
had neither cotton coats nor stoves to keep themselves warm. Their
parents were far away taking part in the steel campaign. The
nursery and crèche personnel did not take sufficient care of the children who were not their own. Thus the nurseries and crèches became the object of many complaints.[40]

Adults had not enough winter clothing either so they could
not work in the fields during frosty weather.[41] Above all the 'production battles' of 1958 had caused such a lack of equilibrium in the national economy that general economic chaos became almost unavoidable. When the following two years brought lower harvest yields
and shortly after a set-back in industrial production,[42] the PR of China
was not in a position to ride the blow. Thus the campaign of 1958
paved the way for the economic crisis of the years 1960-2, causing Lu
Ting-i to state that 'the damage done by the people's communes was
irremediable'.[43] Disorder and the misallocation of materials soon strengthened the resistance which the Chinese peasants in particular began
to undertake against the establishment of the people's communes.
From the middle of October it turned in many places into a general,
if unco-ordinated movement.[44] The peasants refused to go to work in
military formations and secretly cooked their meals at home although
this was forbidden. They took their children out of the nurseries and
crèches. Old people left the old peoples' homes without permission
and returned, often after exhausting marches over long distances, to
their families. The grain harvest did not reach the granaries of the
communes because the 'labour companies' distributed it among themselves. In some communes the peasants even poisoned the wells,
slaughtered their animals on the pastures at night, stormed the stores
of the communes and physically attacked the cadres.

Such acts of resistance were intensified in November and December
1958 in the provinces of Kwangtung, Hupei, Hunan, Kiangsi,
Kansu, Szechwan and Tsinghai into genuine local insurrections of the
people,[45] during the suppression of which the local garrisons of the PLA
proved themselves in some cases to be no longer reliable, particularly
in Mao's home province of Hunan.[46]

The Party leadership at first tried to hold the subordinate organs
responsible for the mounting political and economic difficulties. Thus
the Governor of Shantung, Chao Chien-min, alternate member of
the CC, whose same administrative region had performed pioneering
work for the people's communes, was dismissed from his post on October 23 with the reproach that he had opposed the 'Great Leap'.[47]

But it soon became evident that the reprimanding of industrial functionaries and minor measures of adjustment were insufficient to prevent the imminent crisis. The CCP was obliged to accept a strategic retreat from the radical policies of the year 1958 in order to minimize the destructive consequences to the national economy and the governmental system. This retreat by the Party determined the development of Chinese Communist internal policy from the end of 1958 to the beginning of 1962. It led to new conflicts between the opinion groups within the top leadership and finally prepared the ground for the forming of factions within the CCP.

References

1 Cf. Liu, *loc. cit.*, pp. 11–12; Schurmann, *op. cit.*, pp. 465–7; Mao, first Lushan speech, *loc. cit.*, pp. 25, 411.
2 Liu, *loc. cit.*, p. 25.
3 Li Hsien-nien, in *HC*, No. 2, 1959; cf. *CNA*, No. 265, February 20, 1959.
4 Referring to Mao, *JMJP*, September 29, 1958; Liu, *ibid.*, p. 10; also P'eng Te-huai, in *URI*, Peng Te-huai, *op. cit.*, pp. 11, 400.
5 *JMJP*, September 30, 1958.
6 *NCNA*, Peking, April 14, 1959. Cf. also Robert Michael Field, 'Chinese Communist Industrial Production', in Joint Economic Committee, Congress of the United States, *An Economic Profile of Mainland China*, Washington, 1967, pp. 275–6; also Liu Ta-chung, *The Tempo of Economic Development of the Chinese Mainland, 1949–1965*, *ibid.*, pp. 66–8; also Tang-Maloney, *op. cit.*, pp. 390–5.
7 *NCNA*, Peking, April 14, 1959; cf. *CNA*, No. 281, June 19, 1959.
8 People's Central Radio Peking, December 13, 1958; also Hsia Yi-lun, delegate of the NPC, in *JMJP*, April 30, 1959.
9 Cf. also *JMJP*, November 9, 1958, cited in Domes, *Volkskommune, op. cit.*, pp. 42–3.
10 *Hsin Hunan jih-pao*, Changsha, October 26, 1958.
11 *JMJP*, October 9, November 15, 1958; cf. *CNA*, No. 254, November 21, 1958.
12 Mao, first Lushan speech, *loc. cit.*, pp. 24, 411.
13 Cf. also Cheng Chu-yüan, *The People's Communes*, Hong Kong, 1959, *passim*; also Max Biehl, *Die chinesische Volkskommune, im 'Grossen Sprung' und danach*, Hamburg, 1965, *passim*; also Schurmann, *op. cit.*, pp. 464–500; Tang-Maloney, *op. cit.*, pp. 374–83; also Bettelheim, *La construction . . . , op. cit.*, pp. 57–68.
14 *JMJP*, August 18, 1958.
15 Cf. Schurmann, *op. cit.*, pp. 474–5; Schurmann gives the date of the first mention of the term 'people's commune' (*Jen-min kung-she*) as August 11, 1958 (*Hsin-hua pan-yüeh-k'an*, No. 16, 1958). On p. 477 he legitimately refers to Ch'en Po-ta's article in *HC*, No. 4, 1958, but he maintains that there

the term 'commune' (*Kung-she*) is used 'in a broader sense'. However, a comparison of Ch'en's explanations with the model regulations of the Weihsing (Sputnik)–Commune in Suip'ing, Honan and with the Peitaiho Resolution makes clear that a difference between the terms is not discernible. See below, pp. 131–5.

16 For a survey of the urban people's commune movement see D.C.T. Luard, 'The Urban Communes', in *CQ*, No. 3, July-September 1960, pp. 74–9; cf. also Tang-Maloney, *op. cit.*, pp. 388–90; Schurmann, *op. cit.*, pp. 380–99.

17 The four basic types are characterised by the following examples:

(*a*) The Lota-Commune in Chingfeng, Honan. This was a combination of twenty-two APCs and comprised 5,746 peasant households with 22,568 members and more than 4,500 ha land. There were fifty-three villages in the commune in which 561 medium-size and small factories and workshops as well as tewnty-two centres for raising cattle were in operation. Twenty homes for old people, twenty-two nurseries, and 108 mess halls were made available to the members.

(*b*) The West-T'aikang-Commune in Chengchou, Honan, was a purely urban commune of a specific type. It comprised 10,618 households with 37,432 members who lived in sixty streets of the city of Chengchou. Fifty-four small factories and workshops were attached to it. The commune maintained three basic schools, a so-called 'Technical College' (a vocational training centre), forty-nine mess halls, and 107 murseries, but no homes for old people.

(*c*) The Commune of the Textile Machine Factory in Chengchou, Honan, was a purely industrial commune. Apart from 10,559 peasants in suburban districts who were responsible for the food supply, it comprised the staff and workers of the entire machine factory with their family members. It maintained several basic schools, two secondary schools, and a number of vocational training institutions, mess halls, nurseries, homes for old people, community halls, a theatre, and a clinic.

(*d*) The commune of the rural district of Hsühui in Honan was the prototype of the 'large commune', erected as the ultimate goal of the commune movement, but which *de facto* was realised only in exceptional circumstances. It comprised twenty communities (*Hsiang*) – in a mainly agricultural area – and 283 villages with 64,640 households and 314,444 people. Its militarily organised 'labour power' comprised 65,181 men and 52,622 women as well as more than 53,000 ha. land. The commune maintained 2,400 factories and workshops, 1,498 mess halls, 374 nurseries, and 75 crèches; also a considerable number of schools at all stages, homes for old people, cinemas, and theatres. Cf. Domes, *Volkskommune*, *op. cit.*, pp. 23–4.

18 Among others see for example *WHP*, September 23, 1958; *CKCNP*, September 27, 1958; also *Hsin-hua pan-yüeh-k'an*, No. 16, 1958.

19 *Nung-ts'un kung-tso t'ung-hsün* (*Agricultural Work Bulletin*), Peking, No. 11, 1958: *Ching-chi yen-chiu* (*Economic Studies*), Peking, No. 12, 1958; *JMJP*, August 30 and October 7, 1958.

20 *JMJP*, September 30, 1958; *HC*, No. 7, August 1958.

21 *CKCNP*, *ibid*.

22 Cf. also Schurmann, *op. cit.*, pp. 479–81; Ralph C. Powell, *Jedermann ein Soldat – Die rotchinesische Miliz*, in *Aus Politik und Zeitgeschichte – Beilage zur*

Wochenzeitung Das Parlament, Bonn, No. B4, 1961; *CNA*, No. 291, September 4, 1959.

23 Draft regulations of the Weihsing-Commune in Suip'ing, Honan, in *JMJP*, September 4, 1958, English translation in Chen, *op. cit.*, document XXX, pp. 240–50.

24 *JMJP*, September 10, 1958; English translation in Chen, *op. cit.*, pp. 223–7.

25 *TKP*, September 29, 1958.

26 *JMJP* and Chen, *ibid.*

27 *JMJP*, October 5, 1958.

28 Cf. Domes, *Rotchina*, *op. cit.*, p. 36, 40; source references there.

29 *JMJP*, September 30, 1958.

30 *JMJP*, November 15, 1958; cf. Schurmann, *op. cit.*, p. 493.

31 *NFJP*, September 8, 1958.

32 *JMJP*, September 30, 1958.

33 *CKCNP*, October 2, 1958.

34 *JMJP*, October 1, 1958.

35 Cf. also URI, *Peng Te-huai*, *op. cit.*, p. 203, 478–9.

36 *Anhui jih-pao*, Hofei, December 17, 1958.

37 *TKP*, October 20, 1958.

38 *JMJP*, October 3 and 29, 1958, cited in Domes, *Volkskommune*, *op. cit.*, p. 42.

39 *TKP*, November 16, 1958, cited *ibid.*, p. 43.

40 *KMJP*, October 14, 1958.

41 *TKP*, *ibid.*; also *Honan jih-pao*, December 2, 1958.

42 See below pp. 116, 232.

43 Erik von Groeling, *Widerstand und Säuberungen in der Grossen Proletarischen Kulturrevolution*', doctoral thesis, Berlin, 1969 (hereafter cited as von Groeling, *Widerstand*), p. 273.

44 Data in *JMJP*, *KMJP*, *TKP*, and a number of provincial newspapers from October 15, 1958 to March 31, 1959; cf. Cheng, *op. cit.*, pp. 124–9.

45 *Hupei jih-pao*, January 11, 13, 24, 1959; *Kirin jih-pao*, April 3, 1960; *Hsin Hunan jih-pao*, November 19, 1959.

46 *Hupei jih-pao*, January 14, 1959.

47 *JMJP*, October 23, 1958.

VIII. Opposition and 'Readjustment'

In November 1958 the Party leadership began to ask itself if the effects of the Maoist development policy might in the long run lead to a threat to the political system. Liu Shao-ch'i, who up to then had supported Mao's policy, apparently recognised the threat to the Party from the disorder in many villages and the growing discontent among the people. Gradually he changed his position. Certainly the group around Liu did not yet openly take up a position against the Chairman, but they now began to listen to the warnings of the leading men in planning and economic administration. They were increasingly ready to learn their lesson from their experience in the critical situation and to revise the decisions of spring and autumn 1958. In a speech before representatives of people's communes in Peking on December 25, Liu called for a cautious advance. 'Storming vigour is not to be displayed in the fulfilment of targets from subjective desires but to be shown in true achievements attained by working strenuously, perseveringly and resourcefully.'

Liu had certainly already made this statement of his opinion at the Chengchou and Wuhan conferences at which the 'readjustment' of the 'Three Banner' policy had been initiated. Since then Mao had had not only to face the steadily growing criticism of the opponents of his line from winter 1957–8, but also the scepticism of the men in the civil Party apparatus who, through their growing doubts about the realism of the Maoist conception, came closer to the internal Party opposition. Finally the policy was overthrown by the influence of a growing economic crisis. Although Mao's most outspoken critics were reprimanded, Liu and his followers attracted considerable support with their proposals. Thus apart from the 'old rightists' under P'eng Te-hauai, in three years there developed the more dangerous 'new rightists', headed by Mao's designated successor and number two in the Party leadership.

The Wuhan Plenum, December 1958

After preparatory Party conferences in Chengchou, Honan, from November 2 to 10,[2] and in Wuhan from November 21 to 27, dominated by debates on the situation in the people's communes, the

Sixth Plenum of the Eighth CC was convened, also in Wuhan, on November 28.[3] It conferred until December 10 and adopted fundamental decisions to correct the existing policy of collectivisation. Because even during the Cultural Revolution no detailed material on the debates of this conference has been published, they cannot be reconstructed. Neither Liu, Teng Hsiao-p'ing, P'eng Chen nor the leading men in the economic administration were later reproached with having turned against Mao during the Wuhan Plenum. We only know of P'eng Te-huai that he visited people's communes in Hunan while on his way to Wuhan and that he summarised his impressions in a poem of reproach.

> Grain scattered on the ground, potato leaves withered;
> Strong young people have left for steel-making,
> Only children and old women reaped the crops,
> How can they pass the coming year?
> Allow me to appeal for the people![4]

P'eng continued his criticism, but otherwise the conference took place in the atmosphere of an inventory. A 'Resolution on Some Questions Concerning the People's Communes',[5] which started by lauding this 'new social organisation' in liturgical tones, went on to water down the concept of summer 1958 and was adopted, certainly with the support of the leaders of the civil Party apparatus. The People's Communes Movement in the cities was 'for the time being' interrupted and a general *reinvestigation* of all existing communes was ordered. The accommodation of the people in barracks was forbidden and private ownership of houses, vegetable gardens and small animals was guaranteed 'for all time'. The work in the communes should thenceforth no longer exceed eight hours per day with two hours per day for sleep and four hours of leisure. Wages would again be paid in cash for the most part. The use of nurseries, crèches and canteens became voluntary for commune members and cadres were forbidden to destroy kitchen tools in order to force peasants into the collectives. The 'ultimate aim' of a Communist social order was still described as inevitable, but the resolution stated that it lay in 'the far future'. The CC also refrained from connecting the people's communes with a 'Great Leap' in agricultural production. Rather it confined itself to a declaration that they constituted a 'step forward'.

The Wuhan Plenum initiated the *readjustment* (*T'iao-cheng*) of the 'Three Red Banners' policy with these decisions. It appears that in 1958 the CC proceeded from the assumption that the newly introduced measures would suffice to gain the consent of the people for the new big collectives. However, this assumption soon proved to be wrong. Further corrections became necessary as early as spring 1959.

But the CC's decision to approve the 'wish of Comrade Mao Tse-tung not to stand again as a candidate for the Chairmanship of the People's Republic after the end of his term in office'[6] was of equal importance for the development of the domestic policy of the PR of China as the new decisions concerning the structure of the people's communes.

It meant in practice that Mao resigned from the office of head of state in the middle of a mounting crisis in the very policy he had propagated. Yet there is no evidence that the Party leader had been forced to such a step by the majority of the CC. Even the election of Liu Shao-ch'i as Mao's successor as head of state at the first plenary session of the second National People's Congress on April 27, 1959, should not be over-interpreted in the light of the Cultural Revolution. Mao's intensive activity during the first half of 1959 rather suggested that he in fact wanted to rid himself of the extensive representative duties related to his work as head of state. The Chairman had to allow some revision of his political concept of development in Wuhan, and the majority of the CC had made him compromise in some important aspects. Now it was imperative for him to lead resolutely the Party organisation and to prevent the 'reinvestigation' of the people's communes from turning into a *de facto* liquidation of the big collectives. This required all his attention. Furthermore he could, free from the duties of head of state, devote himself with more care to the supervision of Liu's activities in the Party machine and at the same time attempt, through Liu's designation as head of state, to seek the renewed support of the group around Liu, which in spring 1958 had proved to be so important. Liu, in turn, as Chairman of the People's Republic clearly overtook his rival Chou En-lai and gained an even more favourable position than hitherto as Mao's future successor to the Party leadership. And it is not impossible that the group around Liu regarded Mao's resignation as a demonstrative act of self-criticism which could contribute to the regaining of the people's consent to CCP policy. If this is correct, then Liu was in favour of slowing down the pace of the 'Three Banners' policy around the turn of 1958–9, but not yet of fundamentally revising it. This might explain the behaviour of his group when in spring and summer 1959 the 'old rightists' under P'eng Te-huai started their general attack on the policy and person of the Party leader.

The Situation in Spring 1959

In spite of the manifold difficulties which occurred in the 'Great Leap' and in the People's Communes Movement, the Peking leadership still began the year 1959 with optimism. On January 1 the

Minister of Agriculture, Liao Lu-yen, confirmed that in 1958 altogether 375 million tons of grain and 3·35 million tons of cotton had
been harvested,[7] so that the people need not reckon on shortages of
food and clothes. But during the first months of the new year there
were no signs of a successful solution to the problems which had come
into existence in the communes. On the contrary, the canteens especially were plunged into an ever-growing crisis. In Honan, Hupei and
Szechwan the peasants were still forced to eat their meals in the new
dining-halls,[8] but other provinces began to close them down so that
Mao regarded it as a success that in Honan 90 per cent of them were
functioning, and he declared that it would be 'wonderful if one-third
of the peasants, 150 million' retained this institution.[9]

Peasant resistance increased in intensity and spread further. In the
provinces of Kirin[10] and Shansi[11] resistance organisations were
formed which could not be suppressed by the security forces before
spring 1960. In Kirin open fights occurred in March 1959. Yet while
the world hardly noticed such acts of resistance, the uprising in Tibet
in March 1959, which was not directed against the people's communes
movement, but was caused by a desire for national independence,
received considerable attention outside China.[12]

As early as late 1958, between 25,000 and 30,000 partisans of the
Khampa tribe which had taken up resistance against the occupation of
Tibet by Chinese troops from 1954 approached the region of Lhasa.[13]
On March 10 the population of the city rose up with their support
against the occupying troops. The secular and religious head of the
Tibetans, the Dalai Lama, joined the movement. Apart from the
Chinese garrisons, Lhasa quickly fell into the hands of the rebels. But
negotiations with the Chinese garrison commandant, General Chang
Kuo-hua, for a higher degree of autonomy for Tibet collapsed, and
soon the Dalai Lama escaped through the Himalayan passes into India
at the behest of the leaders of the uprising. In Lhasa a fierce street battle
began on March 19 between 20,000 rebels and 35,000 Chinese soldiers
who only succeeded in regaining control of the town after two days.
In the countryside the fighting continued,[14] and armed incidents still
occur up to this day.

Faced with mounting difficulties the Party leadership was soon
forced to continue to correct the organisational structure and the
social principles of the people's communes which had begun in Wuhan.
At an enlarged Politburo session in Chengchou, the second Chengchou
conference, from the end of February to the beginning of March 1959,
it was decided that the ownership of agricultural land, local industrial
enterprises, tools, cattle and seeds, which up to then had been reserved
for the people's communes, was to be distributed in three levels:
commune, production brigade and production team. Agricultural

land, factories and seeds would remain in the hands of the communes for the time being.[15] The seventh plenum of the eighth CC which – after an enlarged Politburo session at the end of March – was convened in Shanghai from April 2 to 5,[16] confirmed the Chengchou decisions, introduced profit-sharing for commune members, and reinforced the guarantee of private ownership of houses and vegetable gardens which had been made in Wuhan.

The measures of readjustment agreed at Chengchou and Shanghai were caused not least by the results of the 're-investigation' of the people's communes which had been decided upon in Wuhan. As early as February 1959, Teng Hsiao-p'ing demanded that the State Planning Commission and the State Economic Commission should prepare proposals for further 'improvements' in the commune system[17] based on information which the news agency NCNA was to gather in the whole country. Po I-po sent an investigation commission, under the guidance of the vice-chairman of the Planning Commission, Hsüeh Mu-ch'iao, and the director of the Institute of Economics of the Academia Sinica, Sun Yeh-fang, to a number of communes to gather material on faulty planning.[18] The group's report severely criticised the disorder in the canteens and recommended their abolition.[19] On May 30, 1959, Po himself in his speech before leading cadres in the coal industry, referred to the fact that in spite of the record harvest of the preceding year food shortages had been widespread, and he warned against 'exaggerated plan targets' which could not but lead to 'the waste of capital and finally to a break-down'.[20] The Minister of Finance, Li Hsien-nien, also argued openly against the communes, whose establishment had 'undermined the national economy'.[21]

However, it was P'eng Te-huai who again and again marked himself out as Mao's most severe critic. As early as November and December 1958 he made tours of investigation in Kansu and Hunan. In March and April 1959 he visited Kiangsi, Anhui, Hopei and Hunan once more in order to gather evidence from these provinces against the policy of the Chairman.[22] He proved that the commune of Mao's native village, Shaoshan, had reported exaggerated production data, and even worse, that the commune of Hsühui in Hopei, one of the model communes, which the Chairman had visited and praised during his tour of inspection in August 1958, had since 'collapsed'.[23]

These statements constituted a direct attack on Mao, placing him in an open confrontation with the Minister of Defence.

The Case of P'eng Te-huai and the Lushan Decisions[24]

The leading bodies within the CCP discussed the introduction of corrections to the Party line demanded by opposition forces in the

CC, which were to exceed by far the decisions of the conferences of Wuhan, Chengchou and Shanghai, for more than six weeks at the spa of Lushan, Kiangsi. At first an enlarged session of the Politburo was convened from July 2 to August 1.[25] This was followed by the Eighth Plenum of the Eighth CC from August 2 to 16.[26] From the very beginning of the conference, P'eng Te-huai lead the critics of the Maoist course. Other Party leaders too made sharp attacks on the policy of the Chairman, among them the Politburo members Lin Jo-ch'ü and Ch'en Yün, candidate member of the Politburo Chang Wen-t'ien, the Chief of the General Staff, General Huang K'o-ch'eng (member of the CC), and the provincial Party secretary of Hunan, Chou Hsiao-chou. During the first week of the conference, discussions were held in sub-groups divided by regions. P'eng used the meetings of the sub-group for the problems of North-west China to make passionate criticisms of the 'Great Leap' and the people's communes.[27] On the evening of July 13, P'eng summed up his views in an open letter to Mao which was distributed among the members of the conference on the following day.[28] The opening of the letter was couched in a very polite form; P'eng compared himself with the hero Chang Fei of the period of the Three Kingdoms who had been a courageous but uncouth general, and who with his fellow warriors had taken a stand against the cunning and malign tyrant Ts'ao Ts'ao. The parallel to Mao must have been evident to the reader, particularly so since Party propaganda had repeatedly attempted, since spring 1959, to improve the historical image of Ts'ao Ts'ao.[29]

Then P'eng stated that false and exaggerated production data had been fabricated throughout the whole country. He continued:

We have not understood sufficiently the socialist laws of planned and proportionate development, nor have we implemented the policy of walking on two legs in practical work in various fields of endeavour. . . . On the other hand, the objective situation of our country is poor and bleak (there are still a number of people who do not have enough to eat. Last year, there was an average of only 18 feet of cotton cloth for every person, enough for a shirt, one pair of trousers, and two pairs of pants). The people urgently demand a change of the present condition.[30]

The second part of his letter was even more frank:

Petty-bourgeois fanaticism renders us liable to commit 'Left' mistakes. . . . We forgot the mass line and the style of seeking truth from facts. . . . So far as our method of thinking was concerned, we often confused strategic planning with concrete measures, the long-term policies with immediate steps, the whole with the part and the big collective with the small collective. . . . Putting policies in command is no substitute for the economic principles, still less for the concrete measures in economic work.[31]

Finally P'eng demanded that the Party leader exert his influence to reunite the Party for hard work on the basis of economic reality.

Thus the Minister of Defence made it clear that he was aiming at a revision of the political measures of 1958. His attacks on Mao had become so decisive that the latter reacted with extreme anger on July 23, two days after Chang Wen-t'ien had also made frank criticisms.

In an emphatic speech Mao rejected the reproaches of his critics.[32] He declared that the 'Great Leap' and the people's communes movement had brought about more advantages than disadvantages. He would be prepared to accept a break-down of half the communes – 'Up to now none has yet broke down!' – if the others were successful. Mao criticised the leading men in the economic administration, but found friendly words for Chou En-lai, and he threatened an open split if the conference followed the views of his critics:

> If we deserve to perish I shall go away, I shall go to the countryside and lead the peasants to overthrow the government. If you of the PLA will not follow me, then I shall find a Red Army. But I believe that the PLA will follow me.[33]

Mao's sharp reaction apparently gave the group around Liu cause to support the reprimanding of P'eng and his followers as well as making Chou join the majority which was thereby constituted. We do not yet have sufficient details about the process whereby the decision was taken at Lushan, but we know that two ballots took place at the conference and that some of the Party leaders, for example Li Hsien-nien, switched their votes.[34] The first ballot probably revolved around approval for P'eng's criticism. Here Mao seems to have been in the minority. But then the Chairman apparently pressed for a vote of confidence and won over the majority; for although Liu and his followers were in favour of an extensive revision of the 'Three Red Banners' policy, they were not willing to overthrow Mao. A resolution of the Eighth Plenum of August 16, 1959,[35] condemned P'eng and his followers as an 'anti-Party clique' and threatened them with massive sanctions. On September 17, P'eng was dismissed from his post.[36] The Chief of the General Staff, General Huang K'o-ch'eng, the Director of the General Political Department of the PLA, General T'an Cheng (member of the CC), the vice-Minister of Foreign Affairs, Chang Wen-t'ien, member of the CC, Wang Chia-hsiang, alternate member of the CC, Chou Hsiao-chou, and the director of the General Logistics Department of the PLA, General Hung Hsüeh-chih (alternate member of the CC), lost their posts as well. In contrast to the Kao-Jao case, however, none of those reprimanded was expelled from the Party. P'eng himself was sent for some time to a state farm in Tungpei for 'reform through labour'. But from spring 1960 he again made tours of inspection in a number of provinces for the Party leadership.[37]

The outcome of the Lushan conference appears to have been a compromise between Mao and Liu. Chou deserted those of his moderate followers who had come forward too openly, and the *individuals* comprising the internal Party opposition were reprimanded. But the resolution of the eighth plenum concerning the policy of the 'Three Red Banners', to which lip-service was paid again, adopted in essence the elements of the *political measures* proposed by the critics.[38] Military organisation of the communes was abandoned, and the authority of the communes themselves was restricted to the administration of schools, factories, means of transportation, machinery and seed. In future they were only to give directives for the production plan of the production brigade, and to a limited degree they acquire the right to call upon the membership to do public work. But the centre of gravity had already shifted to the brigades, i.e. to the level of the former APCs.

They were entrusted with the ownership of land and were confirmed in the ownership of agricultural tools and animals. They acquired the right to independent accounting and thus to the distribution of profits. Through these measures the leadership expected to master the economic crisis which, autumn 1959, had become even more menacing.

'Three Bitter Years'

After the spring of 1959, reports of a huge increase in agricultural production were followed by news which seemed to confirm apprehension of impending difficulties in food supply. Reports of severe natural disasters in isolated places and of bad weather conditions in larger areas began to appear in the Chinese provincial press. In March considerable parts of Hunan suffered from floods,[39] and soon a portion of the spring harvest in South-west China was lost through drought.[10] In order not to arouse exaggerated expectations among the people, and indeed under the influence of P'eng Te-huai's criticisms and the information collated by the economic planners, the Lushan Plenum had decided in favour of drastically revising the production data originally reported. Thus for 1958 the figures were now 250 million tons of grain harvested, instead of 375 million tons; 1·2 million tons of cotton instead of 3·32 million tons; and 1·2 million tons of peanuts instead of 4 million tons. Steel production data was revised from 11·8 million to 8 million tons.[41] These constituted corrections ranging from 33·3 to 70 per cent. However, even the harvest yield of grain and potatoes which was now reported seemed too high: O. L. Dawson's estimates of the 1958 harvest come to 205 million tons.[42] As for the 1959 harvest, as late as January 1959 the Party leadership had announced a planned target of 525 million tons. In December, Peking reported a total yield of 270 million tons.[43] But in September 1961 Mao stated in a conversation with the British Field Marshal Montgomery that in 'normal years' – and 1959 was regarded as such – an average of 180 million tons had been harvested in China.[44] Western estimates amount to 167·6 to 175 million tons, i.e. below the yield for 1957.[45]

In 1960 the situation deteriorated further. This was the first of the 'Three Bitter Years' (San-k'u-nien) in China. It was a period the like of which the country had not experienced at least since the end of the civil war. Damage caused by bad weather, particularly drought in that year, increased rapidly. At the end of the year the news agency NCNA reported that altogether 60 million hectares of agricultural land, i.e. 55 per cent of the cultivated area, had been hit by natural disasters, 25 million hectares especially badly. In the northern provinces of Hopei, Honan, Shantung and Shansi, 60 per cent of the agricultural land was said to have received scarcely any rain at all, so that there could be no harvest.[46] After that year there are no official Chinese Communist data on harvest yields. The existing estimates for 1960 fluctuate between 142 and 160 million tons.[47]

In 1961 the situation improved only slightly. Estimates vary between 167 and 170 million tons. For 1962 data ranging from 174, 178 to 180 million tons were given.[48] If we follow Dawson's calculations, which are generally regarded as reliable, the per capita production of grain and potatoes came to 258·9 kilograms in 1957, 310·1 kilograms in 1958, but only 232·6 kilograms in 1960 and 254·6 kilograms in 1962.[49]

The resulting food scarcity exceeded the dimensions of a 'bottleneck' in supply from mid-1960 onwards. It meant famine. Food rations for the people fluctuated considerably. They were lower in the countryside than in the cities, generally somewhat higher in north China than in the south of the country, and varied between occupational groups. However, it may be deduced that in December 1961 an average of 220 to 350 grammes of unhusked rice – or a corresponding amount of flour – and three to five grammes of cooking oil per diem was distributed. This was supplemented by 100 to 200 grammes of fish per month and 250 grammes of meat and of sugar four times a year in 1961.[50] At best this amounted to 1,400 calories per day: the Chinese Medical Association had recommended 2,054 as necessary for a 'balanced diet' as early as 1939.[51] Even the average for 1959–61 was calculated at only 1,790 calories.[52] Certainly the food crisis was not of the same magnitude all over the country, but in Anhui entire families died of hunger in some places,[53] and in Hunan, Kiangsi and Shensi functionaries in the propaganda department reported that whole villages were 'desolate and dead'.[54] In 1963 Chinese newspapers called the 'famine' of 1961–2 the 'most severe which had afflicted the country since 1879'.[55] Some estimates of the number of victims of the famine and of the following epidemics reached numbers which are beyond comprehension. At least ten million people died from the consequences of food shortages, but an estimate of even several times this number cannot be entirely dismissed.

The bad weather conditions of the years 1961–2 contributed to the resulting widespread famine; but since 1962, Party leaders, among them Politburo member P'eng Chen,[56] also repeatedly pointed out that misplanning and the consequences of the People's Communes Movement had been a greater cause of the food crisis than the natural disasters.

From 1961 food shortages had obliged the Peking leadership to import great quantities of grain from abroad. In 1957 the PR of China still had an export surplus of 700,000 tons of grain. In 1961 6·2 million tons of wheat were purchased, particularly from Canada and Australia. The deficit in the grain trade reached 4 million tons. In 1962 imports decreased to 5·3 million tons, but the deficit increased to 4·6 million tons. During the five years from 1961 to 1965 altogether 29·7 million tons of grain were imported at a cost of US $2,000 million.[57]

Malnutrition had persistent effects on the work rate in industry, for the production of cotton and of other agricultural raw materials also declined concomitant with food production.[58] Finally, the sudden departure of Soviet technicians from the factories in China in summer 1960 led to further vital disturbances in industrial production. While it was still increasing in 1960, the years 1961 and 1962 showed grave setbacks, as shown in Table VIII/1.

The general index of industrial production had been 88·5 per cent higher in 1961 than in 1956, but in 1962 it was only 9·6 per cent higher than in 1956.[60] The country lost almost entirely the growth initially achieved during the 'Great Leap'. The decline in agricultural and industrial production led to a decrease in the net domestic product of the PR of China to a level below that of 1957 according to the estimates of T. C. Liu and K. C. Yeh and of the Chinese Communists which had been reconstructed by them, is shown in Table VIII/2.

While the official Communist estimates for 1958 to 1962 reconstructed by Liu and Yeh showed a decrease in the net domestic product of 31.4 per cent, the far more cautious estimates of the two Sino-American economists still showed a decrease of 12·9 per cent. Wu Yüan-li

Table VIII/1

THE DEVELOPMENT OF INDUSTRIAL PRODUCTION IN THE PEOPLE'S REPUBLIC OF CHINA, 1960–1962[59]

Item	1960	1961	1962	Average annual decline 1960–62 %
Coal (m. tons)	325	180	180	−14·8
Crude steel (m. tons)	15·2	12	8	−26·4
Electricity (m. kWh)	47	31	30	−10·1
Crude oil (m. tons)	4·5	4·5	5·3	+11·2(!)
Fertiliser (m. tons)	2·48	1·45	2·12	?
Cement (m. tons)	13·5	6	6	?
Wood (m. cubic metres)	33	27	29	?
Paper (m. tons)	2·13	1	1	?
Cotton cloth (m. metres)	6	3	3	−29·3
Sugar (1,000 tons)	920	700	480	?

Table VIII/2

THE NET DOMESTIC PRODUCT OF THE PEOPLE'S REPUBLIC OF CHINA, 1957–1962[61]

(Total in JMP 1,000 million; *per capita* in JMP)

Year	Liu/Yeh estimate	Per capita	Reconstructed estimate	Per capita
1957	95·3	150	104·2	164
1958	108·0	166	145·0	222
1959	104·4	158	176·8	276
1960	95·9	143	155·9	232
1961	92·2	135	127·5	187
1962	94·0	136	99·5	144

commented on these data that the gross national product of the PR of China, which according to his estimates had increased annually at a rate of 6·5 per cent from 1957 to 1960, decreased by about 5·2 per cent per annum from 1960 to 1962 – an extremely dangerous tendency for a developing country.[62]

However, while we are dependent upon estimates with regard to all the above data and cannot do more than show a national economic trend, the balance of foreign trade of the PR of China, concerning which reliable data do exist, also points to the extensive crisis which afflicted the Chinese economy in the aftermath of the 'Great Leap'. The volume of foreign trade, which had attained its maximum level in 1959 of 4,265 million dollars, decreased to 3,975 million dollars in 1960, 3,020 million dollars in 1961 and 2,675 million dollars in 1962.

At the same time the volume of exports decreased 44 per cent from 2,060 million dollars to 1,150 million dollars.[63]

The CCP leaders who were confronted with a severe economic crisis attempted to stabilize the situation from the winter of 1959. As this was obviously not possible by mass mobilisation, which had been initiated by Mao, they thought it necessary to promote a further retreat from the people's communes movement, making concessions step by step, even after the decisions of Lushan.

The Retreat from the People's Communes

While the Party attempted to consolidate the communes according to the decisions of the Lushan Plenum, a new, extensive rectification campaign began in the CCP after the overthrow of P'eng Te-huai in the autumn of 1959; this lasted until 1961. In the course of this 'Second Anti-Rightist Campaign' (Erh-tz'u fan-yu), Ch'en Yün's authority was considerably restricted, and the Vice-Premier and Secretary General of the State Council, Hsi Chung-hsün (member of the CC), was dismissed. At the same time nine of the twenty-eight first secretaries of the provincial Party committees, seven of the twenty-eight provincial Governors and 134 of the 178 members and candidate members of the CC of the Communist Youth League lost their positions, as well as several thousand local cadres.[64] Tendencies towards a new, temporary radicalism also became evident in the attempt to revitalise and to extend the urban communes from January to November 1960.[65] However, these attempts could do no more than slow down the general trend towards demolishing the original form of the people's commune system.

Only a short time after the Lushan Plenum, leading Party and state functionaries – among them the Minister of Agriculture, Liao Lu-yen – in September 1959,[66] began to call for a further strengthening of the production brigades at the expense of the communes. These demands were related to the desire of many members of the leadership group to strengthen the provinces and regions while decentralising planning and economic administration. At a Central work conference at Peitaiho in July and August 1960 they prevailed. It was decided to establish six 'regional bureaux' of the Politburo:

(a) for Tungpei in Shenyang under CC member Sung Jen-ch'iung;
(b) for North China in Peking under CC member Li Hsüeh-feng;
(c) for East China in Shanghai under K'o Ch'ing-shih;
(d) for Central–South China in Canton under the First Secretary of the Kwangtung provincial Party committee T'ao Chu (member of the CC);

(e) for North-west China in Sian under CC member Liu Lan-t'ao;
(f) for South-west China in Chengtu under Li Ching-ch'üan.[67]

The new regional Party leaders soon supported those forces in the top
leadership who – increasingly under the leadership of Liu Shao-ch'i
and Teng Hsiao-p'ing and also temporarily joined by Chou En-lai –
were pressing for further measures of 'readjustment' in the 'Three
Red Banners' policy. The reform decisions taken at a session of the
Politburo in November 1960[68] and at the Ninth Plenum of the Eighth
CC in Peking from January 14 to 18, 1961, initiated such a comprehensive change in the system of people's communes that they hardly
retained any factor in common with the structures of 1958.[69]

Agricultural land, cattle, machinery, tools, and seed were transferred to the ownership of the *production teams*. The *production brigades*
retained supervision over schools, nurseries and local industries. For
the time being they were also responsible for the production guarantees
and for the payment of wages and bonuses. The *people's commune*
itself retained control only over public works and the security organs
as well as a vague right to prepare measures for the 'co-ordination of
the brigades'. From autumn 1960, canteens prepared only one meal a
day, and in February 1961, as Vice-Premier Teng Tzu-hui stated,
they were frequented by only one-third of commune members.[70]
In many communes the old people's homes were closed down
during 1961, and the number of nurseries and crèches rapidly decreased
as well. The principle of 'each according to his needs', which is related
to a Communist social order, vanished completely, and the
amount of political education was reduced from two hours per day to
three or four hours per week. The military training of militia
members was abandoned in the majority of communes. Finally, the
decisions to split up the big people's communes and production brigades, which was not made public by the communications media
before 1964, was of great relevance. Thus the number of communes
increased from about 24,000 in 1959 to 74,000 in early 1962; production brigades increased from about 500,000 to more than 700,000,
and the number of production teams from three to seven million.[71]
The assertion that the people's communes were the basic units for the
'transition to Communism' was no longer mentioned. The communiqué of the ninth plenum still clung to this formula in as much as it
described the people's communes and the policy of the 'Three Red
Banners' as 'achievements of the Chinese people on the *path to building
socialism*',[72] but the communes which were referred to at that point
had little in common with the original type. The state of the
system of ownership and the mode of production once more corresponded to the situation of the APCs of 1957. The people's communes

movement had been liquidated *de facto*. Other changes in the system of agricultural production became discernible too. Since the spring of 1961 in some places the individual farming of small private plots had begun to be conceded to peasants in the communes.[73] Their sizes fluctuated between twenty and fifty square metres for each working member of the family. There was not yet any official decision on the part of the leading organs, but it was a start in further changes of direction in domestic policy, for the toleration of private initiative in agricultural production exceeded by far a simple 'readjustment' of existing policy. Mao himself appeared in public but rarely in 1961. It remains open to doubt whether he had given his consent to the domestic moderation of the years 1960 to 1962. If so, he certainly regarded the 'readjustment measures' as nothing more than an interval which was to be followed by a return to the foundations of 1958 after the recovery of the national economy. However, the men in the civil Party apparatus around Liu and Teng, who were orthodox regarding questions of principle, but governed by pragmatic considerations concerning practical policy decisions, now began to press for a comprehensive revision of CCP policy. The debates on the correction of the policy of 1958 developed into struggles over goals to which ultimately the unity of the Party was sacrificed.

References

1 *JMJP*, December 26, 1958; English translation *URI*, Liu Shao-ch'i, *Collected Works 1958–1967, op. cit.*, p. 43.

2 *JMJP*, December 18, 1958; *JMST*, 1959, p. 37.

3 *Ibid.*; also URI, *Peng Te-huai, op. cit.*, pp. 120, 445.

4 *Ibid.*

5 *JMJP*, December 18 and 29, 1958, English translation in Chen, *op. cit.*, document twenty-nine, pp. 228–39; cf. also *CNA*, No. 258, January 2, 1959.

6 *JMJP*, December 18, 1958.

7 *JMJP*, January 1, 1959.

8 Mao, first Lushan speech, *loc. cit.*, pp. 23, 410.

9 *Ibid.*

10 *Kirin jih-pao*, April 3, 1960.

11 *Nei-meng-ku jih-pao*, April 25, 1960.

12 Cf. *NCNA*, Peking, March 28, 1959; *CNA*, No. 270, April 3, 1959 and No. 282, June 26, 1959, reference sources there; George N. Patterson, 'China and Tibet, Background to the Revolt'in *CQ*, No. 1, January-March 1960, pp. 87–102; Patterson, 'The Situation in Tibet', in *CQ*, No. 6, April–June 1961 pp. 81–6; Tang-Maloney, *op. cit.*, pp. 289–90.

13 *Ibid.*, p. 289.

14 Patterson, 'The Situation . . .', loc. cit., p. 83.

15 JMJP, August 28 and 29, 1959; cf. Schurmann, op. cit., p. 484; Schurmann gives the date of the introduction of the three-level system of ownership as the end of August. In contrast to that see Chang, loc. cit., p. 189.

16 JMJP, April 8, 1959; JMST, 1959, p. 45.

17 Kung-jen p'ing-lun (Worker Revue), Canton, No. 5, June 1968, English translation in SCMM, No. 622, July 28, 1969; cf. Erik von Groeling, 'Der Fraktionskampf in China', Berichte des Bundesinstituts für Ostwissenschaftliche und Internationale Studien, Köln, No. 37, 1970, p. 21.

18 Wen-ko feng-yün (Wind and Clouds of the Cultural Revolution), Peking, No. 4, 1967, English translation in SCMM, No. 635, December 2, 1968; cf. von Groeling, ibid., p. 22.

19 Mao, first Lushan speech, loc. cit., pp. 23–4 410.

20 CB, No. 878, April 28, 1969; cf. von Groeling, ibid.

21 CNA, No. 761, June 20, 1969.

22 URI, Peng Te-huai, op. cit., pp. 120, 203, 204, 446, 479.

23 Ibid., pp. 1–2, 4, 393, 395; cf. Schurmann, op. cit., p. 475.

24 Cf. URI, Peng Te-huai, op. cit., passim; in particular pp. 1–123, 393–448; Dieter Heinzig, 'Von Lushan zur Kulturrevolution', Berichte des Bundesinstituts für Ostwissenschaftliche und Internationale Studien, No. 5, 1968, pp. 6–7; von Groeling, Widerstand, op. cit., pp. 311–16; Lois Dougan Tretiak, Revolt of the Generals, in FEER, Vol. LVIII, No. 9, November 30, 1967; David A. Charles, 'The Dismissal of Marshal P'eng Te-huai', in CQ, No. 8, October–December 1961, pp. 63–76; also J. D. Simmonds, 'P'eng Te-huai: A Chronological Re-Examination', in CQ, No. 37, January–March 1969, pp. 120–38; also Frederick C. Teiwes, 'A Review Article: The Evolution of Leadership Purges in Communist China', ibid., No. 41, January–March 1970, pp. 122 et seq.; Tang-Maloney, op. cit., pp. 102–3; Glaubitz, op. cit., pp. 11–12; CNA, No. 294, September 25, 1959.

25 Peking Review, (hereafter cited as PR), No. 34, August 18, 1967, p. 8.

26 JMST, 1960, p. 158.

27 URI, Peng Te-huai, op. cit., pp. 1–5, 393–5.

28 P'eng Te-huai, 'Letter of Opinion', in Ko-ming ch'uan-lien (Revolutionary Solidarity), Peking, August 24, 1967, English translation, in URI, ibid., pp. 7–13.

29 CNA, No. 274, May 1, 1959.

30 Cited ex Glaubitz, op. cit., p. 191.

31 Ibid., pp. 193–4.

32 Mao, first Lushan speech, oc. cit., pp. 15, 26, 405–12.

33 Ibid., pp. 21, 409.

34 Cf. CNA, No. 761, June 20, 1969.

35 URI, ibid., pp. 38–44, 423–7.

36 JMJP, September 18, 1959.

37 URI, Peng Te-huai, op. cit., p. 390.

38 JMJP, August 26, 1958.

39 Honan jih-pao, March 19, 1959.

40 Among others, for example Yünnan jih-pao, June 3, 1959.

41 Chou En-lai, Report on Adjusting the Major Targets of the 1959 National Economic

Plan and Further Developing the Campaign Increasing Production and Practicising Economy, August 26, 1959, Peking, 1959, *passim*; cf. *CNA*, No. 293, September 18, 1959.

42 Owen L. Dawson, *A Constraint on ChiCom Foreign Policy: Agricultural Output, 1966–1975,* Stanford, Calif., 1967, p. 71.

43 *JMJP*, December 29, 1959.

44 *Sunday Times,* London, October 11, 1961.

45 Cf. also Dawson, *ibid.*; *CS*, No. 27, January 15, 1964.

46 *NCNA,* Peking, December 28, 1960.

47 Dawson, *ibid.*; *CS, ibid.*; also Domes, *Volkskommune, op. cit.,* p. 49.

48 Dawson, *ibid.*; *CS, ibid.*; Wu, *loc. cit.,* pp. 150–1.

49 Dawson, *ibid.*

50 Average amounts calculated from data given by refugees in seventy-three interviews in Hong Kong from April 2 to 11, 1962.

51 Cited in Buck-Dawson-Wu, *op. cit.,* p. 123; cf. also Arthur G. Ashbrook, 'Main Lines of Chinese Communist Economic Policy', in *An Economic Profile . . . , op. cit.,* Vol. I, pp. 31–2; also Wu, *op. cit.,* p. 123.

52 Marion R. Larson, 'China's Agriculture under Communism', in *An Economic Profile. . . , op. cit.,* Vol. I, p. 265; Larson even gives 2,350 calories as a necessary minimum.

53 Cf. *Chung-hua hu-sheng (The Voice of China),* published since 1969 by a group of twenty- to thirty-year-old refugees of different social origin in Hong Kong, No. 1, 1969, pp. 24–5.

54 Cf. *CNA,* No. 630, September 23, 1966.

55 *JMJP,* December 29, 1960, spoke of 'the heaviest catastrophes' since 1879; also *Kung-jen jih-pao,* (hereafter cited as *KJJP*), *(Worker's Daily),* April 17, 1963; *NFJP,* July 5, 1963, spoke of 'a famine'.

56 *JMJP,* October 31, 1966; cf. also Liu Shao-ch'i's speech of January 26 or 27, 1962, English translation, in *SCMM,* No. 652, April 28, 1969.

57 Robert L. Price, 'International Trade of Communist China', in *An Economic Profile . . . , op. cit.,* Vol. II, pp. 600–1; cf. also Ashbrook, *ibid.,* Vol. I, p. 38.

58 *JMJP,* January 1, 1962.

59 Data in Robert Michael Field, 'Chinese Communist Industrial Production', in *An Economic Profile. . . , op. cit.,* Vol. I, pp. 293–4; last column in Wu, in Trager-Henderson, *loc. cit.,* p. 138.

60 Field, *ibid.,* p. 290.

61 Liu, *loc. cit.,* Vol. I, p. 50.

62 Wu, *loc. cit.,* p. 139.

63 Data in Perkins, *CS, loc. cit.,* p. 3.

64 Most of the purges were officially confirmed by personnel replacements at the first plenary session of the third NPC; cf. *CB,* No. 752, February 1, 1965.

65 Cf. Tang-Maloney, *op. cit.,* p. 3.

66 *JMJP,* September 26, 1959.

67 *Chih-k'an nan-yüeh (The Beacon of Kwangtung),* Canton, No. 3, November 1, 1967.

68 *JMJP,* November 20 and 25, 1960; cf. Chester Cheng (ed.). *The Politics of the Red Chinese Army,* Stanford, Calif., 1966, p. 137; Chang, *loc. cit.,* p. 190: Lethbridge, *op. cit.,* pp. 99–100; Schurmann, *op. cit.,* pp. 491–2.

69 *JMJP*, January 24, 1961; also *JMST*, 1961, p. 11; cf. Domes, *Volkskommune, op. cit.*, pp. 62–3; Lethbridge, *op. cit.*, pp. 102–5.

70 *WHP*, February 17, 1961.

71 *TKP*, September 17 and 24, 1964.

72 *JMJP*, January 24, 1961 (author's italics).

73 *TKP*, April 10, 1961; cf. Lethbridge, *op. cit.*, p. 101.

IX. The Road to the Cultural Revolution

In the spring of 1962 another swing in domestic policy became discernible. A new wave of intellectual criticism, which this time – in constrast to the spring of 1957 – was not put forth by non-Party personages but by long-standing members of the CCP, promoted the attack on the Maoist general line and was soon expressed by critical analyses made by non-conformist economists who questioned the policy basis of the 'Three Red Banners'. Party intellectuals and economists, however, did not remain isolated. They received the protection and support of the leaders of the civil Party apparatus, particularly the Mayor of Peking, P'eng Chen (member of the Politburo), as well as Liu Shao-ch'i and Teng Hsiao-p'ing from the winter of 1961–2. Liu and Teng consistently pursued the principle of 'readjustment' and developed an alternative programme, in conjunction with the leaders of the economic administration and planning authorities, which was placed in competition to the concept of the 'Three Red Banners' projected by Mao.

The Party leader attempted to check the impending general revision of his policy by preparing the build-up of the armed forces with the help of Lin Piao as an alternative ruling apparatus. In the autumn of 1962 he succeeded in temporarily preventing the transformation of the 'readjustment' into a comprehensive reform of social and economic policy without, however, achieving a return to the foundations of 1958. While the national economy began to recover, thanks to the correction of the policy of the 'Three Red Banners' which had hitherto been put into practice, opinion groupings inside the leading organs stiffened into factions, and their confrontation shifted to the realms of Party theory and rural Party organisation.

Behind the façade which preserved outward unity the antagonisms intensified until in the summer of 1965 a second, thoroughly prepared and cautiously promoted offensive against Mao was initiated. It threatened the Chairman's vision as well as his position. When the majority of the Politburo openly turned against him, the split in the Party could no longer be avoided.

The 'Small Hundred Flowers', 1960-1962[1]

Tendencies towards a moderation of internal policy were accompanied from the summer of 1960 by the attempt of the Party leadership to introduce greater variety into the intellectual life of the country, through the revival of the 'Hundred Flowers' slogan, especially in the realm of philosophy, historical science and literature. This campaign, whose initiation was prominently undertaken by the deputy head of the Propaganda Department of the CC, Chou Yang,[2] at first evolved in the field of research on Confucius (K'ung-tzu). In July 1960 the leading philosophical historian Feng Yu-lan was, for the first time in a long while, able to express in public the opinion that there also existed 'progressive' elements in Confucian philosophy.[3] He was sharply criticized by some students,[4] but no more than one year later was in a position to restate his views in a discussion with the Maoist theoretician Kuan Feng,[5] and at the same time to criticise the attitude of his opponents.[6] The attempts at a renaissance in the study of Confucianism culminated in a symposium at T'aishan in Shantung, the tomb of Confucius, in November 1962. A great number of papers were presented there which had evidently been prepared in the period after 1957.[7] Apart from reviving objectivity in classical Chinese philosophy, open discussions concerning literary style were permitted[8] at the third National Congress of Writers and Artists from July 22 to August 13, 1960, in spite of demands that literature 'had to serve the workers and peasants'. Although China's intellectuals were extraordinarily reticent at first, recalling the experience of 1957, nevertheless they began to attack Mao's policy in the spring of 1961. Writers and journalists criticised the radical path of 1958-9 in a form that was scarcely veiled. They employed historical allusion and frequently used biting irony to express their opposition.

A group of intellectuals made its appearance as the vanguard of the opposition, centred around the head of the Propaganda Department of the Peking Urban Committee of the CCP, Teng T'o, the Deputy Mayor of Peking, Wu Han (an historian and dramatist) and the head of the United Front Department of the Peking Urban Committee, Liao Mo-sha. From this group, above all from Teng, emanated the satirical essays published in the Peking wan-pao (Peking Evening News) and in the Peking fortnightly Ch'ien-hsien (Frontline) which were compiled in the collections 'Notes from the Three-Family Village' (San-chia-ts'un jih-chi) and 'Evening Talks at Yenshan' (Yen-shan yeh-hua).[9] In order to illustrate the tone of these attacks we may quote from one of Teng's essays of late October 1961 in which he ridicules Maoist terminology:

A neighbour of mine has a child [another possible translation is: A boy is living in my neighbourhood – J.D.] who in recent times, mostly in imitation of the style of great poets, composed a lot of 'empty talk' . . . . Recently he wrote an *Ode on Wild Grass*[10] which is nothing but empty talk. His poem runs as follows:

Heaven is our Father,
Earth is our Mother,
Sun is our Wetnurse,
The East Wind is our benefactor,
The West Wind is our Enemy.
We are a tuft of grass,
Some like us,
Some hate us,
No matter – we don't care,
We keep on growing.

What kind of poem is that? I would really worry about the future of the child if he composed nothing but things like that day after day.[11]

At the same time Wu Han also wrote his play *The Dismissal of Hai Jui* (*Hai Jui pa-kuan*) which describes the downfall through court intrigue of an honest official who had interceded for the peasants, and which ends with a demand that the peasants be given back the land – all set in the historical period of the Ming dynasty.[12] The reader easily recognises in Hai Jui the P'eng Te-huai whose rehabilitation Wu Han had pleaded for in his play.

This group of Peking critics was soon joined by the two leading Marxist economic theorists of China, Lo Keng-mo and Sun Yeh-fang. In articles, and even more so in internal circulars and at meetings, they sharply criticised Mao's concept of development policy, stating that it implied a setback for China rather than an advance.[13] Sun declared that 'Politics in Command' was 'idealism and a disavowal or at least an underestimate of objective economic laws'. The 'Great Leap' had produced 'disproportions', 'undermined the economy' and 'had been nothing but hot air and empty talk'. This criticism culminated in demands for a fundamental decentralisation of the industrial administration, an allocation of investments for profit-making enterprises as well as the extension of free markets and a shift of 'production guarantees' from the production group to the individual peasant household.[14]

Lo's viewpoint contained a potentially even sharper attack on Mao's conceptions of 1958–9. Regarding the 'Great Leap' and the people's communes movement he wrote in July 1961:

If the modes of production are not altered according to the development of productive forces, *or if the modes of production are revolutionised beyond the state of objective productive forces*, then the development of social production will be hindered and the productive forces of society will be ruined.[15]

Although Lo did not openly take up a position against the theory of 'permanent revolution', he called for its combination with the 'theory of *development* of the revolution in stages', thereby making a claim for a general revision of the policy of the 'Three Red Banners'. The arguments of Sun Yeh-fang and Lo Keng-mo provided the rationale for the alternative programme which Liu Shao-ch'i, supported by Teng Hsiao-p'ing, announced in January and February 1962.

Liu Shao-ch'i's Programme

At an enlarged work conference of the CC in Peking, in which about 7,000 Party functionaries took part, Liu made a speech on January 26 or 27, 1962, in which he openly criticised Mao's concept.[16] Erik von Groeling has successfully reconstructed the essentials of Liu's statements from a mass of materials from the Cultural Revolution.[17] Liu began with the statement that the 'struggle against the rightist deviationists among the cadres had been incorrectly carried out' and that it was not justifiable to hold the rightist deviationists responsible for the failure of the people's communes. He continued:

I advise you, comrades, not to be doubtful leftists. . . . Let us not be those leftists who divorce themselves from reality and who are adventurous. Such leftists will not have true, constant zeal. . . Leftists of this kind not only do not deserve respect but should be criticised.[18]

During recent years, Liu argued, too many movements had been launched. The difficulties in agriculture, so the peasants in Hunan had explained to him, were to be blamed 30 per cent on natural disasters, but 70 per cent on 'human error'; 'unscientific and impractical methods had been adopted indiscriminately' and the 'traditional Party style' had been violated. The 'Great Leap' had been launched too early. Eight to ten years would be needed to make 'readjustments for the future'. Basing himself on this unrelenting analysis Liu finally demanded:

1. The transfer of 'production guarantees' to individual peasant households, and 'permission for independent production once more';
2. The cessation of all work on projects from which 'economically relevant results' could not be expected;

3. The closing down of all enterprises which did not make a profit or even made losses;

4. The conceding of the free disposal of surplus production by the peasants;

5. The establishment of free markets and the offering of higher prices to the peasants for their produce;

6. The rehabilitation of the rightist deviationists who had been wrongly reprimanded, and even the reconsideration of the case of P'eng Te-huai.

Liu and his supporters continued their offensive during an enlarged session of the Standing Committee of the Politburo, the so-called 'West Chamber (*Hsi-lou*) Conference', convened from February 21 to 26.[19] Here Ch'en Yün reappeared in public and stated that the state budget showed a deficit of more than JMP 2,000 million.[20] He called for emergency measures to curb the economic crisis, and especially for toleration of larger private plots. Liu took up this demand and proposed to appoint Ch'en the head of the Financial Commission of the CC and to commission him with the restoration of the state budget.[21] Only a few weeks later Liu once more argued for his programme at a session of a Party organ, but we have no details of this. His attacks on Mao and his fundamental position now became even clearer:

A Party member, no matter how capable he is . . . however great the role he plays in the Party, is one element in the apparatus. . . . He should lead and impel the whole Party from within and should not lead the Party from without or above. Democratic centralism within the Party is not who leads whom, but collective leadership' Everyone should . . . submit to the majority. In our Party there are no personal privileges. Unless in the name of the organisation, no one is allowed to lead.[22]

This amounted to a call for the disciplining of Mao by the leading organs of the Party. Simultaneously, in the summer of 1962, Liu reinforced his attempt to rehabilitate the 'right deviationists' who had been reprimanded in the autumn of 1959. He sent the Secretary of the Central Control Commission of the CCP, Mme. Ch'ien Ying, to Anhui to investigate the cases of several thousand inmates of labour camps, many of whom were rehabilitated and returned to their home provinces by plane.[23] P'eng Te-huai, who had gathered new material on the situation in the people's communes during a tour of investigation in 1960–1 through Hunan, Kiangsi, Kiangsu and Anhui, was encouraged by Liu to compile the results of his investigations in a memorandum of more than 80,000 characters, in order to prepare his acquittal of the charges made at the Lushan Plenum.[24]

Thus co-operation between the remnants of the 'Old Right' around P'eng and the 'New Right' around Liu and Teng was getting under way. By publishing a revised edition of his study, *How to Be a Good Communist*, in August and September 1962, alterations in which scarcely disguised a criticism of Mao, the head of state of the PR of China provided a theoretical foundation for the rehabilitation of the 'right deviationists' and for his attack on the Left.[25]

The 'New Right' set itself the task of pressing through its coherent alternative programme. Under the slogan 'Three Freedoms – One Guarantee' (*San-tzu i-pao*), Liu and Teng prepared to present to the Tenth Plenum of the Eighth CC – which was to be convened in September 1962 in Peking – the extension of the peasants' private plots, an increase in privately owned animals and in free markets as well as the decision to transfer 'production guarantees' to the individual peasant household. This actually meant not only the liquidation of the policy of the 'Three Red Banners' but also, generally, of the rural collective economy as it had been practised since 1955.

The principle of developing the national economy through the use of 'agriculture as the basis and industry as the leading factor', which had been made the guideline at the Party conferences in January and February 1962, implied a new concept of development. In contrast to the 'Maoist' one it might be called 'Liuist', since Liu energetically emphasised this concept. The substantial contrasts in these conflicting concepts may be summarised in order to clarify the struggle over goals which encumbered the Party from then on.

1. The Left – or the 'Maoists' – called for the simultaneous development of industry and agriculture; the 'New Right' – or the 'Anti-Maoists' – opted for a new rubric of preferences in development policy whereby agriculture and agricultural auxiliary industries were given priority over heavy and consumer goods industries.

2. While the Left wished to promote modern and traditional methods of production simultaneously, the 'New Right' stressed unequivocally the gradual mechanisation of agriculture and the consolidation of the 'modern, industrial sector'.

3. While the Left decentralised agriculture and local industry at the level of the people's communes *without imparing the system of central administration of the 'modern, industrial sector' practised hitherto*,[26] the 'New Right' favoured the decentralisation of the whole economy at the level of the regions and provinces.

4. The Left regarded the people's communes as the basic units of agricultural production and as the seeds of a renewed process of further collectivisation after the economic difficulties had been

overcome, but the 'New Right' pressed for the recognition of the individual peasant household as the basic unit of production and thus for a reduction of the rural collective economy.

5. While the Left hoped that investment capital could be saved through the mass mobilisation of human labour, the 'New Right' proceeded from the assumption that human labour could replace capital investment only to a limited degree, and that on the other hand, only by forgoing excessive demand could the productive forces of the people be fully realised.

6. The Left wished to elicit a positive attitudinal response on the part of the people by changing their consciousness through mass campaigns; the 'New Right' relied upon the arousing of such a positive attitudinal response through material incentives.

7. While the Left was willing to promote even those projects which would make a loss for a long time to come in the course of building up industry, the 'New Right' made profit the criterion of industrial development.

8. The Left demanded a uniform artistic style – 'revolutionary romanticism' – in its policy towards the intellectuals; this was to be reinforced by continuous indoctrination campaigns. The 'New Right' – here, however, P'eng Chen more strongly than Liu and Teng – favoured an extension of the freedom of expression, providing direct political statements were not involved.

9. While the Left expected that the individual initiative of the Party leader would provide the essential impulse for developing the PR of China into a great industrial power, the 'New Right' stressed the supremacy of collective leadership over the rule of a single person, and of the organisation over the charisma of the individual.

10. The Left wanted to change reality through consciousness and to overcome China's underdevelopment through the revolutionary enthusiasm of the masses, expressing this through the principle of 'Politics in Command'. The 'New Right' started from the orthodox Marxist principle that consciousness is transformed through reality, and it emphasised therefore the priority of 'objective economic conditions'.

In spite of the evolution of both of these relatively coherent programmes, there existed however important differences within both factions. Within the 'New Right', Liu's and Teng's unwavering interest in strict organisational discipline conflicted with the craving for a fundamental liberalisation of the political system among the Peking intelligentsia which was supported by P'eng Chen, Lu Ting-i and Chou Yang. Within the Left the approach of Mao and his closest followers – among them K'o Ch'ing-shih and Ch'en Po-ta – which was primarily theoretical, contrasted with the motivations of the military under Lin Piao, which were primarily oriented towards power politics, upon whose support Mao had to rely *pari passu* with the growing majority which the 'New Right' was acquiring in the leading Party organs.

In the winter of 1965–6 the 'New Right' was weakened by the contradiction between the forces of the intellectual opposition and their protectors on the one hand, and the orthodox apparatchiks on the other to such an extent that it could not prevail over Mao. In the summer and autumn of 1967, however, differing interests within the Left led to the military preventing the victory of the Maoist theoreticians of the 'permanent revolution' after the 'New Right' had fallen from power.

The Indoctrination of the Military Forces 1960–1965[27]

The appointment of Marshal Lin Piao as Minister of Defence[28] did not mean just another change in the Ministry and thus in the power of command over the PLA; rather it was a political turning-point of far-reaching importance with regard to the principles promoted thenceforward, and until late 1971, by the military leadership and the personnel structure of the leading military organs.

Immediately after Lin had taken up his new office, a campaign was started in the Army to serve the glorification of Mao and the widespread circulation of his writings which were now placed on an equal footing with the classics of Marxism-Leninism.[29] This campaign served not only to restore the prestige of the Chairman, damaged by the failure of the 'Three Red Banners' policy, but also the attempt to reinforce political work among the military forces. From early 1964 these attempts were followed by a movement which presented the working style and political behaviour of the PLA as a model for the whole country.

However, Lin Piao did not find a monolithically-structured army. The PLA had come into being in the course of fighting a twenty-two year civil war interrupted by eight years of resistance to Japan. Units with differing regional origins and different combat experience had finally knitted together. The historical formations, however, continued to exist. Although the political options of the Chinese commanders cannot be explained as simply having evolved from their careers in certain units of the civil war army, the personal loyalties which had developed in the course of many years were certainly relevant in the Chinese political scene. In order to understand the attitude of the PLA after 1959 it is therefore of considerable importance to take account of the loyalty groups which William Whitson has termed 'field army systems. The leading Chinese military figures are to be found in them during the civil war, and even after 1949 they remained together.[30] Five such groups may be discerned, originating from the large combat units of the PLA during the last year of the civil war:

1. The group of the First Field Army, commanded by Marshal P'eng Te-huai, also comprising most of the units which had fought under Marshal Ho Lung up to 1947. Their regional centre was in the military districts (*Ta chün-ch'ü*) of Lanchou and Sinkiang.

2. The group of the Second Field Army under Marshal Liu Po-ch'eng with its regional centre in the military districts of Chengtu, Kunming, and Tibet in South-west China.

3. The group of the Third Field Army under Marshal Ch'en Yi, who in February 1958 had been appointed Minister of Foreign Affairs. Its regional centre was in the military areas of East China in Fuchou Nanking, and Tsinan.

4. The group of Lin Piao's Fourth Field Army with its regional centre in the military areas of Canton and Shenyang (Tungpei). With it, in a historically close connection, stood

5. The group of the former 'North China Field Army', under Marshal Nieh Jung-chen, with its regional centre in the military areas of Peking and Inner Mongolia, and with strong representation in the military area of Wuhan in which commanders from the Second and Fourth Field Armies performed their duties as well.

The downfall of P'eng Te-huai and Lin's takeover of the Ministry of Defence reinforced the influence of the loyalty group of the Fourth Field Army in the military leadership. While a general without clear connections with one of the 'field army systems', Lo Jui-ch'ing, was appointed Chief of the General Staff, two members of Lin Piao's loyalty group, Generals Hsiao Hua and Ch'iu Hui-tso, became the heads of the General Political and General Logistics Department of the PLA, and a third, General Han Hsien-ch'u, took over supreme command of the Fuchou military area, i.e. the frontline opposite Taiwan.

Lin's predecessor, P'eng, had devoted himself particularly to the modernisation of the PLA, but political work in the military forces had been neglected under his command. In Mao's interests, the new Minister of Defence wanted to correct this. Only twelve days after taking office he made a clear formulation of the new course for the military forces in an editorial in *JMJP* of September 29, 1959. The Army was to be placed under the command of the Party. The individual would subordinate himself to the 'absolute leadership' of the latter, for the PLA was 'in the service of politics' and must 'never forget politics'.[31]

However, the victory of the 'politicians' over the 'specialists' within the leadership of the military, indicated by Lin's appointment did not solve the profound political difficulties with which the PLA was confronted in the winter of 1958-9. Since 1958 a crisis had begun to develop in the ranks of the Army. The tide of collectivisation and the subsequent food shortages brought about a clear expression of discontent with Mao's policies among the soldiers who came from peasant families. As early as summer 1958 the central organ of the PLA, the 'Chieh-fang-chün pao', complained about widespread 'counter-revolutionary feelings' in the Army,[32] and in October 1960 Lin was obliged to report to the Military Commission of the CC of the CCP that:

> The rightist deviationists in the military forces are sceptical about the general line, the Great Leap Forward and the people's communes . . . , some people in the Army even take counter-revolutionary action to oppose openly the policy of the Party and the State.[33]

In particular those issues of the confidential 'Work Bulletin' (*Kung-tso t'ung-hsün*) of the General Political Department from January to August 1961 which fell into the hands of Western intelligence services in 1962, and were made public in summer 1963, disclosed the phenomena of this crisis. They reported discontent of the troops because their families were short of food, the hunger insurrections of the peasants, which the military suppressed only with hesitation, and 'hostile propaganda' in the units.[34]

Reinforcement of indoctrination was to be the remedy for that. From summer 1960 to 1964 there followed a number of movements for the 'improvement of the working style' and for the ideological education of the troops. The aims of this campaign were defined by those principles of the military leadership laid down at an enlarged plenary session of the Military Commission of the CC in September and October 1960,[35] and at the conferences on political work in the PLA in March 1961, February 1963 and January 1964. These principles obtained particular relevance through the fact that the faction of Mao and Lin attempted to extend them into the realm of civil politics, administration, economy and culture during the Cultural Revolution.

They made the 'living use and living study of Mao Tse-tung's thought' (*Huo-hsüeh huo-yung Mao Tse-tung ssu-hsiang*) the guide-line for political education in the Army. Next to a correct ideological attitude, 'simplicity of life, flexibility and military efficiency' were particularly valued as exemplary virtues.[36]

The working style of the PLA, the 'Three-Eight Working Style' (*San-pa tso-feng*), was described by the slogan 'Three Sentences and Eight Characters'. The 'Three Sentences' called for correct political orientation, hard work and simple life as well as for flexibility in strategy and tactics. The 'Eight Characters' represented the Chinese terms from unity, earnestness, energy and vitality.[37]

In November 1960 the 'Three-Eight Movement' grew out of these formulae. Not more than one month later, around the turn of 1960–1, it was widened to the 'Five Good Soldier Movement' (*Wu-hao chan-shih yün-tung*). Now the leadership attempted to explain to its troops that they had to pursue 'five goods': political thought, military training, the 'Three-Eight Work Style', fulfilment of duties, and physical training.[38] The first four of these five virtues were finally required from and used for entire units in summer 1961, and thus the 'Four Good Company Movement' (*Ssu-hao lien-tui yün-tung*) was initiated. In the context of this campaign, there were competitions between single companies from September 1961, and certain units were recurrently termed 'Four Good Companies'. This usually resulted in financial bonuses for the officers and men and in an increase in food rations.[39]

As a rule after 1960 models played a great role in indoctrinating the PLA. In March 1963 it was the soldier Lei Feng who lived with the works of Mao Tse-tung, and whose short life (he died at the age of twenty-two after an accident) had apparently been under constant observation by photographers. In summer 1963 it was the 'Good Eighth Company of the Nanking Road' in Shanghai which, protected by the *Thoughts of Mao Tse-tung*, resisted all the temptations of the metropolis, such as girls and opium.[40] In January 1964 it was company leader Kuo Hsing-fu who was an 'expert in explaining, demonstrating, teaching and guiding ideological work' – again and again the troops were confronted with real or fictitious models of positive political and social behaviour.

The long duration and the intensity of the indoctrination campaigns of 1960–4 tend to the conclusion that the military leadership encountered considerable difficulties in overcoming the crisis and that the phenomena of this crisis penetrated deeper than had been imagined outside China at that time.

However, many signs point to the fact that Mao and Lin had succeeded by the early summer of 1965 in consolidating the position of the political apparatus in the military forces and in considerably strengthening ideological work among the troops. The extension of the periods for compulsory military service in January 1965,[41] as well as the abolition of military ranks and insignia in May 1965,[42] measures which Lin Piao had called for as early as 1963, demonstrated the temporary victory of the Left in the Army.

Yet one problem remained unresolved. The strengthening of the political apparatus in the armed forces at the level of the military areas and provincial military districts (*Sheng-chün-ch'ü*) at first resulted primarily not in the prevalence of political commissars with a military career – most of them from the loyalty group of the Fourth Field Army – but rather in the strengthening of the influence of the provincial Party secretaries in the civil Party apparatus, many of whom were subordinate to Liu Shao-ch'i.[43] Among the forty-six First Political Commissars of the units at this level there were twenty-nine in the autumn of 1965 who occupied positions in the civilian Party machine and had originated from it. Only seventeen came directly from the political apparatus of the PLA.

Nevertheless, the campaigns had moulded the armed forces into an instrument of the Left which, in the event of an open split in the Party, could be employed as an alternative organisation against the majority of the civilian Party machine. In the beginning of 1964, attempts were made to extend the working style and ideological attitude of the Army to the people as a whole. However, the new campaign under the slogan 'The Whole Country Must Learn from the PLA', was not completely successful for the time being. The hour of the PLA came during the Cultural Revolution.[44]

Mao's First Counter-attack: the Tenth Plenum, September 1962

By the winter of 1961-2, the 'readjustment policy' of the years 1959-61 had not yet achieved the desired improvement of the economic situation in the PR of China. On the contrary, the distribution of food rations reached its lowest point in many parts of the country between December 1961 and the early summer of 1962.[45] Peasant opposition continued to grow and led to further open acts of resistance, and in some places, particularly in South China, to continuous guerilla warfare. Nationalist Chinese agents and commandos infiltrated Kwangtung, Fukien, Kiangsi, Chekiang and for a time even Shantung.[46] In February 1962 the Minister of Security, General Hsieh Fu-chih, reported almost 250,000 cases of 'counter-revolutionary activities' for the year 1961, among them much pillaging of public grain stores, arson, 3,738 cases of 'armed insurrection' and 1,235 murders of Party and administrative cadres.[47] The outside world took cognisance of the obviously desperate situation in many sections of the population with the mass escape to Hong Kong which began at the end of April 1962 and lasted for nearly four weeks. Between 35,000 and 50,000 refugees reached the British crown colony during that time, many of them being sent back again over the frontier by the British authorities.

Because of these mounting difficulties the CCP leadership decided to put into practice a part of those emergency measures proposed by Liu Shao-ch'i and his collegaues in January and February.[49] The pathos of the 'Great Leap' vanished in the publication media and was replaced by calls for working 'step by step', 'taking into consideration place, time and the objective conditions', 'systematically, co-ordinately, persistently and patiently'.[50]

During the whole of 1961 no plenary session of the NPC took place. When it was finally convened from March 27 to April 16, 1962, Chou En-lai officially proclaimed a new policy of 'adjusting the national economy'. An increase in agricultural production, the 'reduction of the number of investment projects', and the improvement of market supply were named as its most important tasks.[51]

During the following months the transfer of private plots to the peasants which had already been put into practice in some places in 1961 was extended to the whole country. A 'tide of individual production' spread, and as early as 1962 the peasants obtained more than 30 per cent of the grain production[52] from these plots, although private land represented only 5–10 per cent of the entire cultivated land. The number of 'free markets' increased from month to month in summer 1962, and there the produce of private plots and of the expanded private rearing of animals could be sold at market prices.

With the help of these concessions and the extension of the system of material incentives, the national economy recovered successfully from the middle of 1962 onwards. According to Chou's statements to Edgar Snow, grain production in 1963 was about ten million tons above that of 1962, and in 1964 it is said to have amounted to nearly 200 million tons.[53] The more cautious and probably more reliable estimates of Dawson still registered an increase from 160 million tons in 1960 to 193 millions in 1965.[54] In the industrial sphere, Wu Yüan-li noted, for the period 1962–5, an increase in coal production from 250 to 300 million tons, in electricity supply from 30,000 to 40,000 million kWh, in steel production from ten to fifteen million tons, and in cotton cloth from 3·0 to 3·9 million metres.[55] The net domestic product rose, according to T. C. Liu's estimates, from JMP 94,000 million in 1962 to JMP108,100 million in 1965, and thereby reached the 1958 level again. According to Chinese Communist estimates, reconstructed by Liu, it rose from JMP99,500 million in 1962 to JMP126,200 million in 1965 and thus still remained 13 per cent below the figure for 1958.[56] The volume of foreign trade in 1965, too, with US$3,695 million, was only slightly (US$40 millions) below that of 1958.[57] Thus the national economy had once more achieved the absolute data of 1958 in important spheres, although the *per capita* data remained below those of 1958 because of a population growth of at least thirty-five million people. The 'readjustment' policy of the Party functionaries and of the economic managers under Liu thus achieved remarkable successes in the framework which had evolved after the summer of 1962.

Nevertheless, they still became for the first time the target for the criticism of Mao and his followers who succeeded in preventing the consistent extension of this policy towards an over-all revision of the general line of the Party at the Tenth Plenum of the Eighth CC in Peking on September 24–7.[58] Earlier the Central Work Conference which (at first in Peitaiho and then in Peking) had been convened to prepare the plenum in August and September had already been the scene of intense confrontations.[59] While Liu and Teng called for a further expansion of the private plots and, even more, for the transference of the 'production guarantee' to individual peasant households, Mao sharply criticised Ch'en Yün, Li Fu-ch'un, Li Hsien-nien, Po I-po and Teng Tzu-hui, demanding that 'the retreat should be continued no further' but rather that 'a restrengthening of the collective economy' should be embarked upon. At the same time the Party leader maintained that the 'class struggle was continuously intensified' and that therefore measures had to be taken against a 'restoration of capitalism'.

During the conference and at the plenum which followed, Mao partly prevailed with his line. Probably a small majority of the CC rejected Liu's and Teng's proposals. The attempts to rehabilitate P'eng Te-huai were defeated, and Teng Tzu-hui was replaced as head of the Agricultural Commission of the CC by T'an Chen-lin, who in contrast to Teng, had emphatically favoured the formation of the people's communes in 1958.[60] Above all the plenum adopted Mao's views on the continued class struggle. The communiqué of the Tenth Plenum said:

> In our own country those landlords, rich peasants and bourgeois rightists who did not reform themselves, and the remaining coutner-revolutionaries were rejoicing in our difficulties. . . . But our people have resolutely shattered and will shatter their activities, be it infiltrations, provocations, aggression or subversion in our country or our Party. . . . The class struggle is intricate. It is going up and down and sometimes takes a sharp appearance. This class struggle finds its inevitable expression in our Party.[61]

The plenum was considerably more reticent in its practical decisions. It rejected the extension of the 'readjustment' policy, yet refused to proclaim the start of a new wave of collectivisation. The leading organ of the Party maintained the *status quo* in economic policy and in the collective organisation that had evolved from 1959 to 1962. Both sides agreed on the re-establishment of control over the rural population which had been shaken during the years of the economic crisis.

The 'Socialist Education Movement' (*She-hui chu-i chiao-yü yün-tung*) was to serve this purpose. It was initiated by a decision of the plenum. But Liu and Teng on the one hand, and Mao and his followers on the other hand, pursued incompatible goals with this movement, which thus became the object of new controversy.

The Conflict over the 'Socialist Education Movement'[62]

The gradual liquidation of the people's communes in their original form, undernourishment and difficulties in supply had led not only to widespread discontent, opposition and acts of resistance in the villages of China up to 1962, but also to a slackening of the enthusiasm for work of the basic cadres (*chi-tseng kan-pu*) who were primarily confronted with the bitterness of the people. Thus the control structure in the rural areas had been considerably damaged.[63] At first the leadership tried to shift responsibility for the critical situation on to the shoulders of the cadres. They were reproached with 'having separated themselves from the masses', with having ill-treated the people and having disregarded the directives of the Party.[64] Thus they became even more insecure, and in many places began to join the peasants in opposing the intentions of the leadership. The 'Socialist Education Movement' was to remedy this. With it the leadership wanted to re-establish better relationships between the different levels of government apparatus and between the cadres and the people. At the same time it hoped to expose and exterminate the forces of resistance in the villages. The campaign started in autumn 1962 in Hopei and Hunan, and in February 1963 at a work conference of the CC, Mao proposed to extend it over the whole country.[65] On May 20, 1963, a second work conference adopted a 'Draft Resolution of the CC of the CCP on some Problems in Current Rural Work'[66] which had been prepared by the Party leader himself and which provided the initial guide-lines for the campaign. The emphasis lay at first on the attempt to reduce the peasants' private production and to check the influence of the old village élites, which had been growing since 1960, through the reinforcement of the social classifications which had been implemented in the course of the land reform movement of 1950–3.[67] The Centre and the provincial Party leadership sent 'work teams' (*Kung-tso-tsu*) to the villages to supervise the implementation of the movement. But the reports of these teams soon made it clear that the campaign encountered considerable resistance among the rural population. The leaders of the civilian Party machine, who had probably been hesitant in agreeing with Mao's plans for the movement, recognised, because of these reports, that the chance existed to undermine the Maoist approach to the 'Socialist Education Movement' through new guide-lines elaborated by Liu and Teng. In September 1963 the Politburo adopted 'Some Concrete Resolutions Concerning the Socialist Education Movement in the Countryside'[68] which differed considerably from Mao's draft of May in substantial aspects. While the latter tried to describe the development of the countryside as one of steady progress since 1950, and thus to cover up the failure of the 1958 people's communes experiment, the September document stressed the importance of the 'readjustment' policy and argued for toleration of the peasants' private plots as well as the establishment of free markets. Mao's document proceeded from the 'sharpening of the class struggle in the countryside', and aimed at preventing the 'restoration of capitalism' (*Tzu-pen chu-i ti fu-p'i*). The September decisions drafted by Liu and Teng, however, interpreted the campaign as a 'Party Reform Movement' which was primarily to serve the strengthening of organisation in the rural areas. While Mao recognised only the 'poor and lower-middle peasants' (*P'in-hsia-chung-nung*) as 'revolutionary classes', Liu and Teng also included the 'upper-middle peasants' (*Shang-chung-nung*) – i.e. those who had already been landowning peasants before land reform. Mao, who evidently no longer completely trusted the civil Party apparatus, wanted to include non-Party individuals in the criticism against the cadres as early as 1962. Liu and Teng, however, aimed at treating this kind of criticism and the resulting reprimands to the cadres as an internal Party affair.

Out of these disputes evolved a confrontation which was no more than slightly mitigated by the fact that it proceeded largely in secret within the Central and provincial leading organs. At first the 'New Right' prevailed. In 1963 and 1964 the 'work teams', delegated to the villages mainly on the orders of the group around Liu and Teng, combined comprehensive rectification measures among the cadres, of whom up to 75 per cent lost their positions, particularly in some places in North China, with the initiation of sustained improvements in the infrastructure: electrification, the construction of cisterns, the supply of pumps and the building of new schools.[69]

Mao's followers, however, wanted to use the movement primarily as an indoctrination campaign in the course of which 'Study classes for Mao Tse-tung's thought' (*Mao Tse-tung ssu-hsiang hsüeh-hsi pan*) were to make a further attempt to transform the consciousness of the peasants in order to build a Communist social order.

As the top leadership could not agree upon an appropriate course the Party did not appear united in the 'Socialist Education Movement'. Thus the campaign neither achieved the objective of consolidating the Party organisation, which Liu and Teng had aimed at, nor was it able to bring about the reduction of the private economy in the villages and the 'revolution' in the consciousness of the peasants in Mao's

sense. Those cadres who had been reprimanded represented a future
reservoir for attacks on the leadership of the civilian Party machine,
while the new cadres who had replaced them tried to preserve their
positions. Thus the movement not only caused an intensification of
the struggle over ends within the CCP, but, instead of strengthening
the basic units of the civil Party apparatus, it weakened them. This
was to become evident to the disadvantage of the group around Liu and
Teng during the Cultural Revolution. The organisational crisis
developed into a comprehensive Party crisis, and crisis of the ruling
system, when the different groups of the 'New Right' once again began
the offensive which in September 1962 had been halted at the Tenth
Plenum.

The Offensive of the 'New Right'

The intellectual Party members who had found support primarily
from P'eng Chen continued their attacks on the policy of Mao and his
followers from the middle of 1963. While, in July 1964, P'eng himself
averted the attempts of the Chairman's wife, Chiang Ch'ing, to introduce a number of modern Peking operas composed by herself in
the style of 'revolutionary romanticism',[70] the Party theorists who
were enjoying P'eng's protection chose the field of dialectical material-
ist philosophy to oppose Mao's views and to impinge upon the foundations of the CCP's *weltanschauung*. The former Director of the Higher
Party School, Yang Hsien-chen (member of the CC), in lectures at
the Academy of Sciences and at the Peking People's University,
made a pronouncement that the combination of antitheses into syn-
thesis was the fundamental principle of Marxism. Yang summed up
his position with the slogan 'Two Combining into One' (*Erh ho erh-i*).
And using the phrase 'One Dividing into Two' (*I fen wei-erh*), Mao's
followers insisted that each entity would always divide itself into antitheses. This controversy, which at first sight appears to be almost
scholastic, acquired considerable political relevance because Yang's
critics accused him of preparing externally a rapprochement with the
'Soviet Revisionists' and internally a 'policy of co-existence between
socialist and capitalist modes of production'.[71]

Liu and Teng obviously sided once again with Mao in the course of
this conflict over Party theory. Yang was severely criticised by the
Party leadership and was probably dismissed from his post without the
opportunity to defend himself. But he was not expelled from the
Party. The mode of reprimanding thus remained the same as in the
summer of 1959 in the case of P'eng Te-huai and his political friends.

The next to be attacked by Maoist critics was the Party philosopher
Feng Ting. In his book *The Communist View of Life*, which had

been re-edited in the summer of 1964, he advocated the idea that the goal of all Communists was the happiness of the general public, but that this constituted nothing but the sum total of all individual happiness. The Party leadership called this idea 'a 100 per cent bourgeois view of life'. Feng's opponents in the Propaganda Department of the CC declared that collective happiness had nothing in common with individual happiness. Even within the Communist social order the interests and aims of the individual remained subordinate to those of the collective.[72] From the end of September 1964 to the beginning of May 1965 further attacks followed against the historians Chou Ku-ch'eng and Sun Ch'a-ming, the writers Shao Ch'uan-lin, Ou-Yang Shan, Ch'u Pai-yin and K'ang Cho, as well as, finally, the film director Hsia Yen, who in March 1965 lost his position as a Vice Minister of Culture. As in the case of Yang Hsien-chen, in all these disputes the same principle held good: the leaders of the civilian Party machine backed the Maoists' attacks on the intellectual critics or at least did nothing to prevent them. They were apparently determined to treat these controversies only as 'contradictions among the people', i.e. not to take any measures involving physical force.

In this context the differences within the 'New Right' once more became evident. The Peking intellectuals around P'eng steadily pressed for a liberalisation of the system; Liu and his followers wanted to preserve the discipline of the Party and were thus unwilling to enter into a humanisation of the system.

However, the downfall of Khruschev and the first successful nuclear test of the PR of China in October 1964 strengthened the self-confidence of the Peking leadership considerably, and now even Liu and the majority of the Politburo were ready to strive for a fundamental relaxation of the internal situation. As early as spring 1964, but even more so from summer 1965, the programme of the internal Party opposition to Mao became once more clearly pronounced.[73] It directed its attacks at the tendency of Mao and his followers to value political reliability and 'revolutionary consciousness' higher than expertise, and it called for sufficient leisure time for the peasants, workers and students.

The Ministry of Education, together with the Department of Education of the Peking Municipal Committee of the CCP, convened a conference of the heads of all the secondary schools of Peking in March or April 1964. It was decided that in future the pupils should be allowed to 'spend their holidays according to their own wishes'.[74]

This perceptible tendency was further augmented in the course of 1965. Teng T'o demanded in Ch'ien-hsien, at the end of April, that in all schools specialist studies should receive priority over political education.[75] On June 21, JMJP itself suggested that the workers should receive the opportunity 'to combine their work with the appropriate leisure'.

It was demanded that male students who were ill and all girl students should be relieved of their duty to perform physical labour, and criticisms were made of political meetings held on holidays. The central organ of the All-China Trade Union Association, the *KJJP*, even maintained, on August 5, that it was the duty of the trade unions to 'improve the standard of living of the masses'.[77] In September the Communist Youth League also joined the chorus of those who favoured a moderation of the course of internal policy. After its organ, the *CKCNP*. had declared on September 7 that the cadres of the student association were 'above all students and then cadres,' it called upon the members of the Youth League, on September 9, to win over even the 'children of the exploiters' to the cause of the League.[77]

Opinions of this kind were only slightly different from those of the leaders of the 'New Right' in 1961 and 1962; what *was* basically new was the fact that they were spoken in public and no longer in closed Party meetings. This was a clear sign that the new attack on the Maoist position had gained the support of the majority in the leading organs of the Party. At the same time there was some evidence that the rehabilitation of the 1959 'right deviationists', the group under P'eng Te-huai, was prepared for a second time – now with evidently more success – after it had failed in 1962.

In the summer of 1965, P'eng appeared as Third Director of the Department of Reconstruction in the South-west China Regional Bureau in Szechwan;[78] a short time later Huang K'o-ch'eng was appointed Vice-Governor of Shansi province.[79] Neither of these was a very influential position, but they still indicated that the Party leadership was willing to revise the view which it had formulated at the Lushan Plenum.

Finally, in spring 1965, the publication media which belonged to the Propaganda Department of the CC began to upgrade the personality of Liu Shao-ch'i to such an extent that he frequently appeared to be in a position equal to that of Mao. Liu had hitherto been called 'Chairman of the People's Republic of China'; now the term 'Chairman Liu' (*Liu chu-hsi*) became more and more frequent, corresponding with the term 'Chairman Mao'. At the closing rally of a national sports event on September 28, 1965, the Peking stadium was decorated with two equally large pictures of Mao and Liu placed side by side,[80] and at a mass rally on the National Holiday, October 1, the pictures of both were carried aloft in roughly equal numbers.[81]

Behind all these signs there proceeded in Peking in September the controversy which led to the open split between the Party leader and the majority of the inner leadership core. At an enlarged session of the Standing Committee of the Politburo, at which the six First Secretaries of the Regional Bureaux took part[82] and which was labelled a 'Central Work Conference', Mao demanded the initiation of a new rectification campaign, to be directed primarily against the intellectual critics in P'eng Chen's Peking Municipal Committee, and to start with the condemnation of Wu Han and his play *The Dismissal of Hai Jui*. But this time the Party leadership refused to follow the Chairman. His motion was turned down by the majority of the top-level body of the CCP.[83] It may be deduced from the attacks on the leaders of the civil Party apparatus in the official mass media and in Red Guard pamphlets during the 'Cultural Revolution' that within the Standing Committe of the Politburo only Mao himself, Lin Piao and the regional Party leaders, Chang Ch'un-ch'iao (East China), T'ao Chu and Li Hsüeh-feng supported the motion of the Party leader. Liu Shao-ch'i, Chu Te, Ch'en Yün, Teng Hsiao-p'ing and the regional Party secretaries Li Ching-ch'üan, Liu Lan-t'ao and Sun Jen-ch'iung, rejected it. Chou En-lai probably abstained.

Thus it was quite clear that Mao could no longer count on the support of a majority in the highest decision-making body of the Party for his policy. A few weeks later, at the end of October, he left for the area around Shanghai, and only after nine months did he return to the capital.

The stage had been set for the struggle over power and goals which the Chinese Communists named *Great Proletarian Cultural Revolution* (*Wu-ch'an chieh-chi wen-hua ta ko-ming*). It evolved as a *struggle over goals*:

(a) between tendencies of differentiation and tendencies towards further levelling of intellectual and cultural life;

(b) between attempts at relaxing internal and probably external policy and the striving for an intensification of the domestic and international class struggle;

(c) between concepts of development formulated by Liu and Mao and their respective followers;

(d) between theories of organisation which on the one hand emphasised collective leadership and Party discipline, and on the other the charismatic leadership of an individual and mass mobilisation, if necessary, even without the control structures of the Party.

As a *struggle for power* the conflict developed in the form of a confrontation between Liu Shao-ch'i and Lin Piao over the succession of the Chairman while he was still alive, and in the form of a confrontation between the alternative machines of the civilian Party organisation and the PLA. Yet in both these organisations there were minorities which stood on the respective opposite side of the split which was cutting through the system of rule in the PR of China.

References

1 Cf. also Glaubitz, *op. cit.*, *passim*; Fokkema, *op. cit.*, pp. 243–55; Dennis Doolin, 'The Revival of the Hundred Flowers Campaign', in *CQ*, No. 8, October–December 1961, pp. 34–40; Merle Goldman, 'The Unique "Blooming and Contending" of 1961–1962', *ibid.*, No. 37, January–March 1969, pp. 54–83; Jürgen Domes, *Kulturrevolution und Armee - Die Rolle der Streitkräfte in der chinesischen 'Kulturrevolution'*, (hereafter cited as Domes, *Kulturrevolution*), Bonn, 1967, pp. 17–18.

2 Cf. *A Collection of Chou Yang's Counter-revolutionary Revisionist Speeches*, English translation of a Red Guard pamphlet of Peking, in *SCMM*, No. 646, March 10, 1969.

3 *KMJP*, July 22 and 29, 1960; cf. *CNA*, No. 398, November 24, 1961.

4 *KMJP*, August 26, 1960.

5 Kuan Feng and Lin Yü-shih, 'K'ung-tzu (Confucius)', in *Che-hsüeh yen-chiu (Philosophical Studies)*, Peking, No. 4, July 1961.

6 Feng Yu-lan, 'On Confucius' Concept of Jen', in Ch-hsüeh yen-chiu, No 5, September 1961; cf. *CNA*, November 24, 1961.

7 *Ibid.*, No. 1 and 4, January and April 1963; cf. Hellmut Wilhelm, 'The Reappraisal of Neo-Confucianism', in *CQ*, No. 23, July–September 1965, p. 130.

8 Cf. Fokkema, *op. cit.*, pp. 243–50; also Jerome Chen, 'Writers and Artists Confer', in *CQ*, No. 4, October–December 1960, pp. 33–40.

9 Teng T'o, *Yen-shan yeh-hua hsüan-chi (Evening Talks at Yenshan)*, A Collection, Hong Kong, 1966; Teng T'o, *Teng T'o shih-wen hsüan (Selected Poems and Essays of Teng T'o)*, Hong Kong, 1966; Teng T'o, Wu Han, Liao Mo-sha, Hsia Yen, Meng Ch'ao, *Ch'ang-tuan lu (Long and Short Essays)*, Hong Kong, 1966; Wu Han, *Wu Han wen-chi (Collected Writings of Wu Han)*, 3 vols., Hong Kong, 1967;

10 A reference to a poem of Mao Tse-tung.

11 *Ch'ien-hsien (Front)*, Peking, October 2, 1961.

12 Wu Han, *Hai Jui pa-kuan (The Dismissal of Hai Jui)*, Peking, 1961; English translation in extracts, in *Union Research Service* (hereafter cited as *URS*), Hong Kong, Vol. 25, No. 2.

13 Cf. also Lo Keng-mo, 'The Nature of the Rural Communes in the Present Stage', in *KJJP*, Peking, July 19, 1961; English translation in *CB*, No. 669, November 16, 1961; Meng K'uei-Hsiao Lin, *Commentary on 'Sun Yeh-fang's reactionary political viewpoint and economic programme'*, in *HC*, No. 10, 1966; English translation, in *SCMM*, No. 539, August 29, 1966; Hsüan

Mou, 'The "Great Cultural Revolution" of the Chinese Communists and the Intellectuals on the Mainland (14) – Sun Yeh-fang's "First Thesis" to the Law of Value, in *Chung-kung yen-chiu* (*Studies on Chinese Communism*),' (hereafter cited as *CKYC*), T'aipei, Vol. 4, No. 9, September 10, 1970, pp. 55–71.

14 *HC*, No. 10, 1966.

15 *KJJP*, July 19, 1961 (author's italics).

16 *HC*, No. 13, 1967, *PR*, No. 34, August 18, 1967. Cf. Chang, *loc. cit.*, pp. 170, 190.

17 von Groeling, *Fraktionskampf*, *op. cit.*, pp. 31–4.

18 *Ibid.*, p. 33.

19 *Peking kung-she* (*Peking Commune*), No. 19, April 27, 1967; also Liu Shao-ch'i's self-criticism of October 23, 1966; English translation in URI, *Collected Works . . . 1958–67*, *op. cit.*, p. 361; cf. von Groeling, *ibid.*, p. 35; also *CNA*, No. 609, 642, 663.

20 *Special Edition Concerning the Counter-revolutionary, Revisionist Crimes of Liu Shao-ch'i*, Red Guard pamphlet, Tientsin, April 1967, English translation in *SCMM*, Nos. 651, 652, April 22 and 28, 1969, in particular No. 652, pp. 22–3.

21 *URI*, *ibid.*, p. 360.

22 *Ts-ai-mao hung-ch'i* (*Red Flags in Finance and Trade*), Peking, February 23, 1967, English translation in *SCMM*, No. 651 p. 21 and No. 652, p. 5; cf. von Groeling, *ibid.*, pp. 35–6.

23 *SCMM*, No. 651, p. 39.

24 *URI*, Peng Te-huai, *op. cit.*, pp. 206–7, 481; the memorandum itself is not yet available outside China.

25 *HC*, No. 15–16, August 1, 1962; cf. Dieter Heinzig, *Mao contra Liu*, *op. cit.*, pp. 29–35.

26 Cf. *Talks at the Expanded Central Committee Meeting, January 30, 1962*, distributed by the CC of the CCP on February 12, 1962, and published by Red Guards in the Cultural Revolution, English translation, in *Joint Publications' Research Service*, (hereafter cited as *JPRS*), Washington, No. 128, December 21, 1970, pp. 1–21.

27 Cf. also Cheng, *op. cit.*, *passim*; Samuel Griffith II, *The Chinese People's Liberation Army*, New York, 1957, and London, 1968, pp. 214–64, 279–96; John Gittings, *The Role of the Chinese Army*, London and New York, 1967, pp. 225–62; Ellis Joffe, *Party and Army: Professionalism and Political Control in the Chinese Officer Corps, 1949–1964*, Cambridge, Mass., 1955, pp. 114–46; Domes, *Kulturrevolution*, *op. cit.*, pp. 73–80.

28 *JMJP*, September 18, 1959.

29 Cf. James T. Myers, 'The Fall of Chairman Mao', in *CS*, Vol. VI, No. 10, June 15, 1968.

30 Cf. in particular William W. Whitson, with Chen-hsia Huang, *The Chinese High Command: A History of Communist Military Politics, 1927–71*, New York, 1973, Chs. 9 and 12; Jurgen Domes, 'The cultural Revolution and the Army', *ibid.*, Vol. VIII, No. 5, May 1969, pp. 350–1; Gittings, *op. cit.*, p. 307.

31 *JMJP*, September 29, 1959.

32 *Chieh-fang chün-pao*, (PLA-Newspaper, hereafter cited as *CFCP*), Peking, July 1, 1958.

33 *CFCP*, October 21, 1960.
34 Twenty-nine issues of the *Kung-tso t'ung-hsün* are available in English, in Cheng, *op. cit., passim*; cf. also *CNA*, No. 510, 511, 512, April 3, 10, 17, 1964.
35 *Kung-tso t'ung-hsün*, No. 3, January 7, 1961, English translation in Cheng, *op. cit.*, pp. 65–94.
36 *NCNA*, Peking, January 17, 1964.
37 *Ibid.*
38 *CFCP*, September 16, 1961.
39 *CFCP*, October 13, 1961.
40 *Lei Feng's Diary*, Peking, 1963, *passim*; cf. *CKCNP*, November 8, 1965.
41 *NCNA*, Peking, January 19, 1965; cf. Gittings, *op. cit.*, pp. 149–50.
42 *NCNA*, Peking, May 24, 1965.
43 *Peking k'ung-ta hung-ch'i* (*Red Flag of the Air Force Academy Peking*), April 17, 1967.
44 *JMJP*, February 1, 20, 24, 1964.
45 Cf. also Wang Hung-chih (Secretary of the CCP District Committee of Lien-chiang, Fukien) 'Carry out the Decisions of the Tenth Plenum of the Eighth CC of the CCP Concerning the Consolidation of the Rural People's Communes and the Development of the Agricultural Production', speech reported, in *Fan-kung yu-chi-tui t'u-chi Lienchiang lu-huo fei-fang wen-chien hui-pien* (*Collected Documents seized in a Commando Operation in Lienchiang, Fukien*), forty-two documents, edited by the Ministry of Defence of the Republic of China, T'aipei, 1964; cf. also Li Tien-min, *Crisis of the Chinese Communist Régime – as seen from Lienchiang Documents*, T'aipei, 1964, pp. 25–6.
46 Cf. Domes, *Volkskommune, op. cit.*, pp. 72–5.
47 *HC*, No. 3, February 1, 1962.
48 Cf. in particular *CNA*, No. 422, May 25, 1962.
49 See above, pp. 126–7.
50 Among others for example an article on water conservancy projects in Sinkiang, in *JMJP*, March 29, 1962.
51 *NCNA*, Peking, April 17, 1962.
52 Wang, *loc. cit.*
53 Edgar Snow, in *The Washington Post*, February 3, 1964; also in *Asahi Shimbun*, Tokyo, February 27, 1965.
54 Dawson, *op. cit.*, p. 71.
55 Wu, in Trager-Henderson, *loc. cit.*, pp. 150–51.
56 Liu, *loc cit.*, p. 50.
57 Perkins, *loc. cit.*, p. 3.
58 *JMST*, 1963, p. 1.
59 *Peking kung-she*, No. 19, April 27, 1967; Liu Shao-ch'i, 'Self-Criticism', in URI, *Collected Works . . . 1958–67, op. cit.*, p. 361; text of Mao's speech at this conference on August 9, 1962, in English in *JPRS*, No. 128, December 21, 1970.
60 *JMST*, 1963, p. 1; also Richard Baum, Frederick C. Teiwes, *Ssu-ch'ing: The Socialist Education Movement 1962–1966*, Berkeley, 1968, Appendix B; cf. Chang, *loc. cit.*, p. 191; text of Mao's speech of September 24, 1962, in *JPRS, ibid.*

61 *NCNA*, Peking, September 28, 1962 (italics, J.D.); also in *URI*, Peng Tehuai, *op. cit.*, pp. 329–37.

62 Cf. Baum-Teiwes, *Ssu-ch'ing, op. cit., passim*; also Richard Baum, 'Revolution and Reaction in the Countryside: The Socialist Education Movement in Cultural Revolutionary Perspective,' in *CQ*, No. 38, April–June 1969, pp. 92–119; Baum, Teiwes, 'Liu Shao-ch'i and the Cadre Question', in *AS*, Vol. VIII, No. 4, April 1968, pp. 323–45; Charles B. Neuhauser, 'The Chinese Communist Party in the 1960s: Prelude to the Cultural Revolution', in *CQ*, No. 32, October–December 1967, pp. 3–36; also von Groeling, *Widerstand, op. cit.*, pp. 325–44.

63 Cf. Wang, *loc. cit.*

64 *NFJP*, November 26, 1960.

65 Baum-Teiwes, *Su-ch'ing, op. cit.*, p. 63.

66 'The First Ten Points', English translation, in *Issues and Studies*, (hereafter cited as *I and S*), Taipei, Vol. II, No. 9, June 1966, pp. 34–5, and No. 10, July 1966, p. 36 *et seq.*; cf. also *JMJP*, November 23, 1967.

67 See above, p. 47.

68 'The Later Ten Points', English translation in *I and S*, Vol. I, No. 10, July 1965, pp. 1–12 and No. 11, August 1966, pp. 27–43; cf. von Groeling, *Widerstand, op. cit.*, pp. 329–33.

69 *JMJP*, July 30, 1967.

70 Chiang Ch'ing, *Wei jen-min li hsin-kung* (*To earn new merits for the people*) Peking, 1967, pp. 3–4.

71 The materials concerning the criticisms made against Yang Hsien-chen are made available, in *HC*, Nos. 16, 17, 18, 21–22, 23–24, 1964; cf. also *CNA*, No. 535, September 25, 1964; David Munro, 'The Yang Hsienchen Affair, in *CQ*, No. 22, April–June 1965, pp. 75–82; also, Joachim Glaubitz, 'Chinas proletarische Kulturrevolution', in *Europa-Archiv*, No. 19, 1966, pp. 685–6.

72 *HC*, No. 21–22, 1964; also *CKCNP*, December 5, 1964.

73 Cf. Jürgen Domes, Ch. IV: 'Party Politics and the Cultural Revolution', in Trager-Henderson, *op. cit.*, p. 73.

74 *KMJP*, March 27, 1964; also *JMJP*, April 12, 1964; cf. *CNA*, No. 618, June 24, 1966.

75 *Ch'ien-hsien*, No. 8, 1965, reproduced in *KMJP*, May 10, 1965.

76 Cf. also *KMJP*, July 31, 1965; *KJJP*, August 5, 1965; *JMJP*, August 10 and 24, 1965; cf. *CNA*, No. 617.

77 *CKCNP*, September 7 and 9, 1965.

78 People's Radio, Ch'engtu, September 23, 1967.

79 *The China Mainland Review*, Hong Kong, No. 4, March 1966, p. 41.

80 *NCNA*, Peking, September 28, 1965.

81 Documentary film of the PR of China, released in Hong Kong cinemas from mid–October 1965.

82 'Party Centre of the CCP, May Sixteen Circular', in *JMJP*, May 17, 1967; also in Union Research Institute, *CCP Documents of the Great Proletarian Cultural Revolution, 1966–1967*, (hereafter cited as *URI, Documents*), Hong Kong, 1968, pp. 20–41.

83 *HC*, No. 7 and No. 9, 1967; cf. Franz Michael 'Moscow and the Current Chinese Crisis', in *Current History*, Vol. 53, No. 313, September 1967, p. 147; also Philip Bridgham, 'Mao's Cultural Revolution: Origin and Development', in *CQ*, No. 29, January–March 1967; p. 16.

Part Three
Crisis 1965–1972

X. The Early Phase of the 'Cultural Revolution'

Open conflict began with a literary dispute of which the world outside China at first hardly took notice. It became evident in the course of this controversy that the majority of the civil Party leadership in the capital, and Mao and his followers in Shanghai, issued contradictory directives until the Party leader's faction succeeded in gaining complete control over the loci of command in the central military apparatus.

Under the influence of the Maoist domination in the armed forces at the turn of 1965-6 the 'New Right' felt obliged to change its tactics. They too appeared to be turning against those intellectual critics who had been most sharply attacked by Mao's followers. They subsequently consented to the initiation of a 'rectification campaign' and tried to deflect the movement at the right time by taking control of it and carrying it out as a 'contradiction among the people'. But this time they did not prevail with their strategy developed in the 'Socialist Education Movement' through which they changed the *content* of a campaign drawn up by Mao by means of the civilian Party machine. Above and beyond the structures of formal organisation the Maoists mobilised parts of the younger generation in *ad hoc* units which Liu and his followers could not control. They therefore decided to keep the Chairman within bounds through a majority decision of the CC. But this attempt too could not but fail when Lin Piao regained control over the capital by staging a demonstration of military power for Mao. The split in the CCP thus became obvious. The combined general attack of the PLA, Maoist youth organisations and the basic cadres who had become embittered by the behaviour of the Party Centre in the 'Socialist Education Movement' initiated the break-up of the Party organisation.

Two Centres: Peking and Shanghai

At the end of October 1965, after the Party leader had left the capital for Shanghai, there and in the nearby city of Hangchow the circle of his closest followers came together. This number included especially Ch'en Po-ta, Mao's wife Chiang Ch'ing, and Chang Ch'un-ch'iao as the successor to the First Secretary of the East China Regional Bureau

and of the Politburo, K'o Ch'ing-shih, who had died in April. Without any previous discussion with the Party Centre the Maoist circle
began its counterattack against the forces of the 'New Right'[1] in an
editorial in the Shanghai newspaper *Wen-hui pao* of November 10,
directed against the Vice-Mayor of Peking, Wu Han. The author of
this editorial, Mao's son-in-law Yao Wen-yüan, described Wu Han's
play, *The Dismissal of Hai Jui* as a 'great poisonous weed which must be
eradicated and rooted out'.

It seems that Peking had at once realised that the gauntlet had
been thrown down with this attack. As early as November 11, P'eng
Chen complained in Shanghai about its publication,[2] and the publication organs of the Party Centre at first refused to reproduce the editorial.
Only after it had been published as a pamphlet in Shanghai on November 26[3] and after the journal of the PLA, the *CFCP*, had reproduced it
on November 29[4] did the *JMJP* at last follow suit on November 30.[5]
However, the central organ of the Party added a footnote which labelled the article as contributing to discussion, and calling for a general
expression of opinions. Up to the beginning of December only fourteen of the more than thirty-five regional newspapers had reproduced
Yao's critique without comment. They were those of Shanghai and
the provinces of Chekiang, Fukien, Kiangsu, Shantung, Anhui, Kiangsi,
Hopei, Honan and Kwangtung. Apart from the *JMJP*, the *KMJP*
and the *Pei-ching jih-pao* also added comments of interpretation or
mitigation. The rest of the newspapers did not take any notice of the
article at all.[6]

The Party Centre had made it clear through the comment in the
JMJP that it was determined to treat this controversy as a 'non-antagonistic contradiction', and indeed the debate was relatively open at
first. The *JMJP* itself and the publication media under the control
of the Peking Urban Committee published several articles in
December which defended Wu Han against Yao's attack.[7] The self-
criticism which he finally published on December 30, 1965, in the
JMJP was equivalent to a defence of his position, and as late as January
1966 the central organ of the CCP published a reader's letter which
condemned the criticism of Wu.[8] Thereafter, however, his defenders
became quiet, and the demand that workers should combine their
work with sufficient leisure was also heard of for the last time at the
end of January 1966.[9] Decisive changes within the military leadership
had meanwhile effected a shift of balance in favour of Mao's faction.

The Purge of Lo Jui-ch'ing[10]

Since the summer of 1965 contradictions had evolved in the central
military leadership between Lin Piao and the Chief of the General

Staff, General Lo Jui-ch'ing, who, representing the professional officers, protested more and more frequently against the mounting influence of the political commissars and the strong emphasis on political work in the PLA.[11] When Lin and Lo had become the heads of the PLA in September 1959 they had been united in their rejection of P'eng Te-huai's conception. While the latter had been striving for an accumulation of military power while building up the general economy under the shield of the Soviet deterrent potential, they believed that the PR of China might obtain a sufficient degree of security by preparing a defence strategy of 'people's war' and by developing a nuclear potential independent of the Soviet Union. However, when in the summer of 1965 the PLA leadership was confronted with new strategical problems in the context of the growing engagement of the USA in Vietnam, the Minister of Defence and the Chief of the General Staff began to develop differences of opinion which were made public by both of them. Comparing Lo's article *Commemorate the Victory over German Fascism! Carry the Struggle against US Imperialism through to the End!*[12] and Lin's work *Long Live the Victory of the People's War!*[13], Helmut Dahm came to the conclusion that both of them argued for the theory of the 'people's war' which had evolved from Mao's thoughts on guerilla warfare, but that Lo wanted to employ this theory only for the defence of China against an external attack,[14] while Lin conceived it as a means by which each country could defeat 'imperialism' *through its own strength*. Thus one could eventually achieve the encirclmeent of the 'world's cities' by the 'world's villages' – of the industrial nations by the developing countries – in the course of a chain of 'people's wars'. In the long run, and *in principle*, Lin attributed an offensive character to the theory of 'People's war', whereas Lo understood it, under all circumstances, as a means of defensive war. Regarding the practical policy of the PR of China in the Vietnam conflict, however, the Defence Minister's position implied limitation of support to moral support for North Vietnam and the Vietcong who had to lead their 'people's war' by themselves, whereas the Chief of the General Staff included *conventional* aid from Socialist countries for Vietnam as well. But such action, would have required the settlement of the conflict between the PR of China and the Soviet Union. Thus a controversy over strategy and foreign policy was added to the fundamental conflict over internal development policy, and the 'New Right' appeared to gain an influential ally.

However, Lin Piao soon won his cause against Lo. On November 27, 1965, the Chief of the General Staff was affirmatively mentioned in the press for the last time.[15] From December 30, 1965, to January 18, 1966, a conference on political work in the PLA took place in Peking. Lo no longer took part in it, and two close followers of Lin Piao, the Director of the General Political Department, General Hsiao Hua, and the Vice-Chief of the General Staff, General Yang Ch'eng-wu, dominated the scene. Both of them clearly argued for the views of the Minister of Defence and directed sharp attacks against the purely 'military thinking' of the professional officers.[16] It may therefore be assumed that Lin Piao succeeded by December 1965 in expelling the Lo opposition group from the centre of the PLA. The harshness of the action against Lo pointed to the severe nature of the conflict which had now begun to develop within the CCP. In January 1966 the Military Commission of the CC formed an investigation committee which began to prove into Lo's case. The self-criticism which Lo made before the commission on March 12 was regarded as insufficient and his arrest was ordered. An attempt at suicide by the Chief of the General Staff on March 18 failed, and on April 24 Mao himself approved the report of the investigation committee which recommended Lo's dismissal from office.[17]

With Yang Ch'eng-wu, an unconditionally loyal follower of the Maoist faction became the acting Chief of the General Staff and head of the PLA which during the following months became Mao's most important weapon, in spite of the hesitancy of some regional military commanders, in the fight against the intellectuals and the opposition of the civil Party apparatus.

The 'February Report' and the Shanghai Protocol

Although the opposition to Mao had been deprived of its chance to influence effectively the armed forces through the downfall of Lo Jui-ch'ing, the leadership of the civil Party apparatus under Liu Shao-ch'i and Teng Hsiao-p'ing continued to prevent the extensive purification campaign for which the Maoists were pressing. They could certainly no longer protect completely intellectual critics from attacks made by the Left, but they tried to define the dispute in the field of literature and art as a 'contradiction among the people' and wanted to resolve it through open discussion. It proved useful to them that Liu had, in Mao's absence, become the head of the Standing Committee of the Politburo in Peking and could thus exercise temporary but unopposed control over the central Party apparatus. On February 5, 1966, the Standing Committee decided to form a 'Cultural Revolution Group' (Wen-hua ko-ming hsiao-tsu) of five members to elaborate the guide-lines of the discussion now proceeding under the label of the 'Cultural Revolution'.[18] Three committed representatives of the 'New Right' (Lu Ting-i, Chou Yang and the director of the news agency NCNA, Wu Leng-hsi), under the guidance of P'eng Chen, and no more than one Maoist, alternate member of the Politburo K'ang Sheng, were elected to this body. As early as February 7, the group offered the result of its discussions in the so-called *February Report (Erh-yüeh t'i-kang)*.[19] Without waiting for the comments of the vacillating K'ang Sheng, P'eng ordered the reproduction of the report and its release for distribution among Party cadres.[20]

The *Report* called the dispute over Wu Han's play *The Dismissal of Hai Jui* and the Maoist critique of other leading Party intellectuals an 'academic discussion' through which a 'contradiction among the people' would be resolved. Although the 'monopoly of the old intellectuals' should be broken through this discussion, the critics should be persuaded and not deprived of their individual liberty. It would be imperative to prevent the establishment of 'academic tyrants' (*Hsüeh-fa*) – a clear reference to Maoist cadres who tried to regulate the behaviour of the intellectuals. Stating that construction was more important than destruction and that 'everyone was equal before the truth', the *Report* was directly aimed against the Party leader and his followers who wanted 'Mao Tse-tung's thought' to be regarded as universal truth.

In this respect the 'New Right' had manifestly challenged the Chairman. Mao and Lin Piao instantly took counter-measures. In the course of a trade union conference which lasted from the end of January to March 5, the Minister of Defence successfully secured, albeit temporarily, the support of the leadership of the 'All-Chinese Federation of Trade Unions, the organ of which, the KJJP, began to publish readers' letters from soldiers which, from mid-January onwards praised the policies of the army leadership.[21] As early as January 16, the First Secretary of the Central-South China Regional Bureau, T'ao Chu, had placed himself on the side of Mao and Lin Piao.[22] During the following months the organ of this Bureau, the *Yang-ch'eng wan-pao*, became the main mouthpiece of the Left apart from the CFCP[23]. At the instigation of Lin Piao, who now took the initiative for the Left more and more obviously, Chiang Ch'ing convened a forum on art and literature in the armed forces from February 2 to 20 in Shanghai. In the course of this forum the participants, several of the leading political commissars of the PLA, drew up a protocol which described the confrontation on the 'cultural front' as a 'sharp class struggle'. It was not a 'contradiction among the people' but an 'antagonistic contradiction between the enemy and ourselves'. A 'black gang' (*Hei-pang*) had started an attack on the dictatorship of the proletariat. It would have to be destroyed.[24] Thus both sides had stated their views in diametrically contrasting documents. After Mme. Mao had transmitted the Shanghai Protocol to Lin Piao on March 19, he succeeded on March 20 in having the Military Commission of the CC declare it obligatory for the whole PLA.[25]

Mao himself convened a session of the Standing Committee of the Politburo in Hangchow from March 17 to 20. There he made a sharp criticism of the *February Report* and of the work of the Propaganda Department of the CC.[26] This completed the split in the leadership group. In Peking, Liu and the majority of the civilian Party machine continued to prevent the purge of critical intellectuals. In Shanghai and Hangchow, Mao and Lin, supported by the PLA, the Federation of Trade Unions and the Central-South China Regional Bureau, called for a 'revolutionary storm'. As early as April and May the Left proved itself superior and the PLA stronger than the civilian Party machine.

The Overthrow of P'eng Chen

The Left used the absence of Liu, who made state visits to Pakistan, Afghanistan and Burma from March 24 to April 19, 1966, to enlarge its influence in the Centre. At a plenary session of the CC of the Communist Youth League, which took place from April 1 to 20 in Peking, army officers successfully demanded in a number of speeches that Lin Piao's formula of 'living study and living use Mao Tse-tung's thought' be incorporated in the documents drawn up by the conference.[27] The attacks of the Left on the leadership of the Youth League remained, however, without success. The League, whose support both sides were bent on obtaining, confined itself to nominal support for the Left. At the same time the conflict in the central Party bodies continued. At a session of the CC Secretariat from April 9 to 12 K'ang Sheng and Ch'en Po-ta made sharp attacks on P'eng Chen and the 'Group in Charge of the Cultural Revolution', whose dissolution was proposed to the Politburo by the members of the Secretariat who were present. From April 16 to 20, Mao again gathered his followers in the Standing Committee of the Politburo in Hangchow – probably only Lin Piao and Chou En-lai who was now beginning to throw in his lot with the Left – and he instigated a decision to condemn P'eng.[28] On April 12 the army journal began its own endeavours at literary criticism in a regular column;[29] and finally, on April 14, the thirtieth session of the Standing Committee of the Second NPC proclaimed the beginning of the 'Great Cultural Revolution' which at that time was still called 'Socialist'.[30]

Although the group around Mao and Lin had already decided upon P'eng's overthrow and upon the dissolution of the 'Group of Five', an additional demonstration of armed power was necessary after Liu's return to press this decision through. Foreign correspondents in

Peking noticed, on April 28, that the offices of the Urban Committee of the CCP were guarded by military patrols.[31] Under the influence of this action Liu and Teng appear to have decided to dissociate themselves from P'eng and from the Peking intellectuals under his protection. The varying values ascribed to the need for free expression in art and literature within the 'New Right' caused a fission process in the opposition which was skilfully exploited by the Left.

On May 4 and 8 the army journal gave the signal for the general attack on the leaders of the intellectual opposition of 1961–2. Teng T'o, Wu Han and Liao Mo-sha were called 'poisonous revisionist weeds', because of their attacks on the Party leader and his policy,[32] and 'vexatious counter-revolutionary rats' which had to be 'crushed and beaten till they were stinking'. They had formed a 'black gang of counter-revolutionaries' and had tried to restore capitalism.[33] On May 4, Mao convened a further session of the Standing Committee of the Politburo in Hangchow in which a number of leading members of the Left who did not belong to this body took part.[34] In two weeks of discussions the leadership circle of the Left decided definitely on P'eng's dismissal and the dissolution of the 'Group of Five'. It adopted the so-called *May 16 Circular* (*Wu-i-liu t'ung-chih*) which revoked the *February Report* and was set forth as the new guide-line for the 'Cultural Revolution'.

It was clearly stated in this document that the 'present situation' is one of 'extremely sharp class struggle', of a 'contradiction between the enemy and ourselves'. The members of the intellectual opposition were now denounced as a 'bunch of counter-revolutionaries opposing the Communist Party and the people' against whom must be waged a 'struggle of life and death'. The 'Representatives of the bourgeoisie' had 'sneaked into the Party, the Government and the Army,' and established 'a faction of power-holders in the Party who take the capitalist road' (*Tang-nei tsou tzu-pen chu-i tao-lu ti tang-ch'üan-p'ai*). They had infested the 'press, radio, magazines, books, textbooks, platforms, works of literature, cinema, drama, ballads and stories, fine arts, music and dance with their bourgeois thought'. They had to be 'unmasked' and 'destroyed' in all realms of intellectual and political life.[35]

A new 'CC Cultural Revolution Group' (*Chung-yang wen-ko hsiao-tsu*, CRG), which thenceforward acted as the leading organ of the genuine Maoist forces of the Left, was entrusted by the conference with the implementation of the purge. Ch'en Po-ta became the head of this group. T'ao Chu and K'ang Sheng functioned as advisers, and Mao's wife was first deputy head. Chang Ch'un-ch'iao and the First Secretary of the provincial Party Committee of Hupei, Wang Jen-chung, as well as the Deputy Director of the General Political Department of the PLA, General Liu Chih-chien, functioned as deputy heads. Among the eleven additional members, the Party theoriests Wang Li, Kuan Feng, Ch'i Pen-yü, Mu Hsin, Yao Wen-yüan and Lin Chieh were particularly outstanding.[36]

The Hangchow decisions were followed by the formal dismissal of P'eng Chen and of seven of the eight secretaries in the Peking Committee between May 16 and June 2, probably before May 25.[37] This fact, however, initiated the second stage of the purge which was now shifted into the Party organisation itself. During the first period, from mid-April to mid-May, most of the victims of the purge were intellectuals who had belonged to the CCP but had not occupied top-level positions. Among them, apart from the three already mentioned, were the head of the association of Chinese dramatists and the author of the words of the National Anthem, T'ien Han, as well as the national economists, Sun Yeh-fang and Lo Keng-no, the Chancellor of 'Peita', Lu P'ing and fourteen other university heads.

After the expulsion of the opposition from the Peking Urban Committee during the second half of May, the propaganda apparatus of the Party became the next objective leftist drive to seize power. On June 9 the dismissal of its head, Lu Ting-i, was announced, and at the same time Chou Yang and Lin Mo-han also fell.[38] New for the first time General Yang Ch'eng-wu was publicly mentioned as 'acting Chief of the General Staff', and thus the downfall of Lo Jui-ch'ing was officially confirmed.[39]

But Liu and his followers did not take the measures of the Left lying down. While Mao and his followers started to mobilise the pupils and students against the 'New Right', the latter made a last attempt to get the movement under its control. The conflict shifted to the secondary and high schools.

The Struggle for the Schools

From mid May, in the course of the campaign against the intellectuals, the Maoists concentrated on the universities and colleges. Strict discipline throughout the Party had caused widespread frustration among the students for years. Moreover, since the mid-1950s, the great expansion in secondary education had steadily diminished the career opportunities of college graduates, for the creation of new job opportunities for scientific and advanced technical personnel had not corresponded to the expansion of the educational system. Many graduates had to reckon with being unemployed or being employed in agricultural work as soon as they graduated from university. At the same time conflicts grew in the schools between pupils from the cities and the children of peasants, who were boarders, and who were often hardly able to cope with the intellectual demands made on them. The Left tried to mobilise these frustrations and conflicts for their own 'drive' to seize power. In a number of colleges and secondary schools the students and pupils were instigated to take up the Left's criticism of their teachers; to attack them in 'Big Character Posters', and in many cases to use physical violence against them. In order to release the energies of the young for such actions all schools were closed from the middle of May, at first in the cities, shortly afterwards in most other parts of the country as well. This measure was confirmed by a directive of the CC on June 13, 1966, and by the State Council which postponed indefinitely the entrance examinations for universities and colleges.[40] In fact the primary schools were reopened only in spring and summer 1967, the secondary schools between autumn 1968 and spring 1969 and one-third of the colleges in September 1970.

The 'Peita' and Tsinghua universities – also in the capital – became the first centres of conflict between the Left student movement and the forces of the anti-Maoist opposition. At 'Peita' the conflict started on the evening of May 25 with an attack on the Chancellor, Lu P'ing, who had been supported by the old Peking Municipal Committee under P'eng Chen, by Nieh Yüan-tzu, a female lecturer in philosophy aged about thirty. When the *JMJP* published the text of the Big Character Poster signed by Mme. Nieh on June 2,[41] the Maoists at the colleges regarded it as evidence that the Party leader and his followers completely approved of their actions. The movement rapidly spread to other universities. Heavy clashes between the followers of the Left and the functionaries of the Party machine occurred at Tsinghua as well as at 'Peita' universities.[42]

On June 8 the first Big Character Posters appeared in the Canton schools.[43] A short time later the Chancellor of Nanking University, K'uang Ya-ming, was physically attacked by Maoist students, and at the end of June attacks began on the Chancellor of Wuhan University, Li Ta, who was a founding member of the CCP in 1921 and who was, in spite of a call for help to the Party leader, finally beaten to death.[44]

In order to check the witch-hunt of critical intellectuals, and at the same time to consolidate the Party's wavering control over the universities, a Central Work Conference of the CC under Liu's guidance decided in Peking at the beginning of June to send '*work teams*' to the schools. However, at a meeting of his followers in the Politburo at Hangchow on June 9, Mao demanded that this decision be revoked.[45] The confrontation of the two centres in the capital and in the region of Shanghai was thus continuing. The 'work teams' responded to the Maoist terror, especially in the Peking universities, with an equally massive counter-terror. Both sides were now looking for a decisive end to this conflict at the highest level of legitimisation, a plenary session of the CC, which had not been used since September 1962.

The Military Putsch in Peking and the Eleventh Plenum

According to a report attributed to the Peking correspondent of the Yugoslav news agency *Tanyug*, Branko Bogunovic, and since fundamentally confirmed by many items of evidence in Red Guard materials,[46] Liu and Teng are said to have planned, in June 1966, a CC plenum at which Mao was to be elected 'Honorary Chairman' of the CCP according to Article Thirty-seven of the Party Constitution, and thus be excluded from making political decisions. Up to mid-June, fifty-one of the ninety full members, and thirty-eight of the eighty-seven candidate members are said to have arrived in Peking. Liu and his followers apparently fixed July 21 as the date for the opening of the planned plenary session. At the same time the Party leader left Hangchow for Wuhan. There he demonstrated his good health, according to a report published by the media ten days later, by long-distance swimming in the Yangtze, returning to the capital after an absence of nine months.[47] Meanwhile, the public railway service from Peking to Tientsin had been temporarily suspended because of big troop movements, and curfew had been ordered in the region of the central station. On July 18 and 19, PLA units under the command of Yang Ch'eng-wu occupied the offices of the Party Centre and surrounded the district where the top leadership had its residence.

Under the influence of this renewed demonstration of power, Mao's opponents cancelled the plenary session. At the same time the Left prepared its own plenum, the Eleventh Plenum of the Eighth CC, which met on August 1 in an atmosphere of gathering conflict and lasted until August 12. This plenum, however, apparently did not constitute a quorum according to the Party Constitution. The communiqué issued on August 12 omitted the usual practice of mentioning the number of full and candidate members present. Instead it referred to the fact that 'representatives of the revolutionary teachers and students of the Peking universities' had also taken part in the session.[48] This corroborates the *coup d'etat* nature of events in the capital of the PR of China around the turn of July and August. There are many indications that no more than eighty of the 173 full and candidate members of the CC had been present.[49]

Essentially the plenum confirmed the policy of Mao and Lin. The 'Decision Concerning the Great Proletarian Cultural Revolution', adopted by the plenum on August 8,[50] created the preconditions for the special organisations which were to replace the regular Party organisation in order to implement the rectification campaign. The

sixteen-point document states that a 'new phase in the socialist
revolution' had been reached, and that it was imperative to carry
through a basic change in the 'superstructure' which could not be
carried out 'without violence'. The 'right deviationists' among the
cadres 'hostile to the Party and anti-socialist' were to be exposed, and
their influence eliminated. The majority of the cadres, however, were
said to be 'good or relatively good'. The revolutionaries should unite
with them. Furthermore, the decision called for a basic reform of the
educational system. The schools would in future have to serve 'proletarian politics and would have to combine study with productive
labour'. Under the guidance of the Party, new mass organisations were
to be established: the cultural revolution groups and congresses whose
organisational structures were to be modelled on the example of the
Paris Commune of 1871. Despite these pointedly Maoist demands the
document was not free of inconsistencies. Apart from the call for revolutionary action, an unequivocal reference can be found to the necessity for Party discipline and a statement that the conflict should in
essence be resolved by means of 'referring to the facts, discussion and
persuasion'. The minority should not be 'suppressed'.

Such statements suggest that the Left had not completely succeeded
in overcoming the opposition to the 'Cultural Revolution' during
the plenary session. However, Mao and Lin prevailed as far as the decisions concerning personnel policy taken by the Eleventh Plenum
were concerned. The Minister of Defence became the sole Vice-
Chairman of the CC and the Politburo. Liu dropped from number two
to number eight in the Politburo and the aging Marshal Chu Te from
number four to nine. P'eng Chen, P'eng Te-huai, Li Ching-ch'üan
and Politburo candidate member Lu Ting-i were expelled from the
leading body. T'ao Chu, Ch'en Po-ta, K'ang Sheng as well as Marshals Hsü Hsiang-ch'ien and Yeh Chien-ying, joined the Politburo as
full members, while the Minister of Security, General Hsieh Fu-chih
and the trade union leader Liu Ning-i became alternate members. The
Standing Committee of the Politburo was enlarged to eleven members.
T'ao Chu, Ch'en Po-ta, K'ang Sheng and Liu Fu-ch'un joined it.

Chou En-lai's position remained unimpaired during this change in
the top-level leadership. He apparently knew, as he had during the
preceding internal Party conflicts, how to side with the stronger
element – which in turn could hardly pass by his great experience
and capacity in diplomacy and administration.

Together with Chou and his closest followers, the Left now possessed
eight of the eleven votes in the Standing Committee. However,
even while in defeat Liu managed to stay in the top-level leadership.
A complete Maoist victory was prevented above all by the resistance
of the regional and provincial Party leadership groups. In order to

defeat them Mao was obliged to make further use of the new, *ad hoc*, mass organisations and of the PLA.

References

1 *WHP*, November 10, 1965.
2 Ch'i Pen-yü, in *HC*, No. 7, May 11, 1966; cf. Bridgham, *loc. cit.*, p. 18.
3 *WHP*, November 27, 1965.
4 *CFCP*, November 29, 1965.
5 *JMJP*, November 30, 1965.
6 Cf. Chao Ts'ung, 'A Report Concerning the Development of the Cultural Revolutionary Movement', in *Tsu-kuo-China Monthly*, (hereafter cited as *TK*), Hong Kong, No. 53, October 1, 1968, pp. 10–11.
7 Li Chen-yü for instance stated in *Peking jih-pao* of December 9, 1965 that 'the *Dismissal of Hai Jui*' was a 'good historical play'. On the same day the *KMJP* published an article by the Head of Nanking University, K'uang Ya-ming, in which he called for a reduction of the political education of the students.
8 *JMJP*, January 19, 1966.
9 *TKP*, January 27, 1966.
10 Cf. von Groeling, *Widerstand*, *op. cit.*, pp. 248–55.
11 Cf. Domes, *Kulturrevolution*, *op. cit.*, pp. 78–82.
12 *HC*, No. 5, 1957.
13 *JMJP*, September 3, 1965.
14 Helmut Dahm, 'Militärpolitische Aspekte der chinesischen Kulturrevolution', *Berichte des Bundesinstituts für Ostwissenschaftliche und Internationale Studien*, Köln, No. 19, 1967, in particular pp. 6–7.
15 *JMJP*, November 27, 1965.
16 *NCNA*, Peking, January 24, 1966.
17 'Commentary of the CC of the CCP on the Delivery of the Report of the Work Team of the CC Concerning the Question of Lo Jui-ch'ing's Mistakes, May 16, 1966', in *URI*, *Documents*, *op. cit.*, pp. 29–32. Initially Lo was not arrested, but on December 20, 1966 he was arrested by Red Guards in Peking and suffered massive humiliations at four mass meetings. Cf. von Groeling, *Widerstand*, *op. cit.*, pp. 254–5. After further accusation rallies he committed suicide according to Japanese newspaper reports in June 1967. Cf. *Asahi Shimbun*, Tokyo, June 7, 1967; one Red Guard journal however reported from Peking in December 1967 that he had been shot according to martial law. Cf. *Chingkanshan*, Peking, December 21, 1967.
18 Cf. Chang, *loc. cit.*, p. 193.
19 'Draft Report of the Group of Five of the Cultural Revolution on the Present Academic Discussion, February 7, 1966', in *URI*, *Documents*, *op. cit.*, pp. 3–12.
20 *I-chiu-liu-pa fei-ch'ing nien-pao* (*1968 Yearbook on Chinese Communism*), Taipei, 1968, p. 573.

21 Cf. *CNA*, No. 627, September 2, 1966.

22 *Yang-ch'eng wan-pao* (hereafter cited as *YCWP*), Canton, February 1, 1966.

23 Cf. Jürgen Domes, 'Generals and Red Guards – the Role of Huang Yung-sheng and the Canton Military Area Command in the Kuangtung Cultural Revolution', Part One, in *Asia Quarterly*, Brussels, 1971, No. 1, p. 15.

24 *Minutes of the Forum on Literature and Art in the Armed Forces Convened by Comrade Chiang Ch'ing on Comrade Lin Piao's Request, February 2 to 20, 1966*, English translation in *SCMP*, No. 3956, June 9, 1967.

25 *Ibid.*; also *JMJP*, May 29, 1967.

26 Cf. Chang, *ibid.*

27 *Communiqué of the Third Plenum of the Ninth CC of the Communist Youth League, April 20, 1966*, in *JMJP*, May 4, 1966.

28 Cf. Chang, *ibid.*

29 *CFCP*, April 12, 1966.

30 *KMJP*, April 28, 1966; the last (thirty-second) session of the Standing Committee of the third NPC took place on April 26, 1966.

31 Branko Bogunovic, 'The Storm in July', in *Politika*, Belgrade, translated from the Chinese, in *Ming-pao* (*The Light*), Hong Kong, January 1 and 2, 1967. Bogunovic's report must be taken with caution, especially as the Tanyug news agency frequently revises the reports of its correspondents considerably. But a number of his statements were later confirmed by Red Guard sources. Only where this is the case has he been cited here.

32 See above, pp. 124–6.

33 *CFCP*, May 4 and 8, 1966.

34 *JPRS*, No. 42, 349, August 25, 1967.

35 *Circular, loc. cit.*

36 Among others on *I-chiu-liu-chiu fei-ch'ing nien-pao* (*1969 Yearbook on Chinese Communism*), Vol. I, Taipei, 1969, Ch. III, pp. 3–4.

37 *JMJP*, June 2, 1966.

38 *JMJP*, July 9, 1966.

39 *JMJP*, July 12, 1966.

40 'Directive of the CC of the CCP and of the State Council Concerning the Postponement of the Entrance Examinations for Universities and Colleges, June 13, 1966', in *JMJP*, June 18, 1966.

41 *JMJP*, June 2, 1966.

42 *KJJP*, June 5, 1966; cf. 'A Foreign Expert, Eyewitness of the Cultural Revolution', in *CQ*, No. 28, October–December 1966, pp. 2–4; also A. Schelochowzew, *Chinesische Kulturrevolution aus der Nähe – Augenzeugenbericht eines sowjetischen Beobachters*, Stuttgart, 1969, pp. 74–116.

43 *Hung-se tsao-fan-che* (*Red Rebel*), Chiangmen, No. 25, November 12, 1967.

44 *Nan-han chan-pao* (*Combat Journal 'Cry'*), Wuhan, February 1968; English translation in *SCMP*, No. 4141, March 19, 1968.

45 Chang, *loc. cit.*, p. 194.

46 Bogunovic, *loc. cit.*

47 *JMJP*, July 25, 1966.

49 Franz Michael, 'The Struggle for Power', in *Problems of Communism*, Washington, May–June 1967, p. 19.

48 'Communiqué of the Eleventh Plenum of the Eighth CC of the CCP, August 12, 1966', in *JMJP*, August 14, 1966; also *URI*, *Documents*, *op. cit.*, pp. 55–70.

50 'Resolution of the CC of the CCP on the Great Proletarian Cultural Revolution, August 8, 1966', in *JMJP*, August 9, 1966; also *URI*, *Documents*, *op. cit.*, pp. 33–54; cf. also von Groeling, *Widerstand*, *op. cit.*, pp. 136–9.

XI.   The Offensive of the Left

The accusations made against the chief representatives of the intellectual opposition, which filled the columns of the Chinese press from
early July 1966, as well as a number of basic statements, particularly
the editorials of the *JMJP* and of the army journal on August 1, Army
Day, and the 'Decision Concerning the Great Proletarian Cultural
Revolution' elucidated the programmatic principles of the Left.
—Henceforward, political reliability was to be of greater importance
than expertise.

—The country should become a 'Great Revolutionary School of
Mao Tse-tung's Thought'. It was the duty of the army to concern itself
as well with culture, agriculture and industry. The people's communes,
sales co-operatives, factories and schools should be organised on military lines and be activated politically and culturally. Small factories
should be built in the villages. Industrial workers should help during
the harvest and pupils and students should 'carry out productive
labour'. Thus the differences between the villages and cities, the factories and the land, and intellectual and manual labour would cease
to exist, and the country could be brought nearer to a Communist
social order.[1]

—The years spent in study at college and university should be
drastically shortened through a 'great educational reform', and study
at all kinds of educational institutions should be combined with long
periods of manual work.

—'Old thought, old culture, old customs and old habits' should be
replaced by a 'new proletarian ideology, new culture, new customs
and new habits' – a demand which was directed above all against the
traditional Chinese family order, the cultivation of the classical cultural tradition and Western cultural influences.

—The intellectual critics of Mao's policy should be dismissed from
their positions in the realm of education and publication, and experience the 'full harshness of the dictatorship of the proletariat'.

—Agriculture should once more be undertaken by mass labour
organised on military lines. There were growing indications that the
abolition of private plots and free markets was on the way.

Substantial parts of this programme were designed to restore the
principles of the 'Three Red Banner Policy'. Mao was determined to
launch another great revolutionary tide aimed directly at revolution-

ising consciousness, at chaos (*luan*) out of which the 'New Society' and 'New Men' would ultimately arise. In this process the expectations of the Party leader and of his most devoted disciples relied upon the innovatory enthusiasm of the younger generation which, with Mao's support, was now setting out on its offensive against the Party machine.

The 'Red Guards'

Thus the 'Red Guards' (*Hung-se hsien-feng pao-wei-ping*; Chinese abbreviation, *Hung-wei-ping*) were the first to come into existence among the Maoist mass organisations which became the most important instruments in the Leftists' struggle for power.[2] The origins of this organisation can be traced back to spring 1966. As early as April 9 and 11 there were reports of student meetings at Peking's Tsinghua University and in Tsinan, the capital of Shantung, during which there were discussions on an 'educational revolution'.[3] From mid-May, the political apparatus of the PLA assembled pupils and students who were regarded as politically reliable in various parts of the country for indoctrination courses.[4] Many indications suggest that the cadres of the 'Red Guards' came from these groups, probably altogether more than a million young people between twelve and twenty-five years old, most of them secondary school pupils, students and young professional soldiers. On May 22 there appeared for the first time in the press the name used for the Red Guards, 'little revolutionary generals',[5] and on June 26 the term 'Red Guards' is mentioned for the first time in the signature of a leaflet distributed in Peking.[6] It is significant that only a month later, on July 27, the Communist Youth League was positively mentioned for the last time for more than two years.[7] The 'Red Guards' were obviously to replace the Youth League as the youth organisation of the CCP. After the Left had successfully secured control over the capital, from the beginning of August tens of thousands of Red Guard cadres were brought to Peking from almost every city in China, by public transport or by military transport facilities under the guidance of political commissars and officers of the PLA. Mao Tse-tung welcomed them on the evening of August 10 in the courtyard of the Party Centre building.[8]

After Ch'en Po-ta had called for the unleashing of a 'merciless revolutionary storm' on August 16, at a meeting of more than 10,000 leading cadres of the new organisation,[9] among them many cadets from the Peking military academy, the 'Red Guards' had their first public appearance on the morning of August 18, at a mass rally of more than a million people.[10] Such rallies were repeated in the capital on August 31, September 15, October 1, October 18, November 3, November 10 and November 25. At almost all of them the Party leader appeared in person, remaining silent and leaving speech-making to Lin Piao, Chou En-lai, Ch'en Po-ta and his wife, Chiang Ch'ing. In all, more than ten million Red Guards are said to have taken part in the rallies, and from the second half of August, their organisation rapidly extended over large parts of China. The local groups of the movement, often led by political commissars from the PLA and by 'worker and peasant students', accepted only children of the 'five red elements' ('workers, poor and lower-middle peasants, revolutionary cadres, revolutionary soldiers and revolutionary martyrs') during the first phase, but in the course of the extension of the mass organisation this regulation soon ceased to be observed. Thus, from the end of August, the most disparate forces gained admittance to the Red Guards. In some places the Party functionaries who had been attacked by Red Guards even established their own youth units which came into conflict with those supported by the Centre. The more the movement grew, the more it disintegrated into a number of rival groups.[11] Attempts to create a central organisation remained unsuccessful. Certainly, after August 31, Mao became their 'Supreme Commander' (*T'ung-shuai*) and Lin Piao his deputy, but this was mainly symbolic. The nearest thing to a centralised organisation was a network of Red Guard units centring around the 'Third Headquarters of the Red Guards of the Capital' which was under the direct influence of Mme. Mao and the CRG. From the end of August the Red Guards used a great number of newspapers and journals which – shortlived for the most part – acted as organs in the struggle with the Party apparatus and in factional struggles amongst themselves. These were published in most of the cities and in many rural areas. It was only during the second half of 1968 that they became more infrequent.[12]

During the weeks following August 18, the Red Guards dominated not only most schools, but even the streets of Peking, Shanghai, Canton and a number of other cities. They destroyed temples, Christian churches and several museums, and made 'domiciliary visits' during which 'bourgeois luxuries' such as pendulum clocks, aquariums and musical instruments fell victim to them. Critics and opponents of the Party leader they dragged through the streets, beating, humiliating and torturing them; in many cases even killing them. Thus the Minister of Foreign Affairs, Ch'en Yi, stated in his 'self-criticism' speech on January 24, 1967, that in the late summer and autumn of 1966 alone, more than 400,000 members of the 'work teams', established in the summer of that year, had been physically liquidated.[13] Although the top-level functionaries of the CCP, against whom the purge had by now been directed, generally did not suffer physical attacks, at the lower level a great number of victims died.

However, the Leftist vanguard soon encountered resistance. As early as June, 'revolutionary students' were apprehended in the province of Kweichow, and on August 3 and September 5 there were further incidents there, which the central organ of the CCP later labelled the 'White Terror'.[14] On August 19 and 20 the situation deteriorated into street battles in Changsha between Red Guards and members of the 'Red Workers' Guards' (*Kung-jen ch'ih-wei-tui*) mobilised by the local Party leadership as a counter-organisation. The end came only after military units had intervened in favour of the Maoists.[15] From August 25 to September 1 there were reports from Tsingtao of the outbreak of 'White Terror' against Red Guards,[16] and on October 31 the publication media reported acts of sabotage against Red Guard railway transportation for the first time.[17] In five other cities and in two rural districts in the province of Kwangtung clashes had also occurred between Red Guards and peasants and workers during September. In some cases this early resistance to Red Guard activities appears to have been spontaneous, but in many places it was organised by the local Party cadres.

The obviously unexpected violence of the opposition soon forced the leadership of the Left to call for greater discipline from the Red Guards. In the ten days following the August 18 rally the army journal and the *JMJP* had continued to laud the actions of the Red Guards,[18] but on August 31 Lin Piao was already calling on them to refrain from violence.[19] On September 8 a decree of the CC and State Council forbade the Red Guards to storm the archives and remove secret files,[20] and on September 14 the CC prohibited all cultural revolutionary activities in the villages during the period of the autumn harvest.[21] While an increasing number of troops took part in the mass rallies of the Red Guards in the capital, after early October the leadership of the PLA attempted to make use of the so-called 'revolutionary exchange of experience' (*Ko-ming ta-ch'uan-lien*) as well to discipline the Maoist youth units. The Red Guards marched in groups of between fifty and 300 men through large parts of the country, especially in North China, to agitate among the rural population for the 'Cultural Revolution' and, at the same time, to strengthen themselves physically. On these marches a 'PLA delegate' was appointed to every twenty or thirty Red Guards.[22] If the assertion that 'far more than six million' took part in the marches is correct[23] then nearly 300,000 soldiers must have been employed. But despite all attempts by the central army leadership to gain a tighter grasp on the Left's youth movement, rivalry among the ranks of the latter grew stronger. Liu's and Teng's group tried in October and November to utilise this situation in a last attempt to curb the Maoist counter-offensive.

Resistance in the Centre

At a Central Work Conference held in Peking from October 2 to 25 to discuss previous developments in the rectification campaign, new conflicts broke out between the factions. Although Liu was prepared to make a 'self-criticism',[24] he spoke merely of 'mistakes' (*Ts'o-wu*) which he wished to 'correct', at the same time hinting at his resolve to maintain his position in the Politburo. Mao's comments on the conference discussions, made on October 24, show that there had been sharp criticism of the Red Guards' activities to which he could only answer that one should not 'be afraid' of the 'nice, young people'.[25] Not later than the end of October, opposition was once again strengthened. Apparently disappointed by the radicalism of the young Maoists, T'ao Chu, Marshal Ho Lung and probably Che'en Yi as well, began to co-operate with Liu and Teng. A *Hung-ch'i* editorial at the beginning of November represented the attempt of this group to channel the movement back into a sound path. The 'Cultural Revolution', it said, had spread over the whole country. The 'bourgeois line' was bankrupt. Now the cadres should be given the opportunity to reform themselves. Thus it would be necessary to discriminate between 'those who had ordered the wrong line and those who had only implemented it', and to 'destroy the sickness but save the patient'.[26] At a party given to celebrate the hundredth anniversary of Sun Yat-sen, at which Liu and Teng still took part, Sung Ch'ingling, the widow of the founder of the Kuomintang and Vice-Chairman of the People's Republic, even praised the Chinese classics.[27] On the same day, November 12, the Red Guards were for the first time, in a joint decree issued by the General Office of the CC and the Secretariat of the State Council, called upon to interrupt their 'revolutionary exchange of experiences' for the time being and to return to their homes.[28] The CC and the State Council repeated this demand with greater emphasis on November 16,[29] but it went unheeded by the Maoist youth organisations, probably under the influence of the CRG. The central leadership organs of the Party and state thus felt obliged to demand once again, on December 1, the departure of the Red Guards from Peking. Now a time limit up to December 20 was fixed, and at the same time it was decreed that as from December 21 they should no longer be allowed to use public transport free of charge.[30]

But the Red Guards ignored this decree as well; even when, on December 21, the municipal authorities declared that Peking was a 'closed city',[31] many of them refused to depart. In their refusal they could feel assured of the support of the CRG, who since mid-November had launched an open attack on the leaders of the 'New

Right'. This after their attack on leading intellectual critics at the end of April, the conquest of the Peking Urban Committee and propaganda apparatus in May and June, the establishment of military control over the capital in July and the replacements made in the top levels of the Party in August.

The Victory of the Left in the Centre

As early as October 20 the Red Guards had for the first time demanded the resignation of Liu and Teng from all positions in the Party and the State,[32] a demand which was steadily repeated from the beginning of December. But above all the radicals, as whose spokesman Mme. Mao increasingly distinguished herself, were concerned with the expansion of the 'Cultural Revolution' from the schools to the factories, mines and rural people's communes. At the behest of the CRG leaders, the Red Guards should transfer their 'revolutionary exchange of experience' to the loci of production. There they were to establish new leadership organs modelled on the Paris Commune and thus prepare the Maoist attack on the regional and Party leadership' On November 17 a circle of CRG members produced a draft of a 'Twelve Point Directive for a Further Advance of the Left'.[33] However, considerable efforts were necessary before the CRG prevailed, especially as the leadership of the Federation of Trade Unions put up an energetic resistance to the plans of Ch'en and the Party leader's wife. Thereby the support of the central apparatus of the PLA proved useful to the Left. On November 28 Chiang Ch'ing had been appointed 'Adviser for Cultural Affairs in the PLA',[34] and during the following weeks the army repeatedly offered a forum for her demands to transfer the movement to the factories and the people's communes. Simultaneously, at the beginning of December, the Red Guards started committing acts of open attack against opposition leaders. During the night of December 3–4 a Red Guard patrol arrested P'eng Chen;[35] shortly afterwards Lo Jui-ch'ing, Lu Ting-i, P'eng Te-huai and a number of other leading members of the opposition were also arrested. On January 4 and 5, 1967 they were for the first time arraigned before a 'mass court' in Peking.[36] A *JMJP* editorial of December 26 finally proclaimed the triumph of the Left with an official call for the initiation of a 'high tide in the Cultural Revolution in industrial and mining enterprises'. Only one day later, December 27, the followers of the CRG, at Chiang Ch'ing's instigation, proclaimed that the leadership of the All-Chinese Federation of Trade Unions had been dismissed from office.[37] Its central organ, the *KJJP*, closed down on December 31.[38]

In the course of the Maoist actions around the turn of 1966–7, new organisations appeared on the scene: the 'Revolutionary Rebels' (*Ko-ming tsao-fan p'ai*). Mainly they comprised apprentices, contractual and seasonal workers, who in many factories were in conflict with skilled labour and willing to follow the egalitarian slogans of the extreme left.[39] With their help the Red Guards and the CRG succeeded not only in enlarging their influence in the Centre, but in bringing about the overthrow of the leaders of the 'New Right'. On New Year's Day 1967, Red Guard newspapers in Peking openly attacked Liu, Teng and Po I-po as 'enemies of the Party' (*Fan-tang fen-tzu*).[40] On January 4 T'ao Chu was dismissed from his position as head of the Propaganda Department of the CC.[41] During the following weeks Marshal Ho Lung, Li Ching-ch'üan, Yang Shang-k'un, Li Wei-han and at least eight, and probably eleven other full members and nine candidate members of the CC were also expelled.[42] The purge did not stop even at the central army leadership, The Commanders-in-Chief of the armoured troops and infantry, three Vice-Directors of the General Political Department and a number of other leading cadres were dismissed and some arrested. Most of them had been former subordinates of Ho Lung and P'eng Te-huai.[43]

The victory of the Left in the Centre appeared complete. But in order to translate it into a comprehensive 'seizure of power' (*To-ch'üan*) by the faction of Mao, Lin Piao and Chiang Ch'ing, the regional Party leaders who had supported Liu had first to be overthrown.

The 'Storm in January'

As early as the first half of December 1966, Ch'en Po-ta had called for an attack on the provincial secretaries of the CCP because they had mobilised, 'out of fear of loosing their positions and prestige', workers and peasants to 'fight the students'.[44] The Party leaders in the provinces had actually begun, with greater and greater frequency, to organise 'Red Workers Guards' modelled on those of the Changsha Municipal Committee of August[45] to protect themselves from the actions of the Maoist youth units. Furthermore, as the latter were often split, in many regions, and as it could not be determined which Red Guard faction enjoyed the trust of the Centre, even the majority of the regional commanders, during the last weeks of 1966, refused to support the Left in the same way as the central leadership of the PLA in Peking. On the contrary, in some military areas explicit orders were given not to intervene in the factional struggle but to remain neutral.[46] Faced with this situation the top-level leadership of the genuine Maoist movement, the CRG, decided, at the end of December, to send groups of militant Red Guards to the provinces in order to establish loyal 'Red Guard' and 'Revolutionary Rebel' units and with their help, to seize power.[47]

In this way the conflict between the Maoists and the opposition spread rapidly from the capital to large areas of China. The Left started the year 1967 with an unexpected success. On January 4 the followers of a 'General Headquarters of the Revolutionary Worker Rebels' (*Kung-jen ko-ming tsao-fan tsung-ssu-ling-pu*) in Shanghai occupied the *Wen-hui pao* building and took over the editorial offices of this newspaper.[48] The following day they deprived the Municipal Party Committee of its control over the *Chieh-fang jih-pao*, the biggest newspaper in the city as well, and finally the First Secretary of the Committee, Ch'en Pi-hsien, and the Mayor, Ts'ao Ti-ch'iu, were removed from office and arrested.[49] When the anti-Maoists consequently called upon the workers to strike, paralysing water and electricity supplies as well as public transport,[50] the 'General Headquarters' and thirty-one other Maoist units, in an 'urgent notification' (*Chin-chi t'ung-kao*), asked the Centre and the 'Rebels' of the whole country for help on January 9.[51] The Shanghai summons was answered with a letter of greetings on January 11 from the four central bodies which during the following months generally acted as the joint leadership of the Party and State – the CC (represented by the Standing Committee of the Politburo), the State Council, the Military Commission of the CC and the CRG – and the action of the Shanghai Maoists was defined as a model for the whole of China.[52]

Thus supported by the top-level leadership, in the next four weeks the Maoist mass organisations often proceeded violently against the local and regional Party leadership groups in many parts of China. The 'storm in January' (*I-yüeh feng-pao*) was to effect the definitive victory of the 'Cultural Revolution' in a great campaign. 'Seizure of power' through Leftist committees – in Shanghai and Shansi initially named *Communes* (*Kung-she*) and organised along the lines of the Paris Commune – took place not only in these two administrative areas but also in Kweichow, Heilungkiang, Shantung, Chekiang and Kiangsi as well as in several cities in Fukien, Hupei, Kirin, Hopei and Anhui.[53] However, the open attacks on the regional leadership groups, and to a greater degree the concomitant invasion of the factories and many villages by Red Guards and 'Revolutionary Rebels', provoked a great wave of popular resistance in many parts of the country in the second week of January. Thus the new offensive of the extreme Left collapsed.

References

1 Mao's Letter to Lin Piao, May 7, 1966, in *I-chiu-ch'i-ling*, *op. cit.*, Vol. II, Ch. VII, p. 46; this document, originally drawn up by the General Logistics Department of the PLA, became the basis of the educational programme of the Left under the name of 'May Seventh Instruction' (*Wu-ch'i chih-shih*). The re-education courses for the Party cadres and the cadres of mass organisations were therefore called 'May Seventh Schools' (*Wu-ch'i hsüeh-hsiao*) after the spring of 1968.

2 Cf. also *A Foreign Expert*, *loc. cit.*, pp. 4–7; John Israel, 'The Red Guard in Historical Perspective: Continuity and Change in the Chinese Youth Movement', in *CQ*, No. 30, April–June 1967, pp. 1–32; Giovanni Blumer, *Die chinesische Kulturrevolution, 1965–67*, Frankfurt/Main, 2nd. revised ed., 1969, pp. 187–216; von Groeling, *Widerstand*, *op. cit.*, pp. 140–4; Domes, *Kulturrevolution*, *op. cit.*, pp. 87–88; *KMJP*, May 20, 1966.

3 *NCNA*, Peking, April 9, 1966; *JMJP*, April 11, 1966.

4 Cf. the statement of a refugee, in Domes, *Kulturrevolution*, *op. cit.*, pp. 87–8; also *KMJP*, May 20, 1966.

5 *YCWP*, May 22, 1966; reproduced in *JMJP*, May 27, 1966.

6 *CNA*, No. 634, October 28, 1966.

7 *JMJP*, July 27, 1966.

8 *JMJP*, August 11 and 12, 1966.

9 *HC*, No. 11, 1966.

10 *NCNA*, Peking, August 18, 1966; *JMJP*, August 19, 1966.

11 An incomplete list compiled by the author comprises 1,417 Red Guard organisations for Peking, Shanghai, Kwangtung, Kwangsi, Hunan, and Hupei only.

12 List in *I-chiu-liu-chiu* . . . , *op. cit.*, Vol. I, Ch. III, pp. 21–9. It gives 264 Red Guard newspapers and journals of which copies have found their way to the West.

13 *Ch'en's Self-criticism*, English translation in *Facts and Features*, T'aipei, Vol. I, No. 11, March 20, 1968, p. 28.

14 *JMJP*, February 1, 1967.

15 Author's interview with a refugee from Hunan on December 14, 1966, in Hongkong, confirmed by a report of People's Radio Hunan on June 3, 1968. The Party Secretary of Changsha, Li Jui-shan, who had organised the Red Worker Guards was recalled from his position because of this, but he was appointed Chairman of the Revolutionary Committee of the province of Shensi on May 1, 1968.

16 *JMJP*, January 30, 1967.

17 *NCNA*, Hangchou, and *JMJP*, October 31, 1966.

18 *CFCP*, August 23, 1966; *JMJP*, August 23, 26, 28, 29, 1966.

19 *NCNA*, Peking, and *JMJP*, September 1, 1966.

20 'Decisions of the CC of the CCP and of the State Council Regarding Protection of Party and State Secrets in the Great Proletarian Cultural Revolution, September 8, 1966', in *URI, Documents*, *op. cit.*, pp. 71–2.

21 *Ibid.*, pp. 77–8.

22 Anna Louise Strong, in *Der Spiegel*, Hamburg, No. 21, May 15, 1967, p. 102.

23 *CFCP*, January 14, 1967.

24 *URI, Collected Works. . .* , 1958–67, *op. cit.*, pp. 357–64.

25 Chinese text in *I-chiu-liu-chiu. . .* , *op. cit.*, Vol. I, Ch. VII, pp. 72–4.

26 *HC*, No. 14, 1966.

27 *JMJP*, November 13, 1966.

28 *URI, Documents, op. cit.*, pp. 95–9.

29 *Ibid.*, pp. 107–9.

30 *Ibid.*, pp. 125–9.

31 Report of a correspondent based on Big Character Posters in Peking, in *Neue Zürcher Zeitung*, (hereafter cited as *NZZ*), December 23, 1966.

32 *NZZ*, based on *Tanyug* and *AFP*, Peking, October 22, 1966.

33 *Hung-wei-ping-pao* (*Red Guard News*), Ch'iengte, December 23, 1966; also in *URI Documents, op. cit.*, pp. 113–19.

34 *CFCP*, and *JMJP*, November 29, 1966.

35 *NZZ*, December 9, 1966, based on *Tanyug*, Peking, December 7, 1966.

36 *Chan-pao* (Combat Journal), Peking, January 18, 1967.

37 Red Guard leaflet, Peking, December 27, 1966, edited by the National Corps of Red Worker Rebels (*Ch'üan-kuo hung-se lao-tung-che tsao-fan tsung-t'uan*, abbr. *Ch'üan-hung-tsung*), re-edited in Canton, January 4, 1967.

38 *KJJP*, December 31, 1966.

39 Cf. Philip Bridgham, 'Mao's Cultural Revolution in 1967: The Struggle to Seize Power', in *CQ*, No. 34, April–June 1968, pp. 6–37; here p. 9.

40 *Chingkangshan*, Peking, January 1, 1967.

41 *Sheng-chih hung-ch'i* (*Red Flag of the Provincial Organs*), Canton, No. 1, January 1968.

42 A first list of overthrown Party leaders was given by a cartoon in *Hung-wei-ping* (*Red Guards*), Peking, February 22, 1967; it was reproduced in *CFCP*, March 8, 1967 and in *CFJP*, March 10, 1967; cf. Kuo Heng-yü, *Mao's Kulturrevolution – Analyse einer Karikatur*, Pfullingen, 1968, *passim*.

43 Cf. Domes, *Kulturrevolution, op. cit.*, pp. 92–3.

44 *Tung-feng chan-pao* (Combat Journal 'East Wind'), Peking, December 11, 1966; cf. Bridgham, *loc. cit.*, p. 7.

45 See above, pp. 168–9.

46 *Tung-fang-hung* (*The East Is Red*), Peking, January 28, 1967. The term 're-gional commanders' refers to the commandants of the Military Areas as well as to the Military Districts which are identical with the provinces.

47 Ch'en Po-ta and K'ang Sheng for instance sent a 'Revolutionary Rebel Regiment' to Canton on January 4, 1967. Officially they were to arrest Wang Jen-chung (who was in Wuhan); in reality, however, they were to prepare the 'power seizure' in the South Chinese metropolis; cf. *Ko-ming kung-jen pao* (*Revolutionary Workers' News*), Peking, January 12, 1967.

48 *WHP*, January 4, 1967.

49 *Chieh-fang jih-pao*, Shanghai, January 5, 1967.

50 For reports on strikes cf. *KMJP*, January 25, 1967; cf. Bridgham, *loc. cit.*, p. 8; von Groeling, *Widerstand, op. cit.*, p. 153.

51 *NCNA*, Peking, January 11, 1967.

52 *URI, Documents, op. cit.*, pp. 155–8.

53 For more detailed data see Domes, *Kulturrevolution, op. cit.*, pp. 101–8.

XII.   Resistance and Military Intervention

With regard to the events in China of January 1967, contradictory reports were at first published. In the Western and East European press there was news of armed confrontations between followers and opponents of Mao Tse-tung, of strikes, severe disorder in the national economy and of widespread active resistance by the people. At times the impression was even provoked that China was on the brink of a huge civil war. On the other hand some Western observers, who up to then had cultivated the myth of the 'monolithic' nature and stability of the rule of the Party, tried to propagate the idea that the disturbances in China were nothing but a calculated and planned *mise en scène*.

Certainly, some press reports concerning the events caused by the 'storm in January' were sensationally exaggerated, but soon an abundance of reports from official publications media in the PR of China confirmed the unrest and the extensive resistance to such a degree that there could not be any doubt about the proposition that China had encountered its most severe crisis since 1949.

The control structures of the Party and State machine collapsed, and the Maoist drive to seize power failed because of the resistance of the people. Mao and his colleagues were eventually obliged to call on the army for help, this being the only pillar of the governmental structure that was relatively intact. The army, which up to then had been regarded as the gun of the Party, was to become the gun of a faction, a demand which could not but expose the armed forces to considerable stresses and strains. Thus the response of the PLA to the appeal for help from the Maoist Centre remained ambiguous. But no matter what the attitude of the regional commanders towards the collapsing Leftist offensive might be, they overthrew the old Party committees and provincial governments in nearly every part of the country, and took control over the regional and local organs of the Party, the state administration and the economic machine. A second offensive by the genuine Maoist forces after May 1967 was therefore directed particularly against the army. Under the influence of this action the crisis was transferred to the PLA itself. When the loyalty of the armed forces thereby became questionable the consensus between the two subsystems of Mao's and Lin Piao's factions, between the CRG-led mass organisations and the military, broke down.

Strikes and Unrest, January 1967

The Party functionaries who had been attacked by the Maoist organisations responded to the Left's challenge by mobilising the workers in Shanghai, Tientsin, Wuhan and a number of other cities. While hitherto only Red Guards and 'Revolutionary Rebels' had travelled through the country, from January 1967 onwards, the means of transportation were crowded with large groups of industrial workers supplied with tickets and travel expenses by local cadres in order to demonstrate in Peking and other administrative centres for a sustained improvement in living conditions.[1] This led to the appearance of severe disturbances in the economic structure, with the result that the leading bodies in the Party and the state administration felt forced to condemn the actions of the opposition cadres as 'economism' (Ching-chi chu-i).[2] 'A small handful of those in authority in the Party who take the capitalist road' had, so it was said, 'instigated the masses to put forth demands for promotion and higher wages' and other 'unreasonable demands'. With particular anger the Centre turned against any attempt to establish 'independent workers' organisations' – an indication that in some places free trade unions were being spontaneously created.[3]

But such appeals had only limited success. The urban workers continued their resistance to the actions of the Maoist organisations unflinchingly, and soon this resistance could no longer be controlled even by the opposition cadres. If we refer simply to reports from the official publications media of the PR of China, then strikes, the closing down of factories and attacks on transport facilities occurred in twenty-six out of the twenty-nine administrative areas of the country.[4] The railway lines between Shanghai, Nanking and Peking, as well as those between Canton and Wuhan, were temporarily interrupted. Ships in the harbours waited for a long time to unload their cargoes or load up with new cargo.[5] From mid-January on, the numbers of bloody clashes between Maoist organisations and 'Red Worker Guards' also increased in several cities, with the Left generally getting the worst of it. 'Urgent appeals' for help from their units to the Centre became more and more frequent.[6]

Acts of resistance did not, however, remain confined to the urban population. In at least twenty-one of the twenty-nine administrative areas the peasants stormed rural grain godowns and banks, drove our members of the state's purchase organisation, established free markets without authority and turned violently against the

Red Guards.[7] In some places they even began to liquidate the people's communes and production brigades in order to distribute agricultural land among themselves and return to individual production with the result that the Party Centre, the State Council and the Military Commission of the CC felt obliged explicitly to prohibit 'infringements against collective property' in a joint circular of March 16, 1967, which was published throughout the whole country.[8]

The resistance of the people, which began locally, had been felt as early as autumn 1966 and was intensified in January 1967 until it became a tide which swept over many parts of the country. Within a few weeks it halted the Maoist faction's offensive. Although, because of its largely spontaneous nature and because of the lack of a central organisation, it did not lead to the breakdown of the governmental system, it nevertheless forced the leaders of the Left to make initial corrections to the previous course of the 'Cultural Revolution'. The Party leader had to call on the military for help in order to restore law and order and to save Communist rule in China which appeared to be in immediate jeopardy.

The Call for the Gun and the Response of the PLA

As early as the first half of January 1967 there were growing indications that the military, whose leadership groups had supported the Maoist position in the spring and summer of 1966, while later taking a more neutral stance, was again intervening more actively in politics. However, the trend of this new activity at first remained unclear. While Lin Piao and the central military machine continued to support the Maoist organisations' drive to seize power, some regional and local commanders used their troops in the interests of 'revolutionary law and order' (*Ko-ming chih-hsü*) against both anti-Maoist and Maoist organisations. Others, however, clung to the 'non-intervention' orders issued in November and December 1966. But the central leadership bodies called upon the PLA to assume control in the non-military sphere. On January 11, 1967, an order of the day from the Party Centre, the State Council and the Military Commission of the CC laid down that military units had to protect banks in the whole country.[9] On the same day the whole of the broadcasting service was put under military control by a circular of the Military Commission.[10] Three days later another directive from the Party Centre prohibited action by mass organisations which 'turned the spearhead of the struggle against the armed forces', and it further decreed that the Party archives should be transferred to the care of the army.[11] Chou En-lai had already pointed out the growing importance of the PLA in a speech before Red Guards in Peking on January 10 when he declared that the Military Commission of the CC constituted the 'Supreme Headquarters of the Great Proletarian Cultural Revolution' and that the CRG was its 'general staff', whereas the State Council, led by himself, was 'nothing but an executive organ'.[12] Only one week later Mao himself demanded that the PLA should abandon its previous reserve. During the night of January 17–18 he gave the following written directive to Lin Piao:

Comrade Lin Piao!
It is necessary that the PLA intervene in order to support the broad masses of the Left! Mao Tse-tung.

P.S.: From now on, whenever the genuine revolutionary faction calls on the troops to assist and save it, then they must all act accordingly. The so-called 'non-intervention' is wrong. If it has been ordered previously then new orders must be issued. The former orders are null and void. I ask for implementation.[13]

At a plenary session of the Military Commission of the CC which was unexpectedly convened on January 20 and 21, the Party leader repeated this call with the same urgency.[14] Mao's appeals brought about on January 23 the decree, in the form of a joint resolution of the Party Centre, the Military Commission, the State Council and the CRG, which was issued to all Party organs and to the army, and by which the PLA units were ordered to support the 'Revolutionary Rebels' everywhere, to break active resistance, by force if necessary, to secure the functioning of industrial production, and means of transportation, and the first sowing in the countryside.[15] On January 25, in even more urgent terms the central organ of the PLA repeated the order to the military to support the Left absolutely:

It is impossible . . . for the PLA to hold back under the conditions which now prevail. . . . The political power of the proletariat, conquered by the gun of the people's army, must also be defended by the gun of the people's army.[16]

The new directives of the central leadership put the regional commanders in a dilemma. Even if they had remained neutral hitherto, they had to show their colours now. If they clung to their neutrality then it meant open disobedience to Peking thenceforward. But if they were willing to follow their orders then the officers and political commissars had first to be sure of the co-operation of the rank-and-file. The widespread uncertainty concerning the outcome of the conflict within the Party and which of the numerous rival factions and groups of 'Revolutionary Rebels' should be recognised as the 'genuine Left' aggravated their difficulties.

The Centre tried to overcome the reluctance of the generals, which became evident during the first days after the promulgation of the resolution of January 25, by extending further the authority of the military. On January 26 civil aviation was put under the control of the PLA.[17] An order of the day from the Military Commission on January 28 forbade all mass organisations to commit any 'infringements against the military leadership organs' and thus offered the regional commanders the opportunity of turning, if necessary, even against Maoist organisations.[18] Also on that day the Centre gave the order to 'postpone temporarily the movement of the Great Proletarian Cultural Revolution' in the military areas of Tsinan, Nanking, Fuchou, Canton, Wuhan and Sinkiang so that these regions, which comprised fifteen of the twenty-nine administrative areas, could 'at first be stabilised'.[19] At the same time military units in Peking began to occupy factories and stores, and on February 11 the police and security machines in the capital were put under military control.[20] On February 13 and 14 the ministries and Party offices of the central organs were placed under the protection of the army.[21]

The growth in power of the armed forces was followed by the leadership's attempts to restrain the Maoist groups. On February 22 the theoretical organ of the CC, *Hung-ch'i*, published an editorial which must be interpreted as the first sign of a retreat in the 'Cultural Revolution'. Under the headline 'Cadres Must be Treated Correctly', the journal stated that 'most cadres at all levels in the Party, government, army, industry, agriculture, commerce and education' stood 'generally behind the Party'. The number of anti-Party elements should by no means be 'exaggerated' and 'the attack' should not be 'extended in the wrong way'. For the first time the leadership criticised the Red Guards who 'naturally' also had 'their faults and deficiencies': 'therefore they often lose their sense of direction in the turns of the revolution. Thus deviations appear among the young such as factionalism, ultra-democratism, individualism and anarchism. In short all forms of bourgeois ideology.'[22]

Simultaneously a significant change took place in the structure of the organisational models recommended by Peking for the new 'provisional power organs' (*Lin-shih ch'üan-li chi-kou*) which were to fulfil the functions of the old provincial Party committees and provincial governments in all those places where the Left had seized power. As late as January 22–3, at a symposium of the CRG in Peking, Ch'en Po-ta had recommended the establishment of Soviets following the example of the Paris Commune of 1871.[23] This proposal was followed up by the 'Revolutionary Rebels' in Shanghai at the beginning of February when they proclaimed the 'Shanghai Commune' (*Shang-hai kung-she*) under the guidance of an executive committee

G

elected by the Maoist mass organisations.[24] A 'General Command of the Revolutionary Rebels', which had been organised in a similar way, had already taken over the leadership in Shansi during the second half of January.[25]

However, on January 31 an organisational model which differed considerably from the 'Commune' was created in the north-eastern Chinese province of Heilungkiang with the establishment of the first 'Revolutionary Committee' (Ko-ming wei-yüan-hui; RC).[26] There is no information available about any formal election, and in the 'Standing Committee' of the RC only one representative of the Maoist mass organisations was faced with two PLA representatives and one Party cadre. Within a few weeks the RC model had prevailed over that of the 'Commune', and on February 24 the 'Shanghai Commune' itself was transformed into an RC.[27] On March 18 Shansi also established an RC.[28] On March 10 the Centre had already declared, in a Hung-ch'i editorial, that the RC was the compulsory model for the new leadership organs in the provinces. The followers of the Left were called upon to establish 'provisional power organs' everywhere in China in the form of RCs based on 'revolutionary trinities' (Ko-ming san-chieh-ho) of 'revolutionary cadres' – i.e. Maoist Party functionaries – representatives of the respective PLA garrisons and delegates from the 'revolutionary mass organisations'. The PLA was to play a leading role thereby, for the editorial goes on to say:

> From the top to the bottom, all those institutions which require the seizure of power need the participation of representatives of the PLA and the people's militia in the provisional power organs of the revolutionary trinity. Factories, villages, finance and commerce, education – including universities, secondary and primary schools – Party and administrative organs, and mass organisations must proceed accordingly. . . . If there are not enough PLA repesentatives then their positions may remain vacant for the time being.[29]

But despite this barely veiled proclamation of military rule at local and regional levels, the reaction of the armed forces to the appeal for support for the Left remained fragmented. Although the regional commanders of some provinces – Heilungkiang, Shansi, Shantung and Kweichow – assisted the Maoist Left to a large degree, the vice-commander of the Tsinghai military district, General Chao Yung-fu, for example, used his troops against Maoist units in February.[30] The Commander-in-chief of the Canton military area, General Huang Yung-sheng, created his own 'Left' with the help of pupils and students from the families of senior officers and the workers' militia in order to oppose the organisation which was guided by the CRG.[31]

An investigation into the attitudinal response of the PLA to the orders of Mao and the central leading bodies from January 17/18 to 23, 1967 leads to the following conclusions for the period from the end of January to July of that year:[32]

In six of the twenty-nine administrative areas the regional commanders supported the Maoist drive to seize power up to the establishment of an RC: Heilungkiang, Shantung, Shansi, Kweichow, Shanghai and Peking.

In four administrative areas they were neutral, tending to assist the Maoist units: Hopei, Anhui, Kiangsi and Fukien.

In nine administrative areas they were strictly neutral: Kiangsu, Kwangsi, Inner Mongolia, Chekiang, Yünnan, Ninghsia, Tientsin, Sinkiang and Tibet.

In another ten administrative areas they refused to support the Maoist units at all or even turned against them openly: Kirin, Liaoning, Honan, Shensi, Tsinghai, Hupei, Hunan, Kwangtung, Szechwan and Kansu.

But without exception the generals removed the previous leadership groups of the Party and the state apparatus. In twenty-three administrative areas where the creation of RCs did not at first succeed, 'Military Control Commission' (Chün-shih kuan-chih wei-yüan-hui), consisting exclusively of army representatives, headed the Party and state apparatus, whereas 'Provisional Production Headquarters' Lin-shih sheng-ch'an chih-hui-pu), placed under the respective regional commands, took over the management of the economic machine. The Party leader's call for the gun had not produced the expected results. Instead of lending its full support to the Maoist movement in the whole country, in most provinces the army used the chaos which originated in the 'storm in January' to seize power itself.

This was contrary to the concept of the genuine Maoist forces, the CRG under Ch'en Po-ta, Chiang Ch'ing and their colleagues. At the end of March they recognised that a new offensive by the Left would have to be launched if the programme of the 'cultural revolutionary' movement were to be carried through. This new offensive could not but be directed against the new regional leaders, the generals of the PLA. Thus the conflict within the camp of the Left had become unavoidable.

The Second Offensive of the Left

The CRG was alarmed by the measures of several regional commanders against its mass organisations, as well as by the attempts of some Party leaders in the Centre to rehabilitate a number of leading cadres who had already been purged. In these attempts T'an Chen-lin was particularly prominent; he had repeatedly demanded in February and March that an end be made to attacks on Liu Shao-ch'i by Red Guard units.[33] Once more the CRG successfully gained the support of Lin Piao and the central army leadership, and with their help it arrived at a narrow majority of six votes to five in the Standing Committee of the Politburo in the second half of March to initiate a campaign against Liu.[34] It started on March 30 with the publication of an article by Ch'i Pen-yü in the journal *Hung-ch'i* which sharply criticised Liu's behaviour since 1945.[35] During the following weeks the other central publication media also took part in the campaign. Although Liu was still not named in these attacks – as he was in the Big Character Posters and Red Guard Leaflets – there remained no doubt who was being referred to as the 'top person in authority who took the capitalist road' and as 'China's Khruschev'.[36] At the beginning of April Liu's wife, Wang Kuang-mei, was arrested by Red Guards and exposed to physical ill-treatment and humiliation in Peking.[37] Liu's efforts to justify himself were rejected by the leaders of the Left.

Energetic attempts by the Centre to foster a more sympathetic attitude on the part of the regional commanders towards the Maoist organisations coincided with the initiation of the new campaign against Liu. On April 6 the Military Commission of the CC issued an order prohibiting the labelling of mass organisations 'arbitrarily' as 'counter-revolutionary', making mass arrests and using firearms in clashes with Red Guard units[38] – or those units controlled by 'reactionary elements'. At an enlarged session of the Military Commission on April 12 Chiang Ch'ing admonished the generals on the grounds that their previous revolutionary merit would not count if they did not earn 'new merits for the people's sake'. Mme. Mao made particularly sharp attacks on the commander-in-chief of the Canton military area. General Huang Yung-sheng, who 'unreasonably and arbitrarily labelled mass organisations counter-revolutionary'.[39]

Shortly afterwards the Centre took the first effective purge measures against regional commanders. The vice-commander of Tsinghai, Chao Yung-fu, whose arrest had been ordered on April 26, was brought to Peking for interrogation.[40] Oh May 7 the Party Centre decreed the dismissal of the commander-in-chief of the Cheng-tu military area and appointed one of the vice-commanders of the Canton military area, General Liang Hsing-ch'u, as the new regional commander in Szechwan. Together with the new First Political Commissar, General Chang Kuo-hua – hitherto commander-in-chief in Tibet – they were to create the preconditions for a seizure of power by the Left in the large south-western Chinese province.[41]

Encouraged by decisions such as these made by the leading bodies of the Centre, from the end of April the Maoist organisations started a new wave of attacks against Party cadres and military officers. At

the same time, however, confrontations between them and the anti-–
Maoist organisations also escalated in a number of provinces, as well
as rivalries between the different factions and groups of the Left.
Violent clashes became more and more frequent. On May 25 the
chairman of the Peking RC, the Minister of Security, General Hsieh
Fu-chih, reported that during the first ten days of May not less than
130 'bloody incidents' had occurred in the capital in which 63,000
people had taken part.[42]

Similar clashes were reported from at least ten other provinces
by the middle of June. They were accompanied by increasingly
vitriolic attacks in Red Guard publications against leading military
officers, particularly Huang Yung-sheng, who, since the beginning of
June, had become the object of a systematic propaganda campaign by
the CRG-led Leftist organisations in Canton.[43]

The large number of local conflicts between the organisations of
the Left and the armed forces approached its climax in July 1967
which became the turning-point in the crisis of the 'Cultural Revolution' when the commander-in-chief of the Wuhan military area,
General Ch'en Tsai-tao, openly mutinied.

The Wuhan Incident[44]

Since the beginning of July conflicts had developed in the central
Chinese industrial metropolis of Wuhan between a mass organisation supported by the military area command and labelled 'conservative' (Pao-shou), which called itself the 'One Million Heroes'
(Pai-wan hsiung-shih), and a number of Maoist groups with close connections with the CRG. On July 12 the Maoists attacked the military
area command building and arrested several senior officers. There-
upon the 'One Million Heroes', partly with the support of the garrison,
took violent steps against the Maoists during the following days.
On July 18 the situation had become so tense that the Centre felt
obliged to send a mediation team to Wuhan comprising Chou En-lai,
Hsieh Fu-chih, the acting Chief of the General Staff, Yang Ch'eng-wu,
the acting head of the Propaganda Department of the CC, Wang Li –
a close follower of Chiang Ch'ing – and the First Political Commissar
of the Air Force, General Yü Li-chin. While Chou tried to avoid a
clear decision and left Wuhan with Yang on the evening of July 19,
at the same time Hsieh and Wang declared at a mass rally of Maoist
organisations that the latter were the 'true Left' and that the 'One
Million Heroes' were 'counter-revolutionary'. But General Ch'en,
who had strongly identified himself with this organisation, did not give
in. During the night of July 19–20 he had Hsieh and Wang arrested by
his troops, and on the morning of July 20 they were brought before a

'kangaroo court' of the 'One Million Heroes'. For the first time a military area commander had openly turned against the Centre, which reacted rapidly. On July 21 Lin Piao declared in a telegram that General Ch'en was dismissed. Parachutists were employed against Wuhan. Five gunboats of the Yangtze Fleet sailed to the city and threatened to shell it. With their help and the support of those units in Wuhan which had remained loyal to the Centre, control over the city was re-established on July 26. Ch'en was arrested and taken to Peking. He was replaced in Wuhan by the former Second Political Commissar of the Shenyang military region, General Tseng Ssu-yü.[45]

Armed Clashes

The Wuhan incident, to which the Chinese gave the same term, *Shih-pien*, which is used to describe the *coup d'etat* against Chiang Kai-shek in Sian in December 1936,[46] evoked strong doubts about the loyalty of the military. The forces of the extreme Left around the CRG were confirmed in their determination to effect an extensive purge of the leading personnel in the PLA, which they had been calling for emphatically since the beginning of July; and the central army leadership under Lin Piao was apparently afraid of further *pronunciamentos* from the regional military commanders'[47] However, not only had the reliability of the PLA been put in doubt, but at the same time armed clashes between Maoist and anti-Maoist groups, as well as between mass organisations and military units, in large parts of the country reached a new stage of escalation with the Wuhan incident. In Canton a number of heavy clashes claimed more than 200 deaths in July and August,[48] and the bloody incidents rapidly spread over large parts of Kwangtung. In Hunan sixty-two Red Guards had been killed in street battles in the provincial capital, Changsha, on July 9,[49] and since then there had been fights in which both sides had used firearms and light machine-guns. Further reports of heavy armed clashes came in from the provinces of Hupei, Kiangsi, Chekiang, Kweichow, Yünnan, Kiangsu, Szechwan, Tsinghai, Kansu, Shantung and Inner Mongolia.[50]

Thus Mao and the other leaders of his faction were confronted with a threefold danger at the turn of July and August 1967: the reinforced attacks on the regional commanders by the extreme Left, the doubtful reliability of the PLA and the fights between mass organisations which, in many provinces, verged on civil war.

References

1 *JMJP*, January 16, 1967; also 'Circular of the CC of the CCP and the State Council Concerning the Prohibition against Corrupting the Masses, January 11, 1967', in *URI, Documents, op. cit.*, pp. 169–70.

2 *WHP*, January 10, 1967; also 'Circular of the CC of the CCP Concerning Opposition against Economism, January 11, 1967', in *URI, Documents, op. cit.*, pp. 163–7.

3 *Kuang-t'ieh tsung-ssu (Headquarters of the Canton Railways)*, Canton, February 1968, English translation in *SCMP*, No. 4729, March 1, 1968.

4 Tientsin had been separated from the province of Hopei in February 1967 and been made a Special Municipality. Therefore it is listed here as an independent administrative unit.

5 Reports on these activities are given in *WHP* and *Chieh-fang jih-pao*, Shanghai, January 9, 1967; *WHP*, January 10 and 12, 1967; *JMJP*, January 9, 12, 20, 1967; *NCNA*, Peking, January 14, 1967; People's Radio Canton City, January 16, 1967; cf. also *CNA*, No. 643, 644, 651, January 13 and 20, March 10, 1967; *CB*, No. 852, May 6, 1968, pp. 39–42; von Groeling (Widerstand, *op. cit.*, pp. 160–1) compiled 139 reports of Chinese Communist media on strikes and disruptions of the communication lines.

6 Cf. von Groeling, *ibid.*, pp. 161–7.

7 Among others, broadcasts from People's Radio Wuhan, January 23, 1967; People's Radio Ch'engchou, January 23, 1967; People's Radio Fuchou, January 24 and February 8, 1967; People's Radio Nanchang, January 20, 22, 23, 25, 1967; also *NCNA*, Taiyüan, January 25, 1967; *Heilungkiang jih-pao*, Harbin, January 23, 1967; *Chieh-fang jih-pao*, Shanghai, January 23, 1967; People's Radio Anhui, February 14, 1967; *JMJP*, January 24, 25, 30, 1967. Cf. also *CNA*, No. 647, 648, 649, February 10, 17, 24, 1967; *CS*, Vol. V, No. 2, January 31, 1967; von Groeling (*ibid.*, pp. 168–73) gives eighty-six pieces of evidence from the official media for the unrest among the peasants.

8 Cf. *URI, Documents, op. cit.*, pp. 365–8.

9 Document *Chung-fa* (67), No. 14, in *URI, Documents, op. cit.*, pp. 159–61.

10 *Ibid.*, pp. 171–2.

11 *Ibid.*, pp. 179–82.

12 Cited from 'Big Character Posters in Peking', in *Asahi Shimbun*, Tokyo, January 13, 1967.

13 *Tung-fang-hung (The East is Red)*, Peking, January 28, 1967.

14 *Asahi Shimbun*, February 4, 1967.

15 'Decision of the CC of the CCP, the State Council, the Military Commission of the CC, and the Group Cultural Revolution Concerning the Resolute Support of the Revolutionary Masses of the Left by the PLA, January 23, 1967', in *URI, Documents, op. cit.*, pp. 193–7.

16 *CFCP*, January 25, 1967.

17 *URI, Documents, op. cit.*, pp. 207–8.

18 *Directive of the Central Military Commission, January 28, 1967, ibid.*, pp. 209–13.

19 *Ibid.*, pp. 215–16.

20 *NCNA*, Peking, December 12, 1967.

21 Cf. Domes, *Kulturrevolution*, *op. cit.*, pp. 97–8; also von Groeling, *Widerstand*, *op. cit.*, p. 181.

22 *HC*, No. 4, 1967.

23 *Hsin Pei-ta* (*New Pei-ta*), Peking, January 28, 1967.

24 *WHP*, February 5, 1967; cf. *CNA*, No. 653, March 31, 1967, No. 658, May 5, 1967, No. 659. May 12, 1967.

25 Central People's Radio, Peking, January 24, 1967.

26 Central People's Radio Peking, February 2, 1967; cf. Jürgen Domes, 'The Role of the Military in the Formation of Revolutionary Committees 1967–1968', in *CQ*, No. 44, October–December 1970, (hereafter cited as Domes, *CQ*), pp. 112–13, p. 116.

27 *JMJP*, February 28, 1967.

28 *JMJP*, March 23, 1967.

29 *HC*, No. 5, 1967.

30 *URI*, *Documents*, *op. cit.*, pp. 383–7.

31 Cf. Domes, Generals, *loc. cit.*, pp. 21–9.

32 Cf. the following studies by the author: Domes, *Kulturrevolution*, *op. cit.*, pp. 97–113; Domes, *CQ*, *loc. cit.*, pp. 120–1; Domes, 'The Cultural Revolution and the Army', in *AS*, Vol. VIII, No. 5, May 1968, p. 356 (hereafter cited as Domes, *AS*).

33 Cf. Bridgham, *loc. cit.*, p. 16.

34 Cf. Heinzig, *Mao contra Liu*, *op. cit.*, p. 12; also von Groeling, *Widerstand*, *op. cit.*, p. 309.

35 *HC*, No. 6, 1967.

36 Among others *CFCP*, April 3 and 8, 1967 and August 1, 1967; *JMJP*, April 8 and 12, 1967, and June 16, 1967; cf. von Groeling, *ibid.*, pp. 310–11.

37 'Triple Interrogation of the great pickpocket Wang Kuang-mei', in *Ching-kangshan*, Peking, n.d., in *I-chiu-liu-pa. . .*, *op. cit.*, pp. 752–69.

38 'Directive of the Central Military Commission, April 6, 1967', in *URI*, *Documents*, *op. cit.*, pp. 407–11.

39 *Chiang Ch'ing*, *op. cit.*, p. 6.

40 *URI*, *Documents*, *op. cit.*, pp. 383–7; *Asahi Shimbun* and *Yomouri*, Tokyo, April 27, 1967.

41 *URI*, *Documents*, *op. cit.*, pp. 431–8.

42 Gordon A. Bennet, 'Hsieh Fu-chih, China's Trouble-Shooter', *in FEER*, Vol. IX, No. 5, 1968, p. 184.

43 Cf. Jürgen Domes, 'Generals and Red Guards', Part Two, in *Asia Quarterly*, No. 2, 1971, pp. 125–6.

44 Cf. also *Wuhan kang-erh-ssu* (*Second Steel Headquarters of Wuhan*), Wuhan, No. 38, August 22, 1967; English translation in *SCMP*, No. 3999, August 11, 1967; *URS*, Vol. 48f., No. 10, pp. 139–49; No. 23, pp. 320–34; *CQ*, No. 32, October–December 1967, pp. 185–90, Domes, *CQ*, *loc. cit.*, pp. 127–8; Domes, *Generals II*, *loc. cit.*, pp. 127–8; von Groeling, *Widerstand*, *op. cit.*, pp. 191–4.

45 Despite his open rebellion, Ch'en Tsai-tao remained in the centre of criticism of the Centre only for a short time. On August 1, 1972, he and his former First Political Commissar, General Chung Kan-hua, appeared in public at an Army Day reception in Peking (*NCNA*, Peking, August 1, 1972).

46 Cf. Domes, *Revolution, op. cit.*, pp. 656–74.
47 Lin Piao, 'What We Are Afraid of is Comrades in the Military Regions Committing Mistakes', Speech before the Military Commission of the CC, August 9, 1967, in *Chu-ying tung-fang-hung* (Pearl River Studio *The East Is Red*), Canton, September 13, 1967.
48 Cf. Domes, *Generals II, loc. cit.*, pp. 126–7.
49 *Ming-pao*, Hong Kong, June 12, 1967.
50 Cf. the collection in *CNA*, No. 676, September 8, 1967.

XIII.   The Change of Course

In early August 1967 the leadership of the CCP faced two alternatives: either to comply with the appeals of the Leftists and try to carry through the 'cultural revolutionary' programme even if it meant going against the regional commanders, or to compromise with the generals in order to consolidate the internal political situation in China and to avert the threat of local civil wars. If Mao, Lin Piao and Chou En-lai followed the proposals of the leading members of the CRG, then they would also have to reckon with events in other parts of the country similar to the Wuhan incident, and it was by no means sure that they would be successful in every case. However, if they sided with the army in the conflict now gathering force between the two sub-systems of the Maoist camp of 1965–6, this would mean breaking with the CRG-led mass organisations of the Left. The CRG misjudged its position in the first weeks after the Wuhan incident and started simultaneous attacks on the army and on those remnants of the central administrative machine which were still intact. Under the influence of these actions a coalition between the regional commanders, the central military machine under Lin Piao, and Chou En-lai came into being. It gained even greater importance when the growing military pressure of the Soviet Union became evident on the northern and western frontiers of the PR of China.[1] Not only the internal but also the external situation of China made the alliance with the army seem more advisable to Mao than continued co-operation with the 'Maoists of the first hour': the Red Guards and the 'Revolutionary Rebels'. Changing course dramatically the CCP leadership thus turned against the Left and paved the way for the army, particularly the regional commanders, to carry through their views about the future of the country which were orientated towards law and order rather than towards revolutionary dynamics.

The Failure of the Leftist Attack

Shortly after the Wuhan incident the Left intensified its offensive in a number of provinces and emphatically called on the leading bodies to allow the arming of the 'Revolutionary Rebels' and their organisations. On July 22, 1967, at a speech before Red Guards from Honan,

Chiang Ch'ing called upon the Maoist groups to take up arms, for the Party leader himself had given the order: 'Arm the Left! Hand over weapons to the Left!'[2] During the following days Chiang Ch'ing and her closest followers in the CRG – Wang Li, Lin Chieh, Ch'i Pen-yü and Kuan Feng – spread the slogan 'Seize the small handful of those in authority in the army who take the capitalist road!' This became the essential argument of an article by Lin Chieh published in *JMJP* and *Hung-ch'i* on July 31 and August 1 – 'The Working Class Must Firmly Grasp the Gun' – in which Lin bluntly called for a comprehensive purge of the armed forces.[3] The followers of the Left in the whole country had clearly understood this call, for a few days later Red Guard pamphlets in Canton started new attacks on Huang Yung-sheng and stated that Lin Chieh's article had 'sounded the trumpet for a general attack' on the Canton commander.[4]

At the same time the head of the Political Department and the chairman of the 'Cultural Revolution Group' of the PLA, Lin Piao's longstanding follower, Hsiao Hua, was dismissed because the CRG accused him of having tolerated for too long the power of the 'conservatives' in the Wuhan military region.[5] Wang Li continued the campaign with a speech before Red Guard delegates in Peking on August 7. He made concrete the hitherto generally formulated call for the purge of the PLA, and demanded that the PLA commanders-in-chief of the military areas of Canton, Nanking, Fuchou, Tsinan and Sinkiang be dismissed.[6] Wang's call, as it became known in March 1968, found support from the acting Chief of the General Staff, Yang Ch'eng-wu.[7]

While the leaders of the Left thus tried to force the Centre to break with some of the most influential regional commanders, in mid-August the CRG-led Red Guard units began to storm and occupy ministries in Peking. On the evening of August 20 they seized the secret archives of the Ministry for Chemical Industries.[8] A few days earlier they had brought the Ministry of Foreign Affairs building under their control. They arbitrarily declared that Ch'en Yi was 'dismissed' and 'appointed' the former chargé d'affaires in Jakarta, Yao Teng-shan, recently been extradited from Indonesia, as the new 'Minister'.[9] For a few days they tried to influence the foreign policy of the PR of China along the lines of 'active revolutionary struggle'. This found its main expression in notes of protest which they broadcast to a great number of foreign states through the broadcasting station of the Ministry which was in their hands. However, these notes were mostly filed without further comment by the parties receiving them. The Red Guard's action against the Ministry of Foreign Affairs was the cause of Chou's definite alliance with the army against the Left. On the evening of August 23 the Red Guards were removed by force from the building of the Ministry by units of the Peking garrison. The attempt by the

CRG to stage a *coup* in the capital had failed. A few days earlier a compromise between the Centre and the regional commanders had already created the preconditions for the new alliance against the Left.

The Compromise with the Regional Commanders

During the critical days after the Wuhan incident an enlarged session of the Military Commission of the CC was to be of particular importance. It was convened in Peking at the beginning of August and most of the military area commanders-in-chief and other regional military leaders apparently took part in it. With regard to this conference there is only one document available, the text of a speech made by Lin Piao on August 9. But the discussions and decisions of this body may be largely reconstructed from this text.[10] Lin feared that the regional commanders might make mistakes in this critical situation, and imploringly he admonished them to discuss all local conflicts with the Centre and to wait for the latter's decision. Certainly he repeated Mao's appeal to arm the Left, but simultaneously he emphasized that local and regional problems should be resolved 'gradually, step by step'; that one should 'not act rashly and be more thoughtful', for 'Heaven does not fall down!' The Party and the Government were paralysed for the time being, Lin continued, and this resulted in 'chaos' which had caused numerous conflicts. In the context of these conflicts it had also happened that 'good people had fought against good people'. Thus the Director of the General Logistics Department, General Ch'iu Hui-tso, had for more than one month been the object of the 'struggle' and had nearly lost his life. The same was true of the Commander-in-Chief of the Air Force, General Wu Fa-hsien. Both of them were fully rehabilitated by Lin as well as the commander-in-chief of the Nanking military area, Hsü Shin-yu, who had not been 'completely correct in his attitude to the Cultural Revolution' but had nevertheless been 'a good general for decades'. Therefore he would not be dismissed from his position. Lin took extraordinary pains to reassure the regional commanders: 'We do not intend to dismiss Chang Tsai-tao and Li Tsai-tao.'[11] It may be further deduced from Lin's speech that a compromise was reached between the central army leadership and the regional commanders at the military conference in Peking. The latter showed their willingness to heed the advice of the Centre in future local conflicts to a greater degree than hitherto and probably also to use their influence more than hitherto to establish RCs in the provinces. Since April no RC had been established. After the military conference a new phase began with the establishment of the Tsinghai RC on August 12.[12] But Lin made a clear promise that

~~Peking. The latter showed their willingness to heed the advice of~~
the regional commanders would not be made the targets of the
purge.

Soon, on August 14, the Party Centre published a circular with the
names of fifty-four leading Party cadres who could be attacked
by name in central and local publications. Attacks on other leading
cadres were therefore forbidden *de facto*.[13] The list did not contain the
name of a single regional military commander.

Apart from these assurances it cannot be directly ascertained whether
the Centre gave in to any of the claims put forward by the regional
commanders for leading roles in the new RCs. However, this might be
a consistent assumption since the percentage of the military in the
standing committees of the RCs rose from less than 32 per cent in
those six which had been established in spring 1967 to about 48 per
cent in the twenty-three created from August 1967 onwards.[14] Even
more important was the fact that Lin Piao had set his face unequivocally
against a further purge of the PLA at the conference. Only a few days
after the conference the Centre went even further. Now the Leftists
of the CRG themselves became the object of a purge.

The Turn against the Left

On August 17 Wang Li was still in a position to publish a new attack
on 'persons in authority in the army' in the journal *Hung-ch'i*.[15] But
only three days later he was surprisingly branded an 'agent of the
Kuomintang' and was arrested by a military patrol in Peking. By the
end of August, CRG members Lin Chieh, Kuan Feng and Mu Hsin
had also been arrested. The four closest followers of Chiang Ch'ing
were accused of having founded, at the end of June 1967, a 'counter-
revolutionary organisation' under the name of the 'May 16 Corps'
(*Wu-i-liu ping-t'uan*) which had connections in all parts of the country
and which was 'left in form but right in essence'. planning to turn
the 'spearhead of the struggle' against Premier Chou and the leadership of the PLA.[16] The purge of the four leading CRG members
had already weakened the top level of the Maoist movement when,
at the beginning of September, the Centre took further measures
to consolidate the position of the military and to discipline the mass
organisations of the Left. Since mid-June Red Guards and 'Revolutionary Rebels' had invaded PLA arsenals in a number of provinces
and had seized arms and other military equipment. In some cases –
mindful of Mao's appeal of July 22 and Lin's corresponding remarks
in his speech of August 9 – the arms had been left for them by the
local military organs. Now on September 5 an order was issued in
the name of the four leading bodies of the Centre which strictly forbade

'all mass organisations and individuals' to seize PLA arms and equipment and forbade members of the military forces to deliver arms to the mass organisations, ordering the return of all military goods then in the hands of Maoist organisations. The PLA became entitled to make arrests and even to use armed force if their return was refused.[17]

On the same day, even Chiang Ch'ing felt obliged to follow the change of course. In a speech before Red Guard delegates from Anhui, the text of which was published in a circular from the General Office of the CC throughout China, the representative of the original cultural revolutionary programme who had previously been the most prominent member of the extreme Left called for a 'great alliance of all forces' and for 'great harmony'. She denounced all armed conflicts, labelling the slogan 'Seize the handful in the military forces', which she herself had put into circulation, as 'reactionary'. She declared that the 'honour of the PLA must be protected'.[18] But Chiang Ch'ing's volte-face plainly did not have the effect she anticipated of ending factional struggles within the Left, the attacks of anti-Maoist groups on Red Guards and 'Revolutionary Rebels', or even stopping the measures taken by the army against the Maoist mass organisations. During the winter of 1967–8 armed clashes continued to occur. From December 15, 1967, to January 15, 1968, alone, such clashes were reported from nine provinces.[19] Attacks on leading members of the CRG subsystem also continued. In the first half of March 1968 another follower of Chiang Ch'ing in the CRG, the journalist and Party theorist Ch'i Pen-yü, was overthrown. For the first time since Wu Han had been attacked from Shanghai the purge of a politician was launched from a province. In Canton a campaign against 'Left extremists' (Chi-lieh tso-ch'ing fen-tzu) had been under way since mid-January 1968 under the guidance of General Huang Yung-sheng.[20] Since the end of February leaflets had appeared calling Ch'i Pen-yü a 'counter-revolutionary disguised as a Leftist'.[21] About two weeks later his opponents also prevailed in Peking. He was stigmatised as a 'Party enemy'. Chiang Ch'ing's attempts to protect her former followers were of little avail. On March 11 she had declared in a dispute with Chou En-lai that the 'May 16 Corps' had 'not consisted exclusively of disguised reactionaries'.[22] The defeat of the Left wing of the faction of Mao and Lin Piao was further aggravated by the fact that in February 1968 there were differences of opinion over the political work of the PLA between Chiang Ch'ing and the acting Chief of the General Staff, General Yang Ch'eng-wu, who up to then had co-operated closely with the CRG.[23] The conflict between Madame Mao and Yang paralysed the Left. It provided the regional commanders with the opportunity to promote Yang's downfall and to replace him with one of their representatives in the central army leadership.

The Overthrow of Yang Ch'eng-wu

On March 22, 1968, Yang Ch'eng-wu, the garrison commander of Peking, General Fu Ch'ung-pi, and the First Political Commissar of the Air Force, Yü Li-chin, were dismissed from their posts by an enlarged session of the Military Commission of the CC which since August 1967 had repeatedly acted as the decisive leading organ of the Centre.[24] The origins of this unexpected purge have not till now been fully exposed. At a session of the Military Commission and ta mass rallies in Peking on March 24 and 25 Lin, Chou and Mme. Mao accused the three generals of having planned a *coup d'état* to be directed mainly against the CRG.[25] This accusation may have been justified, having regard to the controversies between Yang and Chiang Ch'ing, but it seems doubtful that the top-level group of the Left still had enough influence in March 1968 to achieve the overthrow of the number two in the PLA leadership after the position of the CRG had been weakened by the purge of Wang Li, Lin Chieh, Kuan Feng, Mu Hsin and Ch'i Pen-yü. Thus a second accusation made against Yang was probably of more importance. He was accused of having prepared the purge of the Commander-in-Chief of the Air Force, Wu Fa-hsien, and of five senior commanders of military areas, Huang Yung-sheng, Han Hsien-ch'u, Ch'en Hsi-lien, Hsü Shin-yu and Yang Te-chih.[26] These were the same military area commanders who, as has been mentioned, had already been attacked by the CRG in the summer of 1967. Furthermore, a survey of divisional and corps commanders appointed under Yang's command since spring 1966 indicates that the acting Chief of the General Staff had tried to undermine the power basis of the regional military leaders with the help of officers who had served under him for a long time. Thus it is reasonable to assume that Yang was mainly the victim of action by the regional commanders. The choice of a new Chief of the General Staff further substantiates this theory. It fell on an outstanding representative of the regional commanders' group, Huang Yung-sheng,[27] who in summer 1967 had been called the 'T'an Chen-lin of Canton', 'T'ao Chu's Party Killer' and a 'repugnant bandit chief' by the Canton Red Guards.[28]

It is of no importance whether Lin Piao decided voluntarily to sacrifice his long-standing colleague Yang in order to safeguard the unity of the PLA, or whether he was forced to take this step by the session of the Military Commission. Yang's overthrow and Huang's appointment as Chief of the General Staff imply a considerable strengthening of the influence of the regional military machines in the policy-making process.

Since Autumn 1966 the regional commanders, especially General Huang Yung-sheng, had frequently proved that they possessed but

little understanding of the revolutionary enthusiasm and innovatory
zeal of the Maoist groups. Their interests were focused more on discipline, law and order, and a renewed consolidation of government. In
their view the programme of the 'Cultural Revolution', the revolutionary mobilisation of the masses and the shaking up of the bureaucratic
structures had to be subordinated to this interest. Thus they became
the engineers of the liquidation of the Red Guard movement which
started with the change of course in the Centre in August 1967.

The End of the Red Guard Movement

The Red Guards had made substantial contributions to Mao's victory
over his opponents in the Party leadership and had led the attack
against the old Party leadership groups in the provinces, together with
the organisations of 'Revolutionary Rebels', in the name of the Chairman during the first months of 1967. Large sections of Chinese youth
had thereby experienced for the first time the possibility of organising
themselves outside the structures of the Party machine, and they had
become conscious of the concrete power they could exercise. However,
when a coalition was established in the Centre between Lin, Chou and
the area commanders, the 'achievements' of 1966 were to be valid no
longer. Now the PLA received the order to start disciplining the Maoist groups. As early as September 17, 1967, Chou En-lai stated in a
speech before Red Guards in Peking that Chairman Mao had said that
the moment had now come when 'the little revolutionary generals
[a term for Red Guards – J.D.] made mistakes'. They should at once
stop their 'revolutionary exchange of experience' and return to their
schools and universities. 'Those who disobey this order will be
expelled.[29]

Certainly the termination of the Red Guard marches through the
country and the resumption of classes had been ordered by the leading
organs of the Centre several times previously (on February 17, March 7,
March 19, April 17 and 20, 1967[30]) but these orders had remained
ineffectual. This time, however, the army was put into operation. On
October 14 the CC, the State Council, the Military Commission and
the CRG issued a joint circular ordering the immediate resumption of
classes.[31] A short time later military units began 'to help' the pupils
and students in many cities in the country 'to return to the schools', as
the publications media of the PR of China expressed it.[32] Nevertheless,
at first only the primary and secondary schools could be reopened,
supplied with curricula which provided for long periods of political
education and para-military training by PLA troops.

The first group of universities and colleges started up again only in
autumn 1970 after an interruption of more than four years. But by

February 1968 the army had ended the 'revolutionary exchange of experience' in most regions. At the same time the 'Military Control Commissions' for Red Guard units, which had been created in autumn 1966, were reactivated. In future, 'Big Character Posters' and leaflets were to be published only after authorisation from these bodies. In most cases in which the mass organisations disregarded this order the army rapidly and often harshly intervened.

Under the influence of these disciplinary measures, opposition to the Peking leadership began to be rekindled in the ranks of the Red Guards after the autumn of 1967.[33] As early as September 1967 Red Guards in Inner Mongolia had criticised Chiang Ch'ing's speech of September 5 and had called for a 'complete redistribution of power'.[34] During the following months resistance to the army by Maoist youth groups built up in Hunan, Kiangsi, Honan and Anhui;[35] in January 1968 groups of the Left in Canton declared that the city 'still needed great unrest' since the 'old persons in authority' had once more returned.[36] In many provinces the Red Guards now spoke of a 'new trend' (*Hsin ssu-ch'ao*). Thus the dynamic Chinese term for 'trend' (*Ssu-ch'ao*) was contrasted with the static term 'thought' (*Ssu-hsiang*) which is connected with Mao's name. The 'new trend' found its clearest expression in two documents published in December 1967 and January 1968 by the 'Committee of the Great Proletarian Revolutionary Alliance of the Province of Hunan' (*Hu-nan sheng wu-ch'an chieh-chi ko-ming ta-lien-ho wei-yüan-hui*; abbreviated to *Sheng-wu-lien*).[37] The authenticity of the two versions of these documents which have circulated outside China is, when analysed carefully, extremely doubtful; but the essential theses have been quoted polemically so frequently in other reliable sources[38] that the fact of the existence of the former and the essential contents may be regarded as proven.

Therein the 'Rebels' in Hunan complained that the 'storm of the January revolution' had demonstrated to the people 'that China was on the road to a society free from bureaucrats,' but that then the intervention of the army had led to a situation where 'the overthrown bureaucrats had been climbing back to the top again'. When the masses had armed themselves in August 1967 Chairman Mao had 'unfortunately started the retreat' so that the masses could no longer expect much help from the Party. It could not but 'remain a party of bourgeois reformism'. By contrast it was imperative to create a 'Chinese Commune' (*Chung-hua kung-she*) and a Soviet system largely free from government which alone could realise the socialist revolution.

These and similar proclamations (for example, in Canton Red Guard leaflets appeared at the beginning of April 1968 demanding the overthrow of Mao and Chou En-lai because formerly they had been 'high-ranking officials in the Kuomintang'[39]) offered the army the opportunity to proceed against the new Leftist opposition even more harshly than hitherto. Since May 1968 the PLA had used above all those 'Red Workers' Guards', who in January 1967 had put up the toughest resistance to the Left offensive, to support its campaign against the Red Guards. Together with officer patrols they were entrusted with control over the universities. Thus, at the end of July 1968, joint units of PLA members and worker 'commandos' (*Chiu-ch'a tui*) occupied Tsinghua University in Peking which had seen the beginnings of the Red Guard movement in 1966. Several students were killed and many were injured during this action. Yet Mao himself explicitly applauded the workers and soldiers.[40] In Canton, from May to August 1968, the military area command, together with the 'conservative' mass organisations and worker guards, launched a campaign against the Left of 1967 in the course of which hundreds of Red Guards were massacred.[41] However, the harshest clashes between Maoist groups on the one hand and the majority of local troops and members of anti-Maoist organisations on the other hand, which became known outside China, developed between February and August 1968 in the Chuang Autonomous Region, the former Southern Chinese province of Kwangsi.[42] Far more than 50,000 people were killed in four months of incidents resembling civil war. Both sides used heavy arms and the towns of Wuchou and Liuchou were almost completely destroyed.[43] Calls for help by the 'Revolutionary Rebels' and Red Guards to the Centre in Peking went unanswered, and in autumn 1968 Left resistance to the seizure of power by the regional commanders and their followers broke down. At about the same time the Red Guard units in four other administrative areas were also officially declared dissolved.[44]

In order to gain complete control over the 'Maoists of the first hour', from August 1968 the new regional leadership groups began to send down (*Hsia-fang*) former Red Guards to the villages for manual labour. There they were to 'learn from the poor and lower-middle peasants' and to 'exercise revolutionary discipline'. These measures were continued throughout the whole of 1969 and 1970. If they were still insufficient, recourse was had to public executions of 'anarchists, hoodlums and 'Kuomintang agents' – these being the terms which the authorities used for former members of the Leftist mass organisations.[45]

Towards the end of 1968 the defeat of the Left had been organisationally completed. From time to time the Red Guards were still mentioned, but the media of the new provincial leadership did not neglect to point out that although the Red Guards had 'earned merits in the Cultural Revolution' they were now measured 'solely according to their present attitude to the Centre of the revolution' and the 'centre of this centre' was the PLA.[46]

In the course of 1970 reports about the participation of Red Guards in mass meetings became more and more infrequent. From the beginning of 1970 the publications media of the PR of China no longer mentioned the CRG among the leading organs of the Party. The term 'Revolutionary Rebels' had already disappeared in the summer of 1969. The organisation agony of the genuine Maoist Left parallelled the growing strength of the PLA's position. The later created the new regional government structures and also achieved the consolidation of the internal political situation after defeating the opposition of the young vanguard of the cultural Revolution.

References

1 On July 24, 1967, the Chinese Language Service of Radio Moscow started a propaganda campaign in which the Soviet Union called for the overthrow of the Mao–Lin group. Since the beginning of August the Soviet troops in Soviet Asia were considerably reinforced and equipped with more offensive weapons.

2 *An-ch'üan chan-pao* (*Combat Journal 'Security'*), Canton, No. 13, August 1, 1967; also *Wen-kung wu-wei* (*Attack with Words, Defend Yourselves with Weapons*), Lhasa, n.d., probably mid-August 1967.

3 *HC*, No. 12, 1967.

4 Cf. Domes, *Generals II*, *loc. cit.*, pp. 128–9.

5 Lin Piao in his speech of August 9, 1967, *loc. cit.*

6 Extracts of the speech in *Hung-wei-pao*, Peking, October 18, 1967.

7 *Chu-ying tung-fang-hung*, Canton, No. 20, April 1968; also *Kung-lien* (*Workers' Alliance*), Canton, April 1968; cf. Chien Yu-shen, *China's Fading Revolution-Army Dissent and Military Divisions, 1967–68*, Hong Kong, 1969, pp. 104–5.

8 *URI, Documents*, *op. cit.*, pp. 501–4.

9 *Hung-wei-pao*, Peking, September 15, 1967; also *Yeh-chan pao* (*Wild Combat News*), Canton, No. 12–13, March 1968.

10 Lin Piao's speech of August 9, 1967, *loc. cit.*, *passim.*

11 Lin speaks of other regional commanders.

12 Cf. Domes, *CO*, *loc. cit.*, p. 122.

13 *URI, Documents*, *op. cit.*, pp. 495–9.

14 Cf. Domes, *ibid.*, pp. 143–4.

15 *HC*, No. 13, 1967.

16 *Hung-ch'i* (not the Party journal, but a Red Guard journal of the same name), edited by Peking Aviation College, Peking, September 19, 1967; cf. von Groeling, *Widerstand*, *op. cit.*, p. 365 *et seq.*

17 'Directive of the CC of the CCP, the State Council, the Military Commission of the CC, and the Group Cultural Revolution Concerning the Prohibition against Seizing Weapons, Equipment, and Other Military Goods from the PLA, *Chung-fa* (67)', No. 288, September 5, 1967, in *URI, Documents*, *op. cit.*, 505–10.

18 Text of the speech in *Tung-fang-hung*, September 21, 1967; text of the Circular of the General Office of the CC of September 9, 1967, in *JMJP*, September 17, 1967; both documents also in *URI, Documents, op. cit.*, pp. 511–34.

19 Cf. Domes, *AS, loc. cit.*, p. 360.

20 Among others *Ta-han ta- chiao*, Canton, January 30, 1968.

21 Leaflet from Canton, date given February 26, 1968, English translation, in *SCMP*, No. 4317, March 13, 1968; also *T'ao Ch'i (Punish Ch'i)*, Canton, March 1, 1968.

22 *Kuangchou hung-tai-hui (Meeting of the Canton Red Guards' Delegates)*, Canton, April 3, 1968.

23 *Wen-yi chan-pao (Combat Journal 'Literature')*. Peking, No. 11, March 9, 1968.

24 *Chu-ying tung-fang-hung*, Canton, No. 20, April 1968; cf. Chien, *op. cit.*, pp. 104–5.

25 *Ibid.*, also *Kung-lien*, Canton, April 1968; cf. Domes, *Cq, loc. cit.*, pp. 132–3.

26 *Ibid.*, also *Chung-ta chan-pao (Combat Journal of the Chungshan University)*, Canton, No. 47, April 14, 1968.

27 Huang's appointment was officially confirmed in *JMJP*, June 2, 1968.

28 Cf. Domes, *Generals II, loc. cit.*, p. 125 *et seq.*

29 *Chu-ying tung-fang-hung*, Canton, October 1, 1967.

30 *URI, Documents, op. cit.*, pp. 299–302, 341–5, 377–8, 421–3, 429–30.

31 *Ibid.*, pp. 565–7.

32 Among others, People's Radio Peking City, October 14, 1967; People's Radio Tientsin, October 17, 19, December 8, 1967; Peoples' Radio Shantung, November 4, 1967.

33 Cf. von Groeling, *Widerstand, op. cit.*, pp. 197–9, 210–15, 219.

34 People's Radio Inner Mongolia, September 13, 1967.

35 *Hunan jih-pao*, September 16, 1967; People's Radio Kiangsi, March 2, 1968; People's Radio Honan, May 19, 1968; Honan jih-pao, May 29, 1968; People's Radio Anhui, December 25, 1668.

36 Cf. Domes, *Generals II, loc. cit.*, pp. 140–1.

37 'Our Programme, December 21, 1967', in *Kuang-yin hung-chi' (Red Flag of the Printing-Press Canton)*, Canton, No. 5, March 1968, extracts also in *Tung-fang chan-pao (Combat Journal 'The East')*, Canton, No. 19, February 29, 1968; 'Whither China?', January 12, 1968, in *Kuang-yin hung-ch'i, ibid.*

38 Among others *Pa-wu (Eight-Five)*, Canton, February 1968; *Wen-ko t'ung-hsün*, Canton, No. 12, February 1968; also *I-yüeh feng-pu (Storm in January)*, Canton, No. 23–24, March 1968.

39 *Hsing-tao jih-pao*, Hong Kong, April 13, 1968.

40 *JMJP*, August 8, 15 and October 31, 1968.

41 Cf. Domes, *Generals II, loc. cit.*, pp. 148–51.

42 Cf. Victor C. Falkenheim, 'The Cultural Revolution in Kuangsi, Yünnan, and Fukien', in *AS*, Vol. IX, No. 8, August 1969, pp. 585–7.

43 *Ssu-erh-erh t'ung-hsün (Bulletin of April Twenty-two)*, Linchou, No. 6, May 29, 1968; *Hsi-chiang nu-t'ao (Furious Uproar on the West River)*, Wuchou, No. 1, June 1968; *Wuchou lien-chih (United Committee of Wuchou)*, No. 4, June 8, 1968; *Ta-chün pao (Great Army News)*, Canton, July 1970.

44 People's Radio Ch'angch'un, July 21, 1968; People's Radio Honan, August 8, 1968; People's Radio Szechwan, October 24, 1968; People's Radio Sinkiang,

November 21, 1968; cf. *Summary of World Broadcasts*, No. 2912, October 30, 1968, and No. 2934, November 25, 1968.
45 Among others, People's Radio Canton, October 4, 1968; *Hsing-tao jih-pao*, January 14, 1969; also reports of young refugees in interviews with the author, Hong Kong, June and July 1970, August 1971, and September 1972.

XIV.   The Stabilisation of Rule

In the late summer of 1967, the central leading organs of the PR of China had been forced to turn against the Left not only because of growing factionalism among the Maoist organisations, conflict between differing Red Guard and 'Revolutionary Rebel' groups and the impending impairment of the loyalty of the armed forces, but also because of the disintegration of the control and administration structures which, through causing serious disturbances in the development of the national economy, made imperative effective measures to stabilise the political system. However, to achieve this, the utilisation of the only instrument of power that was intact, the PLA, became necessary.

The armed forces took over the task of disciplining the Maoist movement and of building up the new organs of government, the RCs in the provinces, districts, communities, factories and people's communes. Thus the army secured a dominant position in the provinces and counties. Having thus created the foundations for the reconstruction of a functioning state (now, however, far more strongly determined by regional autonomy than before the crisis) the reconstruction of the shattered Party machine began as well. It was started from the top in April 1969 with the establishment of new central decision-making organs at the Ninth Party Congress of the CCP. From December 1970, the PLA again secured a decisive influence within the bodies which it reinforced in the course of establishing the new provincial party committees.

Since then the party organisation has become, in most parts of China, the tool of indirect rule by military officers with a comparatively undeveloped ideological consciousness. While the terminology of the 'Cultural Revolution' remains in use, the practical policy decisions of the leadership groups have become more and more dissociated from the original programme of Mao and his closest followers in the early phase of the 'Cultural Revolution'. Mao's victory in the realm of organisation, achieved by the overthrow of the leaders of the 'New Right', appears questionable in the realm of the political programme. The intellectual criticism of the Party leader and his policy was subdued. Out of the crisis of the 'Cultural Revolution' there emerged a political

system characterised by strict discipline, and by predominantly pragmatic orientations related to medium- and short-term policy decisions.
The degree to which Mao himself is willing or able to influence these
decisions remains unclear. But the difference between the political
principles formulated by himself and the actual policy enacted by the
new leadership group makes it a reasonable assumption that the ageing
leader of the Communist movement in China no longer participates
regularly in the day-by-day decision-making at the Centre.

The Revolutionary Committees[1]

It has already been pointed out that by establishing the first RC in
Heilungkiang on January 31, 1967, an alternative type for the new
provincial leading organs had been created in addition to the concept
of the 'Commune' in Shanghai. The way in which the former had
been created and was related to the mass organisations made it different
from the Shanghai model.[2] The members of the RC were, in contrast
to the 'Commune', only partly elected by the mass organisations, and
since the turn of 1967-8 had hardly been so at all. Thus they could not
even theoretically be voted out of office by the latter. Moreover, the
percentage of old cadres and PLA representatives was considerably
higher from the beginning in the RCs than in the 'Shanghai Commune'.
After the new type of RC had already prevailed over the 'Commune'
in February 1967, in March the publication media introduced the RC
of Shansi province as the model for the future composition of the new
organs of government.[3] It had 245 members of whom 118 represented
'revolutionary mass organisations', sixty-eight the PLA and fifty-nine
the 'revolutionary cadres'. In future about half of the members of the
RC were to represent Maoist groups and the PLA and Party cadres were
to constitute one-quarter each. The real decision-making body, however, the *Standing Committee of the RC*, showed a completely different
picture, even in Shansi. Here four cadres and two military representatives faced one representative from the mass organisations.[4]

At first establishment of the RCs in the provinces, autonomous
regions and autonomous cities proceeded only slowly. From January 31
to April 20, 1967, they could be established in no more than six out
of the total of twenty-nine administrative areas. Then there was an
interruption of nearly four months before the beginning of a second
phase of establishing the new organs of government with the creation
of the seventh RC in Tsinghai on August 12, 1967.[5] Only two weeks
later the leading organs of the Centre changed course, and the army
took responsibility for establishing RCs in the provinces. Nevertheless,
another four and a half months passed before there was a considerable
speeding up of the establishment of RCs. During the last quarter of

1967 only two other Committees had been founded, in Inner Mongolia on November 1,[6] and in Tientsin on December 6.[7] The recurrent delay apparently forced the Centre to reach further compromises with the regional commanders. Reports of a reception given by Mao and Lin Piao for leading military officers from all parts of China in Peking on December 31, 1967,[8] strengthen the assumption that another military conference took place around the turn of 1967–8. No source materials regarding this conference are available yet, but the developments of the following months give rise to the conclusion that on this occasion the Party leader once more gave clear guarantees of the dominant position of the PLA in the RCs, while the regional commanders agreed to advance the establishment of the Committees with greater energy than previously. From January to May 1968 three RCs were established in each month; then there was a break of three months. In August three further Committees followed, and with the establishment of the RCs of the Autonomous Regions of Tibet and Sinkiang on September 5, 1968, the process of constructing the new leading organs of state and economic administration in the provinces of China came to an end.[9]

An analysis of the reconstruction of the administrative machine at the regional level proves to be relevant in many aspects. We shall attempt to systematise it under four aspects.

1. *The chronological order* can be divided into three phases. First, the six Committees established in spring 1967 stand in contrast to the twenty-three created from August 1967 to September 1968. Regarding the *form* of their creation, the latter show more factors in common than differences. However, regarding their composition, the twelve Committees created before Yang Ch'eng-wu's fall on March 22, 1968,[10] differed from the eleven founded after this event to such a high degree that a further caesura should be made at this point. Four of the six RCs established during the *first phase* were initially led by civilian Party cadres and two of them by generals or political commissars from the PLA. Among the seventy-six members of the standing committees of these RCs, twenty-eight were civilian Party cadres (35.4 per cent), twenty-six were representatives of the mass organisations (32.9 per cent) and twenty-five were military representatives (31.6 per cent). Nine of the chairmen of the twelve RCs established during the *second phase* were generals or political commissars and three were civilian Party cadres. Eighty-eight out of the 165 members (63.3 per cent) of their standing committees represented the military, forty-two (25.5 per cent) the civilian Party cadres and thirty-five (21.1 per cent) the mass organisations.

Ten of the eleven RCs established during the *third phase* were initially headed by generals or political commissars, and only one by a civilian Party cadres. But here the mass organisations were more strongly represented in the Standing Committees of these RCs, with sixty-three out of 197 representatives (32 per cent). They faced ninety-two military representatives (46·7 per cent) and forty-two civilian Party cadres (21·3 per cent).[11]

2. Regarding the method or form of establishing the RCs, two different ways may be detected. The *formal way*: regional military leaders brought the mass organisations under their control with the help of the Centre and made them form a 'Great Revolutionary Alliance' (*Ko-ming ta-lien-ho*) which in turn convened a 'Preparatory Group for the RC' (*Ko-wei-hui ch'ou-pei hsiao-tsu*) representing the core of the future RC. Under its guidance representative assemblies of Red Guards (in some provinces simply of 'revolutionary pupils and students'), workers and 'poor and lower-middle peasants' were established to which only those organisations which had placed themselves under the control of the regional commands were allowed access. These assemblies nominated the representatives of the mass organisations who, together with the PLA and the 'revolutionary cadres', finally constituted the RC as a 'revolutionary trinity'. This way, for which the evidence is clearest in the case of Kwangtung,[12] was also followed by Inner Mongolia, Tientsin, Kiangsi, Kansu, Honan, Chekiang, Hunan, Ninghsia and Szechwan.

The *informal way*: the regional military leadership either forced the 'Great Alliance' of the mass organisations into existence without thereafter establishing the 'Preparatory Group' and convening representative assemblies, or the 'provisional power organ', the 'Military Control Commission', was enlarged by the addition of a few Party cadres and representatives of the mass organisations and thus proclaimed an RC. This happened in Tsinghai, Hupei, Kirin, Kiangsu, Shensi, Liaoning, Anhui, Yünnan, Fukien, Kwangsi, Sinkiang and Tibet and – with the PLA having a less dominating position – in Hopei.

3. Regarding the degree of *participation by the PLA*, we may differentiate between three groups:

The *first group* is formed by two of the six RCs of the first phase and one of the twelve RCs of the second phase, Shanghai, Kweichow and Hopei. In these cases the army was only of *assistance*; the Maoist organisations took the lead.

The *second group* comprises the other four RCs of the first phase, two from the second phase and one of the eleven RCs of the third phase, Heilungkiang, Shansi, Shantung, Peking, Tientsin, Honan and Kwangsi. In these RCs the role of the military remains unclear due to the present state of source materials.

The *third group*, by far the largest, comprises nineteen out of the total of twenty-nine Committees. It is formed from nine RCs from the second, and ten from the third phase, Chekiang, Tsinghai, Hupei, Inner Mongolia, Kansu, Kiangsi, Kiangsu, Kirin, Kwangtung, Anhui, Fukien, Hunan, Liaoning, Ninghsia, Shensi, Sinkiang, Szechwan, Tibet and Yünnan. The RCs of all these provinces have practically been *created by the PLA*.[13]

4. Regarding the *patterns of behaviour of the regional military leaders*, in the course of establishing the RCs, the process of seizing power used by the PLA may be demonstrated. Four groups are discernible in this aspect:

1. Those who themselves engaged in establishing the RCs immediately after the appeal to the PLA to support the Left on January 23, 1967. Five of the six RCs of the first phase came into being in this fashion, Heilungkiang, Kweichow, Shanghai, Shansi and Shantung.

2. Those who took part in the establishment of RCs with reluctance, only after measures of discipline had been taken against the Maoist groups. One Committee of the first phase, four from the second and three from the third came into being following this pattern, the RCs of Peking, Honan, Hopei, Kansu, Kwangtung, Hunan, Kwangsi and Tibet.

3. The regional commanders who had been newly appointed to their regions to establish the RCs in co-operation with the Centre. This process effected the establishment of six Committees each from the second and third phases, Chekiang, Tsinghai, Hupei, Inner Mongolia, Kiangsi, Tientsin, Anhui, Ninghsia, Shensi, Sinkiang, Szechwan and Yünnan.

4. Those who either founded the RCs without any co-operation from the Maoist groups or simply proclaimed that the 'Military Control Commission' was the RC. This was the case with two RCs each from the second and third phases, Kiangsu, Kirin, Fukien and Liaoning.[14]

Summing up, in only five of the twenty-nine administrative areas did the regional military commanders give immediate and unconditional support to the establishment of RCs by Maoist groups. Three of them have since been dismissed.[15] In twelve administrative areas the commanders had to be removed from their posts before the RCs could be established, and in another twelve they came into being only according to the terms of the respective regional commanders.

Thus the process of establishing the RCs indeed confirmed the organisational seizure of regional power by the leaders of the PLA. A retrospect of personnel changes after the establishment of the provincial Revolutionary Committees shows that the influence of the representatives of the PLA has not been decreased. From April 1968 to September 1969 altogether twenty-nine members of the Standing Committees of the RCs have been dismissed from their posts. Seventeen were representatives of the mass organisations, ten were civilian Party leaders and two were military representatives. They were replaced by twenty-one military representatives and six representatives of the mass organisations.[16] In two cases[17] a civilian Party cadre replaced a general as chairman of an RC; in two other cases[18] generals replaced civilian Party cadres, and in one case[19] a general replaced a political commissar. Thus twenty-one of the twenty-nine provincial RCs are now headed by members of the PLA.

The Ninth Party Congress of the CCP, 1969

The decision to begin the reconstruction of the Party machine from above by convening the Ninth Party Congress, overdue since 1961, had been made by the Centre no later than October 1967. According to a first announcement the Party Congress was to be convened before October 1, 1968.[29] The original concepts and expectations of the Centre regarding its convention are known from two sources.

Hsieh Fu-chih, the Minister of Security, declared in a speech before delegates from mass organisations in Peking on October 26, 1967, that 'the method of electing delegates from below to above was pseudo-democratic' and that therefore the list of delegates for the Party Congress would have to be 'compiled by the CC'. According to Hsieh the Party Congress was to comprise between 8,000 and 10,000 delegates in order to avoid a 'Congress of old men with about 1,000 delegates'. He emphasized that the majority of the Party Congress should be constituted by 'young forces', particularly from mass organisations.[21] A circular from the Party Centre and the CRG of November 27, 1967, further specified that Liu Shao-ch'i, Teng Hsiao-p'ing, T'ao Chu, P'eng Te-huai, Ho Lung, P'eng Chen, Lo Jui-ch'ing, Lu Ting-i and Yang Shang-k'un could not become delegates under any circumstances. In future only 'genuine Marxist–Leninists' should belong to the Party who were 'loyal to Chairman Mao, loyal to Mao Tse-tung's thought and loyal to the revolutionary line of Chairman Mao'.[22]

From October 13 to 21, 1968, the Twelfth Plenum of the Eighth CC – again not constituting a quorum according to the Party constitution, but comprising nearly all regional commanders and many representatives of the provincial RCs – was convened in Peking. It decided to expel Liu from the CCP 'for all time' and to deprive him (in violation of the Constitution which reserved this right to the NPC) of all his state posts. Regarding the Party Congress the Plenum decided only that it should be convened at a 'suitable date'.[23] However, the draft of a new Party constitution was adopted. This had been prepared under the guidance of Ch'en Po-ta, Chang Ch'un-ch'iao and Yao

Wen-yüan in order to present it to the Party Congress for approval.[24] While the leaders of the Left had still had the opportunity of influencing the drafting of the new constitution of the CCP, the selection of delegates to the Party Congress was reserved for the regional military leadership groups, contrary to Hsieh Fu-chih's statements. Reports about conferences of Party members in the RCs, which were mostly convened by the political apparatus of the PLA, are available for the period November 1968 to March 1969 for eight out of the twenty-nine administrative areas.[25] In only one case is it reported that the selection of delegates to the Party Congress has been 'discussed' at such a conference.[26]

When the Ninth Party Congress of the CCP was finally convened under conditions of the utmost security in the capital on April 1, 1969, there was no further mention of '8,000 to 10,000' delegates.[27] With 1,512 members altogether, the Congress corresponded more closely in size to the Eighth Party Congress of 1956 and thus to the 'Congress of old men' against which Hsieh had so impressively warned in October 1967. About three-quarters of the delegates wore the uniform of the PLA.[28] The Party Congress was opened by Mao who gave a short speech which the first press communiqué described as 'extremely significant'.[29] The Chairman recalled the previous Party Congresses and criticised Liu Shao-ch'i, a 'certain P'eng Chen', Po I-po, Chang Wen-t'ien and Wang Chia-hsiang as well as earlier 'deviationists' like Li Li-san, Ch'ü Ch'iu-pai and Ch'en Shao-yü (Wang Ming) 'who went abroad to fight against us [to Moscow – J.D.]'. Mao called for the preservation of unity. The Party Congress, so he ended his speech, must be a 'Congress of unity, a Congress of victory'.[30]

According to the press communiqué of April 2, 1969, the subjects to be discussed at the Party Congress were to be (in the following order) the *Political Report of the Eighth CC* given by Lin Piao, the adoption of the new Party constitution and the election of the full and alternate members of the Ninth CC.[31] Another press communiqué of April 14 reported the adoption of the *Political Report* and the Party constitution.[32] A third communiqué, of April 24, finally announced that the delegates had elected the new CC on April 15.[33] Together with the list of names of the Ninth CC published on April 27,[34] the *Political Report* and the Party constitution, these three press communiqués constitute the only official documents of the Party Congress which were published. The discussions were not reproduced in the media as they had been in September 1956.

Lin Piao's *Political Report* concentrated on the critique of Liu Shao-ch'i made by the new Party leadership, celebrated the 'complete victory of the Cultural Revolution' and called for the unity of the

Party as well as for permanent criticism and self-criticism from its members. Lin lauded the reform of Peking opera which had been introduced by Chiang Ch'ing, but neglected to mention the Party leader's wife by name. During the discussions of the *Report*, in which the important Party leaders expressed their agreement, Chiang Ch'ing, Chang Ch'un-ch'iao, Yao Wen-yüan and even Hsieh Fu-chih remained silent. This seems significant considering their rank.

The new *Party constitution*[36] is kept much more general than the old constitution. 'Mao Tse-tung's Thought' is now expressly recognised as the theoretical basis of the Party after Marxism–Leninism. The constitution mentions Mao by name as the Chairman of the Party, which is the equivalent of a life appointment. In contrast to the hitherto customary practice of all Communist parties his successor (*Chi-ch'eng-jen*) was also named, Vice-Chairman Lin Piao. Provision has been made for the convening of a Party Congress every five years, but in contrast to the 1956 constitution there are no regulations governing the annual plenary session of the Party Congress. It is stated that the convening of the Party Congress may be 'postponed or held ahead of schedule', and that the CC shall, in future, be convened only once a year, and in this case too the Politburo may postpone the session. Neither the Secretariat of the CC nor the Central Control Commission has been mentioned in the constitution. The formal procedure concerning explusion from the Party formerly practised has been abolished. Above all the new constitution expressly mentions the specific Party organisation of the PLA which in future will not be combined with the civilian organisations at the county level but only at the Centre.

The resolutions of the Ninth Party Congress thus ratified the victory of the faction of Mao and Lin Piao during the crisis of the 'Cultural Revolution'. The new Party leadership also formally obtained comprehensive authority to lead so that in future it will be able to avoid being controlled by the Party Congress even more easily than hitherto. The leading position of the PLA, achieved during the conflicts of 1967 and 1968 and explicitly recognized in the new Party constitution, was clearly reaffirmed by the election of the Ninth CC.

The New Leadership Group—a Coalition[37]

With the establishment of a new leadership group in the PR of China, the 'Cultural Revolution' essentially came to an end. The election of the Ninth CC began on April 15 and required eleven or twelve days, an extraordinarily long period of time. When the election began. Southern Chinese provincial broadcasting stations were still reporting that the number of full CC members would be reduced from ninety-seven to fifty-one, and that of alternate members from ninety-three to seventy-four, in order to 'guarantee a more efficient, more united Central leadership of our great Party'.[38]

In reality, however, the number of full members increased to 170 and that of alternate members to 109. Regarding the long period of time taken for the election, this was probably caused by considerable differences of opinion over the selection of the new leadership group. These differences were seemingly resolved by compromises. An analysis of the composition of the Ninth CC leads to the following conclusions, if compared with the situation in the Seventh CC at the time of the Communist take-over in autumn 1949 and in the Eighth CC at the time of its election in September 1956.[39]

1. The new election effected considerable *changes in the leadership personnel*. Fifty-five of the ninety-two full members of the Eighth CC, who had not been reported dead by April 1969, were not re-elected either as full or as alternate members. Thirty-four were re-elected as full members and three as alternate members. One hundred and thirty-six Party leaders joined the CC as new full members.

2. Nevertheless, the election of the Ninth CC did not bring about the comprehensive *rejuvenation of the leadership group* called for by the Left in the 'Cultural Revolution'. The average age of the full members of the CC, which in 1949 was 54·2 years and in September 1956 had increased to 56·4 years, now amounted to 61·4 years for 118 members. Even if the absent data concerning the remaining fifty-two full members were to be made available, there could not be any decrease below fifty-eight or fifty-nine years.

3. The *regional origins* of the full members are now more balanced. Only thirteen of the twenty-nine administrative areas had been represented in the Seventh CC, and this figure rose to seventeen in the Eighth and twenty-one in the Ninth CCs. Nevertheless, the CC continued to be dominated by southern Chinese. While southern Chinese constitute somewhat over 53 per cent of the population, 83·7 per cent of the members of the Seventh CC and 72·2 per cent of the Eighth CC were southern Chinese. Of the 151 full members of the Ninth CC concerning whom data are available, 72·8 per cent were born in south China. The percentage of those coming from the inland provinces also changed only slightly. In the Seventh CC it came to 76·7 per cent, 76·3 per cent in the Eighth and 68·9 per cent in the Ninth.

The decrease in the percentage of Mao's provincial compatriots from Hunan in the CC is significant. While there were still 37·2 per cent in the Seventh and nearly 29 per cent in the Eighth CCs, only 19·9 per cent now remain. By contrast the percentage of Lin Piao's provincial compatriots from Hupei rose to 17·2 per cent in the Ninth CC whereas it had remained almost stagnant in the Seventh and Eighth CCs with 9·3 per cent and 10·3 per cent respectively.

4. Considerable changes have occurred in the *educational backgrounds* of CC members. Certainly, even in the Ninth CC, 76·2 per cent of the 126 full members for whom data are available attended a college – 88·3 per cent in the Seventh and 79·4 per cent in the Eigth CCs – but the number of university graduates decreased from 58·1 per cent in the Seventh and 41·2 per cent in the Eighth CCs to no more than 23·8 per cent in the Ninth CC. By contrast, the number of military academy graduates, which had amounted to 20·9 per cent in the Seventh CC, increased from 22·7 per cent in the Eighth to 35·7 per cent in the Ninth CC.

5. The number of full members with long *experience abroad* had decreased from 67·4 per cent in the Seventh and 50·5 per cent in the Eighth CCs to 32·5 per cent of the 126 full members of the Ninth CC for whom data are available. While 65·1 per cent of the members of the Seventh and 47·6 per cent of the members of the Eighth CC had been in the Soviet Union for long-term studies, this number had decreased to 27·8 per cent in the Ninth CC; 23·3 per cent of the members of the Seventh CC and 14·4 per cent of the members of the Eighth had had experience of France. In the Ninth CC only 6·3 per cent were left. Only 9·3 per cent of the members of the Seventh and 3·1 per cent of the members of the Eighth CCs had been in the United States, but not one member of the Ninth CC.

6. There were also shifts in *Party seniority* of the full members of the CC. While all forty-three members of the Seventh CC had joined the CCP between 1921 and 1927, and this was still valid for 87·6 per cent of the members of the Eighth CC, only 39·8 per cent remain of the 143 full members of the Ninth for whom data are available in this respect. However, the number of those who had become members of the CCP in the period between 1928 and the end of the 'Long March' in autumn 1935 increased from 10·3 per cent in the Eighth to 40·6 per cent in the Ninth CC. These data do not yet signify a change of élites. No less than 80·4 per cent of the full members of the Ninth CC also came from the group which had joined the CCP before the end of the 'Long-March', i.e. from the first revolutionary generation. The shift in favour of those members of this generation who had joined the Party between 1928 and 1935 is due mainly to the presence of leading military members who turned to the Communist guerilla army during the first period of the civil war between the CCP and KMT. Only 7·7 per cent of the members of the Ninth CC had joined the CCP after the Communist take-over. Among them were some senior politicians who had previously been non-Party individuals or members of non-Communist United Front parties. The leadership

of the PR of China had thus remained in the hands of the *civil-war generation* for the time being. Not a single full member of the new CC came from the Red Guards, and only four of the 109 candidate members had connections with Red Guard units.[40]

7. The 'Cultural Revolution' brought about the most striking change in the *occupational backgrounds* of the members of this CC. Eighty-five (exactly 50 per cent) of the members of the Ninth CC were leading cadres who came from the PLA and possessed a military rank between 1955 and 1965, sixty of them field commanders and twenty-five political commissars. In 1949, 41·9 per cent of the members of the Seventh CC had been military men, and in the Eighth CC this percentage amounted to 40·3 per cent. If one compares this increase with the remaining two pillars of the 'revolutionary trinity' which had been proclaimed in March 1967, then one reaches the conclusion that the percentage of 'revolutionary cadres' from the Party apparatus, state administration and culture decreased from 58·1 per cent in the Seventh and 59·7 per cent in the Eighth to 31·1 per cent in the Ninth CC. For the first time in April 1969, 17·7 per cent of the full members of the CC came from the mass organisations. However, most of the thirty representatives of the mass organisations in the Ninth CC had not made their reputations in the 'Cultural Revolution', but had already distinguished themselves in the middle 1950s as 'labour heroes' or 'model peasants'. They must be regarded as members of the pre-Cultural Revolutionary' élite. What was new was that they were allowed access to the CC.

8. Finally, the *spheres of activity* of the full members of the CC underwent considerable changes. At the end of 1949 strong minorities of 44·2 per cent and 39·6 per cent in the Seventh CC were occupied in the regional organs and in the military machine. In the Eighth CC of 1956 regional organs constituted only 13·4 per cent and the military machine 23·7 per cent. In 1969 this trend towards centralisation and towards the dominance of the influence of the civilian Party machine was reversed. In the Ninth CC 58·6 per cent of the full members represented the military and civilian Party machines in the regions, but only 41·4 per cent represented the central machines of the PLA, the Party and state administration. While the percentage which the central and regional civilian machines represented had decreased from 76·3 per cent in the Eighth to 52·5 per cent in the Ninth CC, that of the military machines at all levels increased from 23·7 per cent to 47·5 per cent. The twofold process which militarised and regionalised the leadership group, the result of the 'Cultural Revolution', may be made even clearer through another comparison. While the percentage of members from the central civilian machine had decreased from 67 per cent in the Eighth CC to 30·4 per cent in the Ninth, that of members from the

regional military machines had increased in the same period from 4·1 per cent to 26·6 per cent.

The 'Cultural Revolution' did not bring about decisive changes either in respect of the regional origins of the leadership group or in respect of its age structure. There was no substantial generational change. The most noticeable changes may be characterised as the decrease in university graduates in favour of the military academy graduates, the diminishing percentage of those members of the leadership group who had had foreign experience, the reinforcement of the influence of the top-level regional functionaries and, particularly, the fact that half of the CC was taken up by members of the PLA.

This tendency was emphasised even more in the *new Politburo of the Ninth CC*. Apart from the members of the old Politburo who were not re-elected to the CC, Li Fu-ch'un, Ch'en Yün as well as Marshals Ch'en Yi, Nieh Jung-chen and Hsü Hsiang-ch'ien also disappeared from the highest decision-making body of the CCP. They were mostly replaced by leading members of the military machine. The new Politburo comprised twenty-one full members and four alternate members:[41]

1. *Mao Tse-tung* (78), Chairman of the CC, member of the Politburo since 1935.

2. *Marshal Lin Piao* (64), Vice-Chairman of the CC, acting Chairman of the Military Commission of the CC, Vice-Premier and Minister of Defence, member of the Politburo since 1935 (died after his purge in winter 1971–2).

3. *Chou En-lai* (73), Prime Minister, member of the Standing Committee of the Politburo, member of the Politburo since 1927.

4. *Ch'en Po-ta* (67), chairman of the CRG, member of the Standing Committee, alternate member of the Politburo since 1956, full member of the Politburo since 1966 (purged in winter 1970–1).

5. *K'ang Sheng* (68), adviser to the CRG, member of the Standing Committee of the Politburo, member of the Politburo 1945–56 and since 1966, alternate member of the Politburo 1956–66.

6. *Chang Ch'un-ch'iao* (62), member, of the CRG, chairman of the RC of the city of Shanghai, First Secretary of the Municipal Committee of the CCP in Shanghai since January 10, 1971; newly elected.

7. *General Ch'en Hsi-lien* (58), supreme commander of the Shenyang military region, chairman of the RC of Liaoning, First Secretary of the Provincial Committee of the CCP of Liaoning since January 13, 1971; newly elected.

8. *Madame Chiang Ch'ing* (57), vice-chairman of the CRG, Mao Tse-tung's wife; newly elected.

9. *General Ch'iu Hui-tso* (63), Director of the General Logistics Department of the PLA; newly elected (purged in autumn 1971).

10. *Marshal Chu Te* (85), Chairman of the Standing Committee of the NPC, member of the Politburo since 1935.

11. *General Hsieh Fu-chih* (74), Vice Premier, Minister of Public Security, Chairman of the RC of the city of Peking, First Secretary of the Municipal Committee of the CCP in Peking since March 15, 1971, alternate member of the Politburo since 1966 (died March 1972).

12. *General Hsü Shih-yu* (65), supreme commander of the Nanking military region, Vice-Minister of Defence, Vice Chairman of the RC of Kiangsu, First Secretary of the Provincial Committee of the CCP of Kiangsu; newly elected.

13. *General Huang Yung-sheng* (63), Chief of the General Staff of the PLA; newly elected (purged in autumn 1971).

14. *Li Hsien-nien* (66), Vice-Premier and Minister of Finance, member of the Politburo since 1956.

15. *Admiral Li Tso-p'eng* (57), First Political Commissar of the PLA navy; newly elected (purged in autumn 1971).

16. *Marshal Liu Po-ch'eng* (79), Vice-Chairman of the Standing Committee of the NPC and of the Military Commission of the CC, member of the Politburo since 1945.

17. *Tung Pi-wu* (85), Vice-Chairman of the PR of China, member of the Politburo since 1945.

18. *General Wu Fa-hsien* (57), supreme commander of the PLA Air Force; newly elected (purged in autumn 1971).

19. *Yao Wen-yüan* (50), member of the CRG, Vice-Chairman of the RC of Kiangsu, Second Secretary of the Municipal Committee of the CCP in Shanghai since January 10, 1971; newly elected.

20. *Marshal Yeh Chien-ying* (72), Vice-Chairman of the Military Commission of the CC, Director of the Training Section of the PLA, member of the Politburo since 1966.

21. *Madame Yeh Ch'ün* (55), Lin Piao's wife and head of the latter's personal bureau; newly elected (purged in autumn 1971).

Alternate members of the Politburo:

1. *Chi Teng-k'uei* (?), Vice-Chairman of the RC of Honan, Secretary of the Provincial Committee of the CCP in Honan since March 8, 1971; newly elected.

2. *Li Hsüeh-feng* (64), Chairman of the RC of Hopei; newly elected (purged in winter 1969–70).

3. *General Li Te-sheng* (62), Director of the General Political Department of the PLA, Chairman of the RC of Anhui, First Secretary of the Provincial Committee of the CCP in Anhui since January 21, 1971; newly elected.

4. *General Wang Tung-hsing* (?), Commander of the Peking Guard Regiment, Director of the General Office of the CC; newly elected.

The average age of the twenty-three full and candidate members of the Politburo whose ages are known came to 64·5 years. Thus it becomes even more evident than in the case of the CC that a genuine rejuvenation of the leadership group was not achieved in the 'Cultural Revolution'.

Nineteen of the twenty-one full and candidate members for whom data concerning their membership of the CCP are available had already joined the Party before the end of the 'Long March'. Only Chiang Ch'ing and Mao's son-in-law, Yao Wen-yüan, had joined the Party after 1937.

If we include Lin Piao's wife, Yeh Ch'ün, in the PLA fold, which seems appropriate if her then position in the former's headquarters is considered, then fourteen out of the twenty-five (twelve full and two alternate members) belonged to the military, while eleven (nine full and two alternate members) may be described as civilian Party cadres.

Nine full members and one alternate member worked in the civilian machines of the Centre, eight full members in the military machine of the Centre, two full members in the military machines of the regions, and one candidate member had a position in the military machine of the Centre as well as in the regional civil and military machine of Anhui province.

Through investigating the organisational connections and political attitudes of the full and candidate members of the Politburo which became known from the crisis of the 'Cultural Revolution', five groups may be distinguished, as of summer 1969:

1. The Maoist Left which was represented by the CRG up to the end of 1969, comprising Mao himself, Ch'en Po-ta, K'ang Sheng, Chiang Ch'ing, Chang Ch'un-ch'iao, Yao Wen-yüan and the alternate member Chi Teng-k'uei. Hsieh Fu-chih had also moved to this group, especially with his speech of October 26, 1967.

2. The state administration group, comprising Chou En-lai, Li Hsien-nien and probably Tung Pi-wu.

3. The central military machine group, comprising Lin Piao, Huang Yung-sheng, Ch'iu Hui-tso, Li Tso-p'eng, Wu Fa-hsien, Yeh Chien-ying, Mme. Yeh Ch'ün, alternate member Li Te-sheng and possibly Wang Tung-hsing.

4. The regional commanders group, comprising Hsü Shih-yu, and Ch'en Hsi-lien, to whom Huang Yung-sheng and Li Te-sheng may also be added because of the former's close links with the Canton military area and the latter's continued activities in Anhui.

5. A group of Party veterans who appear in public only infrequently, and who probably do not take any real part in decision-making any longer. Chu Te and Liu Po-ch'eng, possibly also Tung Pi-wu belong to this group.

The leadership of the PR of China immediately after the 'Cultural Revolution' thus showed itself as a combination of the Maoist Left, the remnants of the old state apparatus around Chou En-lai, the central military machine and the regional commanders. The position of the Left within this set-up became steadily weaker soon after the Ninth Party Congress because it had been deprived of its organisational basis through the Red Guard movement. Ch'en Po-ta no longer appeared in public after July 31, 1970,[42] and must certainly be regarded as 'purged'. Since spring 1971 he has been called a 'pseudo-Marxist political swindle of the type of Liu Shao-ch'i'.

By contrast the position of the military became even stronger at first. Up to summer 1971 the central military apparatus, the regional commanders, and the representatives of the state and economic administration could establish a majority of twelve to at most seven votes. However, this *coalition for stabilisation*, which, with regard to its functional interests and its behaviour during the 'Cultural Revolution' as well, was interested in pragmatic policy decisions and in the consolidation of government, was soon, in the summer of 1971, to be subjected to stresses from which it collapsed – earlier than all observers had anticipated. With the fall of Lin Piao and his closest followers in the central military machine, the latter no longer remains part of the leadership group. Thus the Peking coalition now appears as an alliance between the civil administrative apparatus and the regional commanders whose support has been secured by the fact that the Centre respects their interest in large parameters of autonomy.

The alliance of the military and the bureaucrats, before the Lin Piao crisis had nevertheless been capable of controlling the reconstruction of the Party organisation. Above all the process of establishing the new provincial Party Committees since the end of 1970 has made it clear that the 'post-Cultural Revolutionary' CCP became the Party of the PLA to an even greater degree than had been visible in the results of the Ninth Party Congress.[42]

The reconstruction of the CCP, officially termed the 'Movement for the Rectification and Reconstruction of the Party' (*Cheng-tang chien-tang yün-tung*), has not yet come to an end. It thus appears to be too early to make any definite statements about this process. However, according to material available at the present, it may confidently be assumed that the PLA played a decisive role in establishing the new Party committees at all levels. It still has to come to terms with the resistance of remnants of 'Revolutionary Rebel' organisations, particularly at the basic level, which have tried to preserve, at least on this level, the influence which they gained in the early phase of the 'Cultural Revolution' and have attempted to restrain the old cadres from joining the new leading organs. These attempts by the Left, however, have been unsuccessful in nearly all cases which have become known up to now.[44]

In summer 1969 the Party leadership propagated the principle that the reorganisation should be continued from the bottom to the top, meaning from the Party branches in the people's communes, factories, offices and city quarters to the county and provincial committees. But only slight progress had been made in the basic organisations before the first new county committee was established in Changte, Hunan, on November 18, 1969, and the movement was transferred to the level of counties and municipalities.[45] But even at this level the reconstruction of the Party organs made only slow progress. After one year, in mid-November 1970, only forty-five of the 2,185 counties had set up new Party committees. The Party leadership therefore felt obliged to accelerate the reconstruction by including the provincial level. On November 21, 1970, the first provincial Party congress held after the 'Cultural Revolution' was convened in Chang-sha, Hunan. As in all later cases there is no evidence that the delegates to this Congress had been elected. They formed the first new provincial Party committee on December 4.[46]

By August 19, 1971, the new leading regional organs of the CCP had already been built up in all twenty-nine provinces, autonomous regions and autonomous cities.[47] County committees existed at the same time in 401 local administrative areas.

Twenty-two of the twenty-nine first secretaries of the new provincial Committees were members of the PLA (thirteen military officers and nine political commissars) and seven of them are civilian Party cadres.

Their real decision-making bodies, the secretariats, comprised altogether 158 secretaries and vice-secretaries. Ninety-eight (62 per cent) of them were from the military (fifty-one military officers and thirty-two political commissars). Fifty-two (32.9 per cent) were civilian Party cadres, but only eight (5.1 per cent) were representatives of the mass organisations.

One of the governors who had been overthrown by the Left in spring 1967 rejoined the secretariat of his province.[48] Three former first secretaries of provincial Party committees, denounced as 'Party enemies' in 1967, reappeared – though, at first, in other provinces – as members of secretariats.[49] The new provincial committees of the CCP will, as the publications media emphasise,[50] 'take the leading role' in their provinces over and above the RCs. In reality, however, their secretaries are in nearly all cases also the heads of the RCs. In twenty-one administrative areas the chairman of the RC also became the first secretary. As for the remaining eight, it may be safely assumed that the newly appointed first secretaries have meanwhile also taken over the chairmanships of the RCs,[51] because the chairman of the latter have not appeared in public for a long time.

Up to now the names of ten of the eleven military area commanders have become known. Six of them function simultaneously as first secretaries and chairmen of the RCs in the most important province, economically and strategically speaking, of their respective areas.[52] Another two are members of the provincial secretariats.[53] In nearly all cases the commanders of the military districts belong to the secretariats. In six provinces they were appointed first secretaries, and in nine administrative areas the regional political commissars took over this position.

Thus at the provincial level the leading posts in the Party apparatus and state administration are, as a rule, in the hands of the regional commanders or their political commissars. The percentage of the PLA in the regional leading bodies is now even higher than in the period immediately following the civil war. At that time only 30·1 per cent of all members of the top-level group were from the military and among the Communists at this level only 36·4 per cent belonged to the PLA. Today they constitute more than a half. The consolidation of government after the 'Cultural Revolution' thus – in the provinces, at least – became the consolidation of the leading role of the military.

The purge of Lin Piao and of the other major leaders of the central military machine – Huang Yung-sheng, Ch'iu Hui-tso, Wu Fa-hsien, Li Tso-p'eng, and Yeh Ch'ün – after September 12, 1971, seems not to have enacted major changes in this respect. With this leadership crisis a new stage in the development of Chinese Communism has begun. New and comprehensive research is necessary to detect the dominating features of this stage and it seems too early so far to present any substantiated conclusions. Some observers have held that this crisis has again established the control of the "Party" over the army. But this appears to represent a much too formal and thus somewhat superficial analysis. One could only speak about the re-establishment of "Party" leadership over the military, if there really were a separate sub-system of the civilian Party machine, as had existed between 1953–4 and 1966. But at the regional level, leadership of the Party machine, even in 1972, remains almost identical with that of the PLA. Thus, exhortations to the military to "accept the leadership of the local and regional (ti-fang) Party committees", which dominated in the media between November 1971 and June 1972, for all practical purposes did not mean much more than a quest for the loyalty of the military rank-and-file to the regional military commanders. On the contrary, there are some indications that in the course of the Lin Piao crisis, the major regional military leaders were able to expand their autonomy further. If one considers their en-

hanced powers, there seems to be good reason for assuming that the
evolving political system might display rather strong regional over-
tones.

The Results of the 'Cultural Revolution'

One might try to adapt the Maoist formula of 'unity–struggle–unity'
to the course of events since the beginning of the 'Cultural Revolution'.
This would imply that the development of the crisis followed a pattern
anticipated by the 'augurs'.

If we proceed from such an assumption, then Mao and his followers
had consistently attained in the early phase of the movement the twin
goals of creating new revolutionary experiences in a generation which
had grown up after the Communist seizure of power and of effectively
loosening the torpid structures of the Party and state apparatus. The
Chairman had overcome revisionist and bureaucratic tendencies in the
Party with the help of the tool of youthful rebellion, had imbued the
political system with new revolutionary enthusiasm and thus had
elevated the political consciousness of the masses to a higher level.

A comparison of this theoretical argument with political reality
leads to a number of questions which result from doubts about the
assertions of 'syste-immanment' interpretation.

– Why had the army been entrusted with the restoration of peace and
order in most of the provinces immediately after the high tide of the
offensive of the Left, the 'storm in January' 1967?
– Why had the attempt been made in summer 1967 to supplant the
military leadership groups in the regions with a new offensive by the
Left?
– Why had this attempt been halted abruptly by the Centre after a
few weeks, if not for the reason that it had failed?
– Why were the very same military representatives who had been the
objectives of the Leftist attack shortly afterwards entrusted with the
reconstruction and leadership of the new power organs?
– Why were the delegates to the Ninth Party Congress nominated
by the regional leadership in nearly every place, and not elected by
the Party members?
– Why, finally, did the Red Guards, the vanguard of the 'Cultural
Revolution', become the objects of massive disciplining and even
persecution by the army after spring 1968?

If the pattern of 'unity–struggle–unity' were to be used as an
analytical approach, then one would have to accept that the original
unity had excluded the young 'rebels'. The 'contradiction' would have

existed not only between them and the 'revisionists' and Party bureau-crats, but also between the military and the civilian Party machine and finally between the 'rebels' and the PLA as well. As for the new 'unity', it would not only have excluded Mao's 'New Right' opponents, but also the most active forces of the Maoist movement of 1966-7. Indeed, it would be largely embodied by the military forces plus the old state bureaucrats.

The usefulness of Mao Tse-tung's theory of contradictions clearly lies in the fact that it offers the leadership the opportunity of rationalis-ing desirable political changes as necessities of historical development. This theory provides a clever and power-conscious leadership élite with a myth to legitimise its rule. However, it does not constitute the theoretical framework for understanding the crisis of 1965-9 in the PR of China. The actual contradiction developed between the theoreti-cal concept and reality. If the official programme of the 'Cultural Revolution', which had been derived from this concept, was not been expounded purely to decide a struggle over power and goals, then the outcome of the 'Cultural Revolution' must be regarded as a defeat for Mao. If its function was purely this, then one might talk of at least a partial success for the Party leader. In such a case the use of the theory of contradictions had resulted from an assessment of a situation which required the mobilisation of the masses to safeguard the rule of an alliance between the military and Mao's followers in the Party appara-tus. A misinterpretation of the primarily utilitarian nature of the theory of contradictions among the masses, whose emotions were not to be released but channelled into a predetermined course of struggle, must inevitably have led to the abandonment of the original programme by the Party leader.

The real results of the 'Cultural Revolution' can, rather, be measured against the explicit or undeniably implicit goals of the two subsystems of the Left of 1965-6 when they started their counter-attack on the 'New Right', the genuine Maoist forces under the guidance of the CRG on the one hand, and the military, particularly the members of the Fourth Field Army under Lin Piao, on the other hand. Both groups in the Leftist faction wanted to make changes in three areas jointly:

1. They attempted to interrupt the growing tendency towards a revision of the Maoist development concept of 1958. If we consider the content of Party propaganda since 1966, then this goal was achieved. The practical decisions of development policy since summer 1969, however, and even more so since 1971, lead to the conclusion that the essential results of Liu Shao-ch'i's 'readjustment' policy – the transfer of the 'production guarantee' to the 'production teams', the toleration of private plots for the peasants and a system of material incentives –

have been maintained or reintroduced, and recently are even being expanded.

2. They wished to suppress the intellectual opposition and to prevent the spread of nonconformist ideas. This has undoubtedly been achieved in the realms of art, literature and public discussion. However, it remains to be seen whether the consequent isolation of China, from the intellectual world and from its own intellectual history can be maintained for a long period. The new boom in publications since early 1972, at least, seems to suggest that even in this field, pre-'Cultural-Revolutionary' patterns might soon re-emerge.

3. In the realm of power politics, they planned to overthrow the majority of the civilian Party leadership, which, under the guidance of Liu Shao-ch'i, rejected Mao's policy of mass mobilisation or took at least a critical stance towards it. Here the Left gained its greatest success. Seven of the seventeen full members of the Politburo active in summer 1965,[55] and four of the six alternate members[56] were dismissed from their positions and denounced as 'Party enemies'. Another three full members rejoined the CC in 1969, but they were excluded from the Politburo.[57] In the Secretariat of the CC six of the ten members[58] and all three alternate members[59] were dismissed. Fifty-four out of ninety-seven full members of the CC[60] were affected by the purge; furthermore, four of the six first secretaries of the regional bureaux and twenty-three of the twenty-eight first secretaries of the provincial party committees were also affected. Three of them, however, were rehabilitated in spring 1971. In the Standing Committee of the NPC, twenty-one out of 115 members were purged, and the circumstances of another seventeen remain unclear. Finally, in the State Council, eight of the fifteen vice-premiers, the Secretary General and twenty of the forty-eight heads of the ministries and commissions were denounced as 'Party enemies'. Another four ministers have not appeared in public since 1965. By this purge Liu's faction had been eliminated from the process of political decision-making in the Centre.

The CRG under Ch'en Po-ta and Chiang Ch'ing certainly aimed at three other goals apart from these goals common to the whole of the faction:

1. In the field of cadre recruitment, they wanted to train 'revolutionary successors' whose experiences in the 'Cultural Revolution' corresponded to those of the old leadership group in the civil war. In the period May 1966 to August 1967 this appeared to be successful. But whereas the revolutionary experience of the 'Long March' generation ended in triumphant victory of 1949, that of the Red Guards and 'Revolutionary Rebels' ended in the liquidation of their organisations, in deportation to the villages only thinly disguised as *Hsia-fang*, and in

massive disciplining by the PLA and the workers' militia co-operating with the PLA.

2. In the realm of education (i.e. *integrative mobilisation*), they aimed at a fundamental 'educational revolution' in order to shorten study time drastically, to introduce manual labour as a means of education and to extend political education considerably.

The publication media of the PR of China reported spectacular successes in this sphere from time to time. However, a document published in summer 1970 which emphasised details – the minutes of a discussion on the 'educational revolution' in Shanghai on June 2, 1970[61] – paints a less optimistic picture. It makes it clear that the 'educational revolution' and its measures had been introduced into only nine of the forty-nine colleges in the city at that time; that workers were unwilling to co-operate and that the administration showed scarcely any interest in changing the education system. If the situation in Shanghai three and a half years after the 'storm in January' presented itself in such a way what must it be like in provinces where the influence of genuine Maoist Leftists had been considerably weaker from the beginning? By March 31, 1971, there were reports of success – in some cases too of failure – in the 'educational revolution' from no more than 187 rural people's communes. What is the situation in the 73,800 communes or so which up to then kept quiet and in which about 80 per cent of the population live? The over-all picture remains unclear. The price of transforming the educational system, a transformation which apparently did not entirely succeed, has been the loss of four years of university education.

3. They wanted to rejuvenate substantially the central leadership group. The Party leader himself was not to be affected by that. Without the shadow of a doubt this has not been achieved.[62]

The specific goals of Lin Piao and the other generals in the Fourth Field Army system find scarcely any expression in documents. However, four goals have been clearly discernible from the behaviour of this group:

1. Lin Piao was to replace Liu Shao-ch'i as the number two and heir presumptive. This goal was temporarily achieved.

2. They wanted to enlarge the number of members of the Fourth Field Army in the leading organs of the PLA in the Centre and in the regions. This process had started as early as 1959; however, it was speeded up in the 'Cultural Revolution' when they took over the posts of Chief of the General Staff and of supreme commanders of the military regions of Chengtu and Sinkiang. But it was halted again after the fall of Lin Piao, and it seems that the members of the Second, Third and North China Field Armies have recently come to the fore again more strongly.

3. The system of state security organs was to be placed under the control of the PLA. Complete success was achieved, here, on the provincial level.

4. Those cadres in the military regions and districts who had their bases in the civilian Party machine were to be excluded from the political apparatus of the PLA and replaced by personnel who had grown up in the political apparatus of the military itself or in commanding troops.

In 1965 forty-one of the fifty-three political commissars in the military areas and districts had been 'civilians' in this sense. In 1970 thirty-six of the forty-three political commissars at these levels who had been indentified by then belonged to the PLA. The military thus achieved another success in this sphere.

This summary leads to the conclusion that the goals of the 'Cultural Revolution' had been achieved at least in part in two of the three spheres in which the two subsystems of the Leftist faction of 1965-6 had been in agreement. The military subsystem completely accomplished its objectives. However, the Maoist Left under the leadership of the CRG party failed in realising its specific conceptions of the future and achieved only ambiguous results. Thus it appears as if the counter-offensive of Mao's faction in the 'Cultural Revolution' failed in its programmatic aspects, but was more successful in the aspects related to power politics.

But the internal crisis brought further results which could hardly have been intended by the initiators of the 'Cultural Revolution' and even less by the Party leader himself. This is particularly the case with regard to the undoubted transfer of essential decision-making authority in the provinces into the hands of the military, the growth of the influence of the regional leadership groups in the top-level bodies of the CCP and the remarkable extension of the economic and administrative autonomy of the regions in which the regional commanders represent the decisive political force. Finally, it is of long-term relevance that the younger generation, particularly young intellectuals, have, in the early phase of the crisis, had the experience of being able to organise themselves outside the Party structures and official professional organisations. However, this was only valid before the army intervened in the crisis. And so this young generation learned yet another lesson: the organised rebellion of youth against the Party apparatus and their innovatory enthusiasm had been manipulated by the guiding élite of the Leftist faction under Mao and Lin Piao as a tool in the struggle for power in the Party and State. When this enthusiasm threatened to free itself from the control of the leadership élite, the army successfully turned against the Red Guards and 'Revolutionary Rebels' by using force. Neither the Party leader nor even the CRG wished – or were able – to help the rebellious youth which had come under military pressure. Considering these experiences it seems more than doubtful whether this generation will once more be ready to stand up for Mao and his vision of China's development with the same zeal as in 1966-7.

The fall of Lin Piao in autumn 1971 made it still clearer to the 'Cultural Revolution' generation that even the most intensive support for the Chairman is no safeguard against a purge if the bureaucracy and regional commanders work together. The new leadership crisis, which has not yet ended, produced an interim administration in the Centre under the guidance of Chou En-lai. It thus appears as if the final phase of the Chinese gerontocracy will be determined by the prototype of an educated bureaucrat – indeed an unexpected result of the 'Cultural Revolution'!

If these considerations constitute a correct assessment of the political reality – the results since autumn 1967 seem to confirm this – then the end of the 'Cultural Revolution' also designates, in spite of Mao's victory over Liu and the 'New Right', and in spite of the extreme veneration accorded to him in the media of the PR of China, the end of the phase in which the word of the leader of the CCP authoritatively determined the politics of China, that is, the era of Mao Tse-tung.

References

1 Cf. also Oskar Weggel, *Die chinesischen Revolutionskomitees oder der Versuch, die Grosse Kulturrevolution durch Parzellierung zu retten (Stand 1. Juli 1968)*, Hamburg, 1968, *passim*; Oskar Weggel, 'Die Partei als Widersacher der Revolutionskomitees – (Siegt Lenin oder Rosa Luxemburg in China?', *Mitteilungen des Instituts für Asienkunde, Hamburg*, No. 34, Hamburg, 1970; Domes, *CQ, loc. cit.*, also the case studies in Falkenheim, *loc. cit.*, also Domes, *Generals II, loc. cit.*, pp. 139-44.
2 See above, p. 180.
3 Among others, People's Radio Shanghai, March 23, 1967.
4 *JMJP*, March 23, 1971.
5 *NCNA*, Peking, August 13, 1967.
6 *JMJP*, November 2, 1967.
7 *NCNA*, Peking, December 6, 1967.
8 *JMJP* and *NCNA*, Peking, January 1, 1968.
9 *JMJP* and *NCNA*, Peking, September 6, 1968; cf, Domes, *CQ, loc. cit.*, pp. 114-15.
10 See above, pp. 193-4.
11 Domes, *CQ, loc. cit.*, pp. 143-4.
12 Cf. Domes, *Generals II, loc. cit.*, pp. 139-43.
13 Cf. Domes, *CQ, loc. cit.*, p. 142.

14 *Ibid.*, p, 143.
15 In Kweichou and Shansi.
16 *Ibid.*, p. 144.
17 Hunan and Yünnan.
18 Shantung and Shansi.
19 Kweichou.
20 Cf. Dieter Heinzig, *Die Krise der Kommunistischen Partei Chinas in der Kultur-revolution*, Mitteilungen des Instituts für Asien-kunde Hamburg, No. 7, Hamburg, 1969, p. 41 *et seq.*
21 *Wen-ko t'ung-hsün*, Canton, December 11, 1967, English translation in *SCMP*, No. 4097, January 11, 1968; cf. von Groeling, *Widerstand, op. cit.*, pp. 609–21.
22 Document *Chung-fa* (67), No. 358, in *URI, Documents, op. cit.*, pp. 609–21.
23 'Communiqué of the Twelfth Enlarged Plenum of the Eighth CC of the CCP, October 31, 1968', in *JMJP*, November 2, 1968.
24 *Hung-ch'i t'ung-hsün (Bulletin of the Red Flag)*, Canton, No. 10, January 25, 1969; *Wen-ko t'ung-hsün*, No. 12, February 1968; also People's Radio Inner Mongolia, November 20, 1968.
    The Draft Constitution of the CCP was first published by the Nationalist Information Service, in *FCYC*, Vol. III, No. 1, January 1969, pp. 150–2. This text corresponds, apart from a few minor points, with the Constitution passed by the Ninth Party Congress.
25 Chekiang, Kweichou, Hunan, Hupei, Honan, Kwangtung, Szechwan and Yünnan. Cf. *CNA*, No. 746, February 28, 1969.
26 Hunan, cf. *CNA, ibid.*
27 *JMJP*, April 2, 1969, English translation, in *Peking Review*, No. 14, April 4, 1969.
28 This conclusion is the result of a careful analysis of the film produced by the CCP at the Ninth Party Congress.
29 *JMJP*, April 2, 1969.
30 Speech of Mao Tse-tung at the opening of the Ninth Party Congress, in *Internationales Asienforum*, München, No. 3, July 1970, pp. 444–5.
31 Cf. von Groeling, *Widerstand, op. cit.*, pp. 229–34; also Jürgen Domes, *Chinas spätmaoistische Führungsgruppe – Die sozio-politische Struktur des IX. Zentralkomitees der Kommunistischen Partei China*, in *Politische Viertel-Jahres-schrift*, Köln-Opladen, No. 213, September 1969, (hereafter cited as Domes, *PVS*), p. 191.
32 *JMJP*, April 15, 1969, English translation in *Peking Review*, No. 16, April 18, 1969
33 *JMJP*, April 25, 1969, English translation in *Peking Review*, No. 18, April 30, 1969, pp. 44–7.
34 *JMJP*, April 27, 1969.
35 English translation in Supplement of *Peking Review*, April 28, 1969.
36 English text of the Party constitution in *NCNA*, London, No. 4102, April 29, 1969; cf. Heinzig, *Krise, op. cit.*, pp. 45–8; Erik von Groeling, *Innenpolitik und Organisation im kommunistischen China*, Hanover, 1971, pp. 85–126; von Groeling, *Widerstand, op. cit.*, pp. 230–3.
37 Cf. Domes, *PVS, loc. cit.*, pp. 195–214; Domes, 'The Ninth CCP Central

Committee in Statistical Perspective', in *CS*, Vol. IX, No. 2, February 7, 1971, pp. 5-14 (a revised version of the *PVS* study based on more recent data); Donald B. Klein, Lois B. Hager, *The Ninth Central Committee*, in *CQ*, No. 45, January–March 1971, pp. 37-56; also von Groeling, *Innenpolitik, op. cit.*, pp. 91-114.

38 People's Radio Kwangsi, April 15, 1969.

39 The biographical data of this analysis is given in particular in the following source materials:

Union Research Institute, *Who's Who in Communist China*, Vols. I and II, Hong Kong, 1969 and 1970;

Ministry of Defence of the Republic of China, *Fei-tang cheng-kan-pu jen-shih tzu-liao hui-Pien* (*Collection of Materials on Personnel Matters of the Political Cadres of the Rebel Party*), Taipei, 1966;

Institute for International Affairs, Republic of China, *Chung-kung jen-ming lu* (*Data on Chinese Communist Personalities*), Taipei, 1968;

Huang Chen-hsia, *Chung-kung chün-jen chih* (*Mao's Generals*), Hong Kong, 1968;

Howard L. Boorman (ed.), *Biographic Dictionary of Republican China*, Vols. I and II, New York and London, 1967 and 1969;

K'an Yin-lan, *Chung-kung jen-wu su-miao* (*Chinese Communist Personnel*) Hong Kong, 1954;

Chao Kuan-yi and Wei Tan-po, *Mao Tse-tung chih chu-t'uan* (*Mao Tse-tung's Leadership Corps*), Hong Kong, 1951;

Issues of the *Biographical Service* of the Union Research Institute, Hong Kong, since June 1967; also data collections of the author from newspapers and journals of the Chinese People's Republic, Hong Kong, Taiwan, the Soviet Union, and Western countries.

40 Miss Nieh Yüan-tzu, Ch'en Kan-fêng, Lung Kuang-ch'ien, and Ta Lo.

41 The media of the Chinese People's Republic list the names of the Politburo members, apart from the members of the Standing Committees, according to order of strokes in the ideograms. They are therefore listed in alphabetical order beginning with position six. The age of the members is given as at December 31, 1971.

42 *JMJP*, March 17 and July 31, 1970.

43 Cf. Erik von Groeling, 'Die Volksrepublik China nach dem IX. Parteitag: Einheit oder Dissens?', Berichte des Bundesinstituts für Ostwissen-schaftliche und Internationale Studien, No. 60, 1970, Köln, 1970; von Groeling, *Chinas Generale und ihre Politik*, Manuscript, Köln, 1971, pp. 6-61.

44 Cf. von Groeling, *Die Volksrepublik . . ., op. cit.*, pp. 18-24.

45 People's Radio Hunan, December 2, 1969.

46 *NCNA*, Peking, December 13, 1970.

47 Hunan (see above), Kiangsi, Kiangsu, and Kwangtung (*NCNA*, Peking, December 31, 1970), Shanghai (*NCNA*, Peking, January 14, 1971), Liaoning (*NCNA*, Shenyang, Jan. 16, 1971), Anhui (*NCNA*, Peking, Jan. 21, 1971), Chekiang (*NCNA*, Peking, Jan. 30, 1971), Kuangsi (*NCNA*, Peking, Febr. 20, 1971), Kansu (*NCNA*, Peking, Febr. 21, 1971), Shensi (*NCNA*, Sian, March 8, 1971), Honan (*NCNA*, Peking, March 11, 1971), Tsinghai (*NCNA*, Peking, March 13, 1971), Peking (Radio Peking, German Language Service, March 21,

1971), Kirin (People's Radio Peking, March 30, 1971), Hupei (People's Radio Peking, April 1, 1971), Fukien (*NCNA*, Peking, April 6, 1971), Shantung (*NCNA*, Chinan, April 8, 1971), Shansi (*NCNA* T'aiyüan, April 16, 1971), Sinkiang and Kueichou (Central People's Radio Peking, May 17, 1971), Hopei (*NCNA*, Peking, May 24, 1971), Tientsin (*NCNA*, Peking, May 30, 1971), Yünnan (*NCNA*, Peking, June 9, 1971), Tibet, Szechwan, Ninghsia, Heilungkiang (*NCNA*, Peking, August 21, 1971).

48 Pai Ju-ping (Shantung).

49 T'an Ch'i-lung (Shantung) in Fukien, Chang P'ing-hua (Hunan) in Shansi, and Chao Tzu-yang (Kuangtung) in Inner Mongolia.

50 Among others, Central People's Radio Peking, May 19, 1970.

51 Shantung (Yang Te-chih), Shansi (Hsieh Chen-hua), Kweichou (Lan I-nung) Inner Mongolia (Yu T'ai-chung), Hopei (Liu Tzu-hou), Yünnan (Chou Hsing Tibet (Jen Jung), Heilungkiang (Wang Chia-tao).

52 Ch'en Hsi-lien (Shenyang) in Liaoning, Yang Te-chih (Chinan) in Shantung, Hsü Shih-yu (Nanking) in Kiangsu, Tseng Ssu-yü (Wuhan) in Hupei, Han Hsien-ch'u (Fuchou) in Fukien, and Lung Shu-chin in Sinkiang.

53 Ting Sheng (Canton) in Kuangtung, P'i Ting-chün (Lanchou) in Kansu, Wang Pi-ch'eng (K'unming) in Yünnan, Liang Hsing-ch'u (Ch'engtu) in Szechwan.

54 Cf. von Groeling, *Die Volksrepublik . . .*, op. cit., p. 6 a–b.

55 Liu Shao-ch'i, Teng Hsiao-p'ing, P'eng Chen, P'eng Te-huai, Ho Lung, Li Ching Ch'üan, and T'an Chen-lin.

56 Ulanfu, Chang Wen-t'ien, Lu Ting-i, and Po I-po.

57 Ch'en Yün, Ch'en Yi, and Li Fu-ch'un.

58 Teng Hsiao-p'ing, P'eng Chen, Wang Chia-hsiang, T'an Chen-lin, Lu Ting-i, and Lo Jui-ch'ing.

59 Liu Lan-tao, Yang Shih-k'un, and Hu Ch'iao-mu.

60 Liu Shao-ch'i, Teng Hsiao-p'ing, Lu Ting-i, Lo Jui-ch'ing, P'eng Te-huai, Liao Ch'eng-shih, Lin Feng, P'eng Chen, Ulanfu, Huang K'o-ch'eng, T'an Cheng, Ho Lung, Yang Shang-k'un, Sun Jen-ch'iung, Liu Hsiao, Li Wei-han, Wang Chia-hsiang, Liu Lan-t'ao, Liu Ning-i, Po I-po, Hu Ch'iao mu, Yang Hsiu-feng, Shu T'ung, Chang Chi-ch'un, Ch'eng Tzu-hua, Wu Hsiu-ch'üan, Hsiao K'o, Ch'ien Ying, Wang Ts'ung-wu, Ma Ming-fang, Chang Wen-t'ien, T'an Chen-lin, Ch'en Shao-min, Li Pao-hua, Hsü Kuang-ta, Lin T'ieh, Cheng Wei-san, Hsiao Hua, Hu Yao-pang, Ouyang Ch'in, Hsi Chung-hsün, An Tzu-wen, Chia T'o-fu, Li Li-san, Li Ching-ch'üan, Wu Chih-'pu, Lü Cheng-ts'ao, T'ao Chu, Ch'en Shao-yü, Yang Hsien-chen, Lo Kuei-p'o, Chang Ching-wu, Yeh Fei.

61 *HC*, No. 7, 1970, also *WHP*, Hong Kong, July 24, 1970.

62 See above, pp. 207–8.

XV. Achievements and Perspectives

An attempt to evaluate the internal political developments in the first two decades of Communist rule in China should be made with respect to three aspects:

1. An analysis of the substance of the discernible phases in this development and of the turning-points which will influence the future.

2. An evaluation of the efficiency of the system's development policy as far as the latter can be qualitatively and quantitavely analysed and measured.

3. An investigation into the internal constitution of the determining agents of rule whose influence on the legitimising ideology as an instrument of rule has to be discussed as well as the change in their respective relationships.

Apart from the medium-range perspectives which have to be outlined alternatively in accordance with this approach, consideration must be given to the fundaentmal question of what role may be attributed to the Communist movement in the Chinese modernisation process – i.e. the Chinese Revolution.

Phases and Turning-points in the Development of Internal Politics since 1949

The development of internal politics in the PR of China shows eight phases with specifically differing criteria.

The *first phase* started with the establishment of complete military control by the Communists over the Chinese mainland in winter 1949–50, evolving fully in the early summer of 1950 with the initiation of the land reform and marriage reform movements and ending in autumn 1953 with the proclamation of the 'transition to socialism' by the Party leadership. In the cities it was determined by a policy of co-operation with private enterprise which was brought about by the necessity of reconstructing the national economy damaged in the civil war. In the villages it introduced revolutionary changes in ownership relations, and in the whole country there was established an effective system of control supported by massive psychological and physical terror. There can thus be recognised, side by side, methods of rule

226

resembling those of the period of war Communism in the Soviet Union and measures which showed many factors common to decisions made in the period of the 'New Economic Policy'. This dichotomy in the reality of rule was bridged by the theory of overcoming 'semi-feudalism' and achieving individual ownership in the 'national bourgeois-democratic' stage of revolution.

In the *second phase*, from autumn 1953 to the beginning of 1956, this dichotomy was actually overcome. The complementary processes of agrarian collectivisation, the nationalisation of private enterprise, the transfer of trade and handicraft to co-operative ownership and the disciplining of those technological and intellectual élites trained before the Communist take-over, were to create the preconditions for building a socialist social order. But the remarkable socio-economic achievements of this policy of transition were not matched in the realm of 're-educating' the élites.

The perception of this fact caused the leadership to initiate the *third phase* early in 1956. Although attempts to adjust the diverse branches of the economy to the conditions prevailing in a socialist social order were successfully continued up to the middle of 1957, political pressure on large sections of the populace had, at the same time, been diminishing. A system of 'socialist legality' was tested and the parameters of intellectual differentiation were extended. However, this led to the manifestation of an opposition critical of the system, the size and intensity of which Mao had not anticipated, necessitating a decisive change of course since it increasingly jeopardised the political system.

This change of course represents the first marked turning-point in the exercise of Communist rule in China. In summer 1957 it initiated the *fourth phase*: a renewed stiffening of the control structures, extensive campaigns aimed at the total collectivisation of life, and an experiment in implementing a labour-intensive concept of development. By the end of 1968 the dissociation from the Soviet concept of economic and social development had thus been completed. But the maximally fixed rates of accumulation demanded sacrifices from the peasant masses which lowered the standard of living to the bare minimum. Thus the decline in labour productivity ultimately neutralised the temporary acceleration in growth, and at the same time disseminated passive resistance among the people, which had become the object of mobilisation, threatening to erode the system of Party control. In order to curb this development the majority of the leadership in the civilian Party machine began to correct Mao's concept of development without the decisive participation of the Chairman.

In the *fifth phase*, from the turn of 1958-9 to autumn 1962, these corrections were intensified through a gradual process of reintroducing economic criteria in decisions concerning economic policy, lowering the level of collectivisation and reducing the demands made on the population. The result was a new development concept which, being a coherent alternative to the Maoist programme, offered the ruling élite new options and thereby led to factional struggle.

In the *sixth phase*, from autumn 1962 to autumn 1965, the conflict between the factions still took place as a struggle behind the scenes over power and political direction. It found its particular expression in the controversial objectives in view and in the methods proposed for the 'Socialist Education Movement' as well as in the formulation of opposing political programmes and behavioural norms within the increasingly competitive machines of the civilian Party organisation and the PLA.

When the majority of the Party leadership disobeyed the Chairman in autumn 1965 the *seventh phase* set in with an actual split in the leadership and the open struggle over power and policies. The Leftist faction under Mao and Lin Piao not only attempted to return to the development concept of 1958, but also undertook an experiment in mobilising and organising the young generation outside the control structures of the Party and in shattering the system of the civilian Party machine with its help. However, this attempt at directly revolution-ising consciousness failed because of the resistance of large groups of the population and the realisation by the military leaders – among whom the regional commanders gained more and more influence – that a continuation of the policy of the 'Cultural Revolution' might lead to civil war and thereby the collapse of the political system.

Thus the provisional take-over of the most important government functions of the PLA from January 1967 eventually ushered in the *eighth phase* which ended with the demise of Lin Piao. The protracted but largely successful attempts over nearly two years to stabilise the governmental order have been combined with the renunciation of mass mobilisation against the Party which was initially successful; since summer 1970 the return to the development concept of the 'readjust-ment' policy of 1958–9 to 1962 has become steadily more evident.

Thus the decisive turning-points in Chinese internal politics have been marked by the years 1957–8 and 1965–6. Under the direct influence of Mao Tse-tung there were attempts to introduce a new concept of development and a transformation of the government struc-tures established during the early 'fifties. Both attempts failed from the standpoint of the original Maoist intention. In both cases they grew until they threatened Communist rule, thus necessitating substantial corrections to the socio-economic course at the end of 1958, and, from spring 1967, the incorporation of the military into the political decision-making process.

The initiation of the 'readjustment' policy transformed the essential nature of the *Chinese development concept* from a *voluntarist experiment* by Mao Tse-tung into one of *pragmatic improvisation* which had been developed by the opponents of the Party leader in the camp of the 'New Right'. In the realm of the *political system* the events of the 'Cultural Revolution' brought about the turn which changed the Maoist experiment in transformation into pragmatic measures of improvisation aimed at the preservation of rule and order. But the necessary use of the PLA as a dominant political force introduced the army as an additional authoritative leadership élite which, on the level of the provinces, seems to have turned the Party into a tool of military rule.

The 'Balance Sheet' of the Development Policy[1]

Development policy embraces the total of the developmental measures taken by the leadership in an underdeveloped country that has entered upon the process of socio-economic modernisation. These measures serve to improve the health service, the education of political, scientific and technical cadre élites, to guarantee the basic food supply for the whole population, the construction of an industrial and technological basis for the national economy and the intensification of external economic relations. The concepts on which the development policy is based are themselves oriented without exception towards the enhancement of the standard of living by the expansion of production and the exchange of commodities as well as by the strengthening of the infrastructure in the spheres of education, health and transport. Moreover they are determined by images of the future[2] to which the ruling élite itself feels committed or which it uses to legitimise its rule. In order to judge the success of such concepts, statements concerning quantitative results do not, by themselves, suffice. Rather one must ask to what extent a system led the society nearer to the realisation of the image of the future projected by this system. Such a 'system-immanent' analysis, however, reaches its limits at the point where a gap develops between the implementation of the image of the future and the quantitative efficiency of the system – i.e. its ability to enhance the living conditions of the population. If it is proven that the priorities determined by the image of the future obstruct material development rather than support it then the concept which defined such priorities lacks the capacity for developmental efficiency.

A balance sheet of development policy in the PR of China since 1949 should, therefore, be drawn up first according to the principles which have been establishing the norms of the vision of Communist ideology, the abolition of those structures which cause the self-alienation of man, the achievement of self-realisation by man, and the release of all available productive forces. The collectivisation of agriculture, trade and handicrafts and the nationalisation of the industrial means of production created the preconditions for building a socialist social order which theory called for, i.e. the gradual accomplishment of those principles mentioned. However, the assertion that the dependency of the peasants in the communes on the collective and on the demands of the state has become smaller than that of the poor peasant, tenant and rural worker on the landlord of former times has not yet been convincingly proved. The right of industrial workers to decide about their factories remained limited by the plan data for which the state set norms and by the production campaigns which the leadership initiated. Wherever the workers freely organised themselves – (particularly in spring 1967) – to expand this right of decision-making and to emphasise their demands for an improvement of labour and wage conditions, they were accused of 'economism' and disciplined with the help of the army. Even individual use of leisure time remains limited by the regulations established by the ruling élite in regard to the study of ideology at indoctrination meetings. The leadership assumed from the individual the right to decide which books he wants to read, which pictures he wants to see, which plays he wishes to watch, which music he wants to listen to and which dances he wants to dance. Chinese society is still far short of the implementation of the vision of Karl Marx.

The self-determination and self-realisation of this generation must remain subject to what the élite 'augurs' in the Party and army have defined as the happiness of future generations. Thus the question of the extent to which the people have internalised these claims of the leadership in 'revolutionary consciousness' becomes important. We lack sufficient material to provide a reliable answer. Reports from refugees driven out of the country by their discontent can provide only questionable evidence. The same applies to the stories of those visitors to China who were given the opportunity by the leadership to live for some time in carefully chosen and intensively prepared Chinese villages because they had previously shown their willingness to praise.[3] Considerable doubts about the extent to which the Communist vision has been internalised are raised by the fact that the mass movements of the CCP reached their preconceived goals less and less frequently after the mid-'fifties even as they were being pushed with greater and greater intensity and that the people used every opportunity – particularly in spring 1957, during the 'readjustment' phase, and in 1967 when the control structures collapsed – to evade the collective economy and the discipline imposed upon them by the ruling élite. These doubts have been reinforced by the widespread opposition to the mobilisation of labour in the production and reconstruction campaigns of 1958. If these campaigns had been the expression of spontaneity produced by the voluntary acceptance of the vision then they would not have been abruptly halted because of resistance to them. However, as there was an apparent lack of spontaneity, the mobilisation of the peasants for special performances which went unrewarded over and above their usual production duties represents the highest conceivable degree of alienation.

Nevertheless, the comprehensive restrictions which the political system imposed upon the populace might be justified by the necessity of modernising the largest and most highly populated developing country in the world if the quantitative balance of the development policy of the PR of China were to lead to results which would raise the country far above the level of other East and South-east Asian developing countries.

The achievements of the CCP in the realms of *education and the health service* are particularly notable. It successfully extended the number of pupils undergoing compulsory education to almost three-quarters of those within the relevant age brackets, and it increased the number of pupils and students in primary and secondary schools as well as in colleges to an even greater degree than had the KMT at the time of its greatest success in establishing an educational system.[4] Furthermore, it emphatically supported – especially during the 'Three Red Banners' period, and again after 1968, at least according to press reports – adult education so that the percentage of illiteracy among the population decreased considerably. The reduction of primary education from six to five years as well as of junior and senior secondary education from three to two years respectively, initiated in the later stages of the 'Cultural Revolution', is also aimed at a more rapid expansion of formal education.[5] However, the effect of these measures cannot yet be estimated, nor can that of closing down the universities for more than four years during the 'Cultural Revolution' crisis. Another question must also remain unanswered: will the emphasis on an education orientated to practice actually lead to the creation of a large stratum of workers and peasants with technical expertise? The extension of the public health service, energetically promoted since 1951 has, however, unquestionably produced considerable productive results. Even if the spread of epidemics, especially in the 'three bitter years' 1960 to 1962, and again at the high tide of the internal political crisis in 1967, could not be prevented, the general state of health of the population appears to be much better than before the CCP take-over.

The *communications network* in China has been remarkably improved since 1949. Although the 4,200 miles or so of new railway lines which have been built up to now constitute a little less than that in the period of KMT rule since 1928, nevertheless the extension of the whole railway network, most lines now being double-tracked, brought about an increase in track mileage from 14,750 miles in 1949 to 32,870 miles in 1963,[6] i.e. an increase of 123 per cent. Furthermore, there must be added more than 62,500 miles of new roads, almost half of which have a permanent surface. Thus the preconditions for the internal exchange of commodities and for the extremely important adjustment of food supplies between regions of agricultural surplus and deficit have been considerably improved.

In the realm of the *development of production* the picture is somewhat more ambiguous. The rapid reconstruction of 1949–52, which is among the most impressive developmental achievements carried out under Communist rule in China, was followed by a period of intensive expansion in industrial production and only slow expansion in agricultural production during the course of the first five-year plan, 1953 to 1957. The 'Great Leap Forward' led initially to further success, which surpassed even that of the first plan period, but then its effects led the country into a crisis in the realm of agriculture after 1959 and in industry since the end of 1960, and China's development suffered a set-back of several years. Only after the 'readjustment' policy which had been formulated from 1959 to 1962 had come into full effect did the recovery start. In 1965 most of the 1959 production levels had been reached again. These tendencies in development become even more evident when consideration is given to the annual growth rates of some important indicators which *Wu Yüan-li* calculated on the basis of numerous, varying production estimates:

Table XV/1

Annual Growth Rate of Important Economic Indicators in the People's Republic of China in Various Periods since 1952 (percentages)[7]

	1952–7	1957–60	1960–2	1962–5	1952–65
Coal	14·1	40·8	−14·8	6·25	12·7
Electricty	21·1	34·45	−20·1	10·1	14·1
Crude Oil	27·3	55·6	11·2	13·7	27·25
Crude Steel	24·3	51·1	−26·4	14·45	20·35
Cotton	5·7	5·9	−29·3	9·1	0·13
Grain (Official)	3·7	9·0	−3·0	4·8	2·0
(O. L. Dawson)	1·1	−2·8	6·0	2·35	0·75
Gross National Product	5·8	6·5	−5·2	7·2	4·45

For the period following 1966 there do not yet exist adequate data from which to draw substantiated conclusions. But one must proceed from the fact that the crisis of the 'Cultural Revolution' brought about a noticeable decrease in industrial production in the years 1967 and 1968 while hardly affecting food production.[8] But since the beginning of 1968 these losses have been made good so that in 1969 the economic levels of 1965 were regained and overtaken in 1970, levelling off again somewhat in 1971.

The development of the PR of China's *foreign trade*, for which reliable data is available, reflects the ups and downs for the over-all development of the economy since 1957 as the following table shows:

Table XV/2

The Foreign Trade of the People's Republic of China since 1957.
(US$1,000,000)[9]

	Total turnover	Exports	Imports
1957	4,025	1,595	1,430
1959	4,265	2,205	2,060
1962	2,675	1,525	1,150
1966	4,290	2,245	2,045
1968	3,620	1,860	1,760
1969	3,885	2,060	1,825
1970	4,246	2,063	2,183
1971	4,611	2,364	2,247

In 1971 the volume of foreign trade overtook the level of 1959 and 1965 so that over-all foreign trade, in absolute terms, has expanded by 8 per cent since 1959. But considering the simultaneous development of the rest of the world this means that the share of the PR of China in world trade decreased by about half from 1959 to 1971.

The calculative stagnation since 1959–60, which arose out of the severe set-back of the 'three bitter years' as a result of the 'Great Leap', and the gradual recovery of the national economy since 1962 is also evidence in the rare official and semi-official reports of the CCP leadership on grain production which many observers believe to be exaggerated. After the orginal data had been corrected it is said to have amounted to 250 million tons (metric) in 1958, 185 million tons in 1962, 200 million tons in 1964, 230 million tons in 1967 and finally 246 million tons in 1971.[10] If the tendency which may be discerned from these figures is correct then domestic production provides somewhat less grain than twelve years ago while there was a considerable population growth at the same time. This must be balanced by imports and agricultural side products.

The slowing down of China's economic development after the failure of the 'Great Leap' was a further impediment to the CCP in attaining the goals to which it had committed itself in 1957–8. In 1972 the *per capita* production of Great Britain in the most important heavy industrial products should have been 'caught up with and over-taken'. Even if one takes one of the lower estimates of the Chinese population of 725 million inhabitants, and accepts at face value the data on production yields which have been given recently by Chou En-lai and other Party leaders, British *per capita* production of coal surpasses the Chinese six times, that of steel and cement about fifteen times and that of electricity sixty-five times. In the realm of agricultural production the targets set for 1967 by the Twelve Year Programme for Agricultural Development had been reached in 1968 in only two of the twenty-nine administrative areas and in another three by 1970. Seven administrative areas reported that the plan targets had not been reached and fourteen made no report at all.[11]

The available data, furthermore, clearly show that the set-backs in economic development were the direct outcome of the 'Three Red Banners' campaigns and the 'Cultural Revolution' which Mao had initiated. The first campaign in particular had extraordinarily dis-advantageous consequences. By contrast the first five-year plan, orientated to the Soviet development concept, produced a strong, if lopsided, expansion in production, and the employment of the concept developed by Liu Shao-ch'i and his followers in the period of 'readjustment' facilitated the recovery from the crisis of 1960–2 as well as the expansion of the years 1969–71. The material achievements of the CCP's development policy are thus not the outcome of the application of the Maoist development concept.

These achievements derive an appropriate relevance with respect to an international comparison. If one compares the development of the gross national products of other Asian countries from 1953 to 1963 with that of China in the more favourable period of 1953 to 1965, one comes to the conclusion that the growth rates in the PR of China corresponded to those of Pakistan. They ranged *above* the growth rates of India, Indonesia and Ceylon, but *below* those of Burma, Malaysia, the Philippines, Thailand, South Korea and Taiwan.[12] Perkins states that the results for the period 1957 to 1969, with an annual growth rate of 3–3½ per cent in over-all economic production, which he calculated according to 'favourable estimates', are even less favourable for the PR of China. In this period many other Asian countries attained growth rates of between 7 per cent and 9 per cent. Even India ranges only slightly lower, with an annual average of 3·3 per cent since 1960.[13]

The expansion of the national economy thus remained rather limited on the whole. The gap in the standard of living between China and many of its neighbouring countries widened in the last decade to the clear disadvantage of China.

The respectable achievements in the realms of education and the health service, in developing the communications network as well as in modern nuclear technology are contrasted by progress in the normal economy which, when compared internationally, does not support the conviction that the high demands made on the people by the ruling élite have produced a development policy that is specifically efficient. Rather, it is due to these demands that the optimum rate of accumulation has not yet been reached. The argument frequently propounded that the sacrifices made by the Chinese people since the CCP takeover have benefited an unusually effective development policy appears to be untenable when considering the quantitative results.

Change in the Ruling Agencies

The question of whether the intervention of the army in the political decision-making process and the consolidation of the PLA in this function at the regional level have actually caused a change in the ruling agencies depends essentially on the extent to which the Party and the army may be identified with each other. In the period of the 'Long March' the Party and the army were almost identical. Solid arguments may be evoked to the effect that this close linkage continued during the armed struggle to seize power in the civil war and during the first years of establishing the new government order up to 1953-4. At that time the PLA exercised leadership and control functions in the regional administration. Nevertheless, we must acknowledge that since the *Cheng-feng* movement, if not earlier, a civilian Party machine had been developing which was clearly separated from the armed forces, and which came to a full organisational deployment in 1954. The Chinese Communist movement, being an élite of 'augurs' which acts according to the mandate of an irresistible historical process and being at the same time a military fighting unit, split into two specific systems of functionally determined machines.

The *Party* was led by a leadership group which for the most part sprang from the civilian machines and whose members exercised their functions predominantly in the Centre. It saw itself as the motor of the political, social and economic development of China. It was structured by a rigid, centralised command hierarchy and controlled the mass organisations, the non-Communist United Front Parties and a ramified bureaucracy which as a rule, until 1957, reacted instantaneously and efficiently to the stimuli from above.

The military forces loyally obeyed the orders of the civilian leadership while at the same time concentrating their energies on modernising weapon systems and improving the professional qualifications of their members.

The collapse of the civilian Party machine, the quasi-bankruptcy of the agency for development and modernisation in China in 1967 has to be reconstructed systematically in order to elucidate its historical dimensions.

Since the mid-'fifties internal Party disputes had been steadily growing which made discernible two types of group-formation:

1. *Factionalisation*, i.e. the formation of short- and medium-term *opinion groups* with changing, mostly issue-oriented affiliations.

2. *Factionalism*, i.e. the formation of long-term *factions*, being coherent circles which relied upon alternative programmes and competed for overall control.

As long as the group-formation within the CCP had been determined by changing issue-orientated opinion groups the internal Party disputes were resolved by:

1. The *expulsion* of individual leading cadres *from the Party* – especially in the case of Kao Kang and Jao Shu-shih. The impression of monolithic unity which the CCP sought to present to the outside world was not substantially impaired.

2. The *dismissal* of opposing Party leaders *from their positions* in the State and Party machine, which, however (in the case of P'eng Tehuai) was not followed by their expulsion from the Party so that the outward appearance of unity in the ruling agencies was again maintained.

These methods of overcoming an internal Party opposition were employed up to about 1958–9, in the course of the debate about the principles of the first five-year plan as well as in the dispute over the relaxation of internal policies in 1956–7 and in the confrontations over the policy of the 'Three Red Banners'. The development of opinion groups into integrated, long-term factions after 1961–2 elucidates Mao's vanishing authority in the Party, the failing of his charisma against the background of the crisis which the use of his socio-economic development concept had provoked. However, the fact that the method of resolving *internal* Party conflicts as mentioned above could no longer be adopted, and that an *external split* had to follow can only be understood if one considers that in autumn 1965 a break-down of the *procedural consensus* had been evolving from the breakdown in the *consensus on issues* in the Party. The Party leader refused to subject himself to the majority decision of the Politburo. Rather, Mao induced the conflict between the leadership principle of the charismatic individual and the principle of collective leadership and carried it through in the crisis of the 'Cultural Revolution'. The Party apparatus was reduced to being the organisational weapon of the 'New Right' while Mao and his followers intitially relied primarily upon *ad hoc* organisations which were placed beyond the control of the Party and later relied primarily upon the army.

Despite strict discipline and rigid organisation, the civilian Party machine could not hold its own against the onslaught by Maoist mass organisations. In the ranks of the basic organisations, groups of dissatisfied people had come forth because of the purges which the faction under Liu Shao-ch'i had initiated in the 'Socialist Education Movement'. These groups co-operated with the Maoists in the hope of being rehabilitated. But above all the masses were not ready – in spite of spontaneous resistance to the excesses of the Maoist units – after long years of experience of repression by the Party machine to be organised for the latter's protection.

Thus the resolution of the internal Party conflict in the 'Cultural Revolution' from outside marked the second failure of a Leninist-type cadre party in China and in the leadership of the Chinese Revolution.

The *army* thus became the most powerful new ruling agency. The take-over of responsibility for law and order and the functioning of the economic administration in spring 1967 had been intended to be of short duration, but around the turn of 1967–8 it was succeeded by a medium-term take-over, and since then by a definite proclamation of occupation of the regional leadership positions in the RCs. The third step in the process of transforming the PLA into a ruling agency is marked by the establishment of a majority of military representatives in the CC in April 1969. This process was completed with the expansion of military control over the leading bodies of the newly-established Party organisations in the provinces from December 1970, and has since not been reversed, in spite of Lin Piao's demise.

The army prepared the reconstruction of the Party apparatus at both the local and the provincial levels. It takes part authoritatively in the training of Party cadres and intervenes to correct those tendencies in the new Party organisations which the leadership labelled unorthodox. Thus the Party – on the regional and local level – has indeed taken on the role of a mass organisation of the army, and the army controls itself through the leading bodies of the CCP which are mostly still dominated by the army's representatives. Formally the rule of the military places the political system in the PR of China close to other military dominated governmental systems in Asian and African developing countries, but one must ask whether the nature of the Chinese Communist army does not differ strongly from other armies. The PLA claims to be an army of a 'new type'. Its intensive political work, comprehensive participation in the process of production and extremely close connection with the people constitute, so it is said, the specific nature of the armed forces in the PR of China. Particularly since the indoctrination campaign of the years 1960 to 1965, the PLA has become the most loyal pillar of Mao Tse-tung's Thought, and is already laying the prototypical foundations of the future Communist social order. Without doubt the PLA has been politicised more strongly than many other armies, and the claim that it is closely linked to all sections of society has been put forth with justification. Yet it cannot be overlooked that the leaders of the PLA, which came into existence as an army of civil war, have received a predominantly conventional and professional training since the mid-'fifties. Even during the civil war and the war against Japan Mao repeatedly felt obliged to warn against the dangers of 'purely military thought'. The behaviour of the PLA in the 1965–9 crisis in internal politics, its reservations about the Maoist movement since autumn 1966, its hesitant reaction to Mao's call to support the Left in spring 1967 and its clearly demonstrated interest in discipline, law and order since then offer the conclusion that there has been no considerable change in this respect.

This conclusion is reinforced by a number of public statements by regional commanders since spring 1968. If they spoke at meetings of students, cadres or activists they presented themselves as men used to command, used to being obeyed and expecting to be obeyed in their new leading positions in the Party and state administrative machines. The extent to which their political decisions are determined by logistic considerations cannot yet be reliably verified, but it appears as if these considerations have been growing more relevant with regard to Chinese Communist politics since the end of the 'Cultural Revolution'. Moreover, an analysis of the biographical background of many Chinese military leaders tends to the conclusion that professional qualifications were at least as important for their careers as was their political reliability.

One essential aspect relates the PLA, regardless of its particularities, to the armies of other developing countries. It seems to be a *national integrative élite* which, motivated by a trans-traditional code of moral values, formulates political decisions on pragmatic criteria of modernisation. In the crisis of the 'Cultural Revolution' this élite took over those functions in China which it has been exercising for a long time in many other developing countries.

The change in the ruling agencies has not been without any influence on the *ideology* of the CCP. While the Marxist–Leninist theories of historical determinism and the Communist social order formally define the ultimate goal of the Party, Mao and his followers have developed through their version of the theory of uninterrupted or 'permanent' revolution the specific guiding principles for the exercise of rule, at the centre of which is placed the *theory of contradictions*. This distinguishes the two categories of 'non-antagonistic' contradictions 'among the people' which may be solved through discussion and persuasion, and 'antagonistic' contradictions 'between ourselves and the enemy' which are to be solved by means of force, i.e. by the 'dictatorship of the proletariat'. During the whole period of building and completing the socialist social order, even in the phase of transition to the Communist social order, contradictions 'among the people' could change qualitatively into contradictions 'between ourselves and the enemy'. Faced with this distinction it is essential for the inhabitants of the PR of China to know who belongs to 'the people' and who to 'the enemy'. But the CCP did not develop precise criteria to answer this question. Mao's definition of 1957 that those 'classes, strata and social groups which approve, support and work for the sake of socialism' belong to the people leaves open the question of who confirms this 'approval' and 'support'. At the time of the high point of the 'Hundred Flowers' movement the Politburo laid down that 'non-antagonistic' contradictions had turned into 'antagonistic' ones and that the critics of spring 1957 had become 'enemies'. In the early phase of the 'Cultural Revolution' the majority of the Party leadership under Liu Shao-ch'i declared that the conflict between the CCP and the intellectual opposition was a contradiction 'among the people', while the minority under Mao defined it as a contradiction 'between ourselves and the enemy'. The outcome was not determined by socio-political or philosophical analyses, but by the victory of the Maoists in the Centre, achieved with the help of military demonstrations of power in the capital. Thus the nature of the theory of contradictions was shown to be highly flexible, largely a manipulative tool with which to legitimise the rule of the leadership and finally even of a faction within the Party leadership which had prevailed in the sphere of power politics.

From the time that the army became the most important factor in determining the political decision-making process a growing tendency has been discernible towards reinterpreting substantially the principles of Marxist–Leninist theory with regard to the nature of the phase of socialism and the transition to communism. The function of the 'Three Supports' (workers, peasants and the Left) and of the 'Two Militaries' (leadership by the military and training by the military) which had been assigned to the PLA in spring 1967 in order to define its intervention in the internal crisis, has since turned from a function described as provisional into a 'substantial development of Mao Tse-tung's Thought'.[14] It became a 'fundamental task of our army in the *whole historical period of socialism*'.[15] From there, it is only a small step to the thesis that 'the army is the main element in state power', 'according to the Marxist theory of the state'.[16] This thesis was expressed on the anniversary commemorating the Paris Commune, March 18, 1971.

The ultimate consequence of this definition implies that the transition to a Communist social order will proceed according to the principles of military organisation and according to the norms of political and social behaviour which have developed within the military. The extension of these organisational principles and norms of social behaviour to the whole people is thus being declared to constitute the 'permanent revolution'.

Should this tendency continue or even be reinforced, and this cannot be ruled out in spite of the most recent events in China, then finally the specific form of rule in China, the 'proletarian dictatorship of the military', would find its rationalisation in a truly creative contribution to Marxism–Leninism. The army as the motor of the historical process of development transforms the Party and in practice replaces it. Its position as the ruling agency in the whole phase of the transition to Communism would thus be ideologically legitimised.

However, should the overthrow of Lin Piao and his associates in the central military leadership result in major ideological corrections – and this possibility cannot be excluded either–the organisational doctrine of Chinese communism would have to be redefined along lines which modify the position of the Party as well as the army. This would lead to new definitions, the content of which is not yet distinguishable at all. A protracted period of insecurity in the field of ideological rationalisation would be the inevitable consequence.

Perspectives

The Chinese Communists under Mao Tse-tung were successful, within a few years, in completely reconstructing the national economy which had been heavily damaged by twelve years of war. The political system in the PR of China also developed – but with only the reluctant support of the Party leader or even against his will – the flexibility necessary to start the recovery from the damage caused by the 'Three Red Banners' policy and to lead it to a successful conclusion. The integrating and mobilising capacities of the Party machine, before the crisis of the 'Cultural Revolution', and of the army in the last three years, have undoubtedly contributed considerably to the modernisation of China. Regarding the complexity of the development problems which faced the CCP – and the KMT as well before its take-over – these achievements deserve a positive evaluation. However, they should not deceive the observer of Chinese politics as to at least four central problems as yet unresolved:

1. The Chinese Communists have not yet fully succeeded in overcoming the *disparity between food production and population growth*. Assessing the Chinese population in 1958 at about 650 million and at about 725 million in 1970, then the *per capita* grain production and production of other crops decreased – according to official and semi-official data from the Peking leadership – in twelve years from

385 to 330 kilogrammes. If we use the average data of foreign estimates then there is a decrease from 315 to 290 kilogrammes. As population growth rates have been relatively low this retrogressive development may be traced back to the extraordinarily small expansion in agricultural production, especially if longer periods of time are compared.

2. The practice of CCP rule curbed the necessary *stimulation of a broad range of intellectual expression*. For the young generation at secondary schools and colleges in particular, identification with the system of government was made difficult for a long time. When it finally reacted positively to the Chairman's call for identification in the early phase of the 'Cultural Revolution', it was, after barely a year, subjected to extensive measures of military discipline, in the name of the very person and the very image of the future to whose defence it had come forward. Instead of the 'New Society' under the leadership of the Chairman and the mobilised young rebels for which they had hoped, it is confronted with a shattered old society run by a coalition of cool professional military power engineers, suave diplomats and uncommitted development bureaucrats. It is extremely doubtful whether the young generation in China recognises its vision of 1966. Its identification with the political system now is certainly not much more intense than it was before 1965.

3. The CCP retarded China's *access to the international intellectual exchange* of the world communications culture. The isolation which has also been implemented in regard to national intellectual history impoverished China intellectually and provoked an accumulation of discontent which in the future might lead to political convulsions capable of jeopardising the system.[17]

4. Although the achievements in development policy are clearly noticeable, up to now the *forces of production* of the Chinese people have by no means been sufficiently mobilised. The economic initiative of the individual and of the family, which is specifically characteristic of the Chinese, has, on the contrary, been curbed. Thus the fact that China still belongs to those countries which are severely underdeveloped in the field of peace economy cannot be blamed simply on a century of repression by the imperialist powers and on unfavourable natural conditions, but must also be blamed, to a growing extent, on the use of nineteenth-century doctrines of development which have not yet proved to be particularly efficient for expansion in any country in the world.

Only the resolution of these problems could achieve further fundamental progress in the modernisation of China. Whether or not the Communist system of rule will be able to resolve them in the future depends substantially on its *medium-range development perspectives*.

The coherence of the present leadership group of the CCP is hardly greater then that of the leading bodies of the Party prior to the development of the factions with their alternative programmes in the early 'sixties. The coalition which put an end to the 'Cultural Revolution' and made a start at liquidating its offspring was deprived of the central military machine under Lin Piao in the leadership crisis of autumn 1971. Furthermore, the dichotomy between the Maoist theorists and the alliance of regional commanders and bureaucrats, which now represents the majority of the leadership, appears to have laid down the preconditions for a new struggle over power and policy after the death of the seventy-nine-year-old Party leader. A *victory for the genuine Maoist Left* cannot be rated very probable although this possibility may not yet be excluded completely. The Left lost its organisational basis in most of the provinces through the liquidation of the Red Guard movement. Biological inevitability will in the not so distant future deprive it of its individual symbol whose prestige and charisma it can still claim for the time being.

The leaders of the *state administrative bureaucracy* will be in a position to realise their concepts in the political decision-making process only as long as the regional military authorities are willing to use the capacities of the former. For they too lack an organisational basis. But one may reckon that the military will be willing to co-operate with them for a relatively long period, in the course of which they will be able to turn their indispensability into political influence in the sense of an external and internal course of policy which is shaped by pragmatic considerations.

The medium-range perspectives of the governmental system will thus be determined predominantly by the answers to the question of the coherence of the *regional military leadership group*. The PLA is no more monolithic than the civilian Party machine before the 'Cultural Revolution'. After the fall of the central military leadership the loyalty groups which have traditionally evolved from the five 'Field Army' systems also face each other in the regional military machines.[18] Their common interest in restabilising the system of rule, in developing the defence potential of China and strengthening the international standing of the country has produced a solid consensus among the regional commanders in spite of the severe disturbances in the leadership crisis of autumn 1971. Thus together with Chou En-lai they could defeat Lin Piao. But if the functional and traditional groups within the military forces were to fuse into factions, then China's return to *military regionalism*, naturally different in substance and quality from that of the early phase of the Republic, could be excluded no more than the possibility of the breakdown of the Communist system of rule. In order to prevent this the leadership might probably attempt to check these regionalist tendencies which have now become clearly evident by setting up a *system of federal military rule.*

Only such a system would expose the authoritative myth of Party ideology to the process of differentiation and erosion which might bring about an extensive *liberalisation* of the system and practice of rule. Until then we may probably reckon on a reduction in the demands of the leadership on the population, and on tendencies towards relaxation in the socio-economic sphere, but on scarcely any extension of the extremely narrow parameters of intellectual and political competitition.

Bearing in mind these perspectives one is led to reflect, initially, albeit provisionally, on the role of Communist rule in the context of the *Chinese Revolution,* i.e. the modernisation process which has been proceeding for more than a century. The nature of this Chinese Revolution has been defined by the goals and expectations formulated by the different modernising groups which have since successively prevailed. The leaders of the intellectual reform movement after 1914–15 called for national emancipations, reforms in the social structure and the political emancipation of the individual. Therefore they demanded the revision of the unequal treaties, reform in the relations existing in agricultural ownership, the improvement of labour conditions in the young Chinese industry, but furthermore the guarantee of individual liberty, freedom of thought and freedom for the press, the right of assembly and association as well as freedom of artistic and literary expression. In theory the KMT made similar demands. However, it concentrated on the goal of national emancipation and thus for the most part promoted the unification of the country while neglecting necessary reforms in the social structure and withholding political rights and liberties. The CCP finally viewed change in the social order and the attainment for China of a position in international politics equal to that of the other great powers as its central, pragmatic goals. In the period of KMT rule China achieved legal equality among the nations through the abrogation of the unequal treaties in 1943, and national emacipation was decisively promoted by the defeat of Japan in 1945. Moreover, up to the early phase of the Second World War, the KMT laid substantial foundations for a centralised and rationalised bureaucratic system of rule. This system of rule was the necessary precondition for economic and social development and was fully deployed by the Communists in the period from 1950 to 1965, but it was once more extensively damaged in the crisis of the 'Cultural Revolution'. Furthermore, the Communist government effected substantial changes in the social structure, especially in the first decade, rearranging ownership relations in agriculture and the family system. Finally, it considerably enhanced China's international status. But

I

while the KMT and CCP ruled the country, the quest for personal, intellectual and political freedom for the individual could never be completely suppressed. This quest had first been made by the 'May Fourth' movement around 1920, and was repeated when the young Chinese intelligentsia criticised KMT rule from 1931 to 1936, demanding a freely-elected, constitutional government. It further underlined the attacks of Hu Feng and motivated his followers against the regimentation of art and literature by the CCP, as well as the comprehensive revolt of the Chinese intelligentsia against Party rule in spring 1957, the intellectual criticism of Party doctrine and the Party leader in the early 'sixties and the attempts at a complete revision of the Party line against which Mao and his faction launched the counter-offensive of the 'Cultural Revolution'. It cannot yet be clearly verified to what extent the Red Guard movement was influenced by these calls for freedom, but certainly the Leftist opposition took them up again against the disciplinary measures pursued by the military and the reconstruction of the machines undertaken by the bureaucrats after the turn of 1967–8.

Faced with this clear and continuing longing for freedom it is scarcely to be doubted that the quest for freedom of literature and art, science, speech, press, association and assembly has been an integral part of the programme of the Chinese Revolution. Hitherto in the main it has been expressed by intellectuals, but this was also the case at first in regard to national emancipation and reforms of the social structure.

As long as the quest for substantial guarantees of freedom has not been implemented, the process of the Chinese Revolution has not yet come to an end. Communist rule undoubtedly fulfilled an essential, innovatory function in the course of this revolution, but while the continuity of the Communist system of rule must be taken into account as a factor of medium-range constancy in any analysis of Chinese politics, this continuity becomes questionable in a long-term perspective because it stands in an antagonistic contradiction to the continuing longing for freedom.

The call for freedom and for political emancipation of the individual protracts the process of the Chinese Revolution beyond the phase of Communist rule. This long-term perspective takes on an irrevocable nature, not least because the Era of Mao Tse-tung has left unanswered questions concerning the extensive mobilisation of productive forces, the opening of China to intellectual exchange with the outside world and the reduction of the rulers' demands on the people.

DATE DUE FOR RETURN